IARIA

AA004085

INTERNET 2019

The Eleventh International Conference on Evolving Internet

June 30 – July 4, 2019

Rome, Italy

INTERNET 2019 Editors

Eugen Borcoci, University "Politehnica" of Bucharest (UPB), Romania

Dirceu Cavendish, Kyushu Institute of Technology, Japan

Nicola Fabiano, Studio Legale Fabiano, Italy

Printed from e-media with permission by:

Curran Associates, Inc.
57 Morehouse Lane
Red Hook, NY 12571

Some format issues inherent in the e-media version may also appear in this print version.

Printed by Curran Associates, Inc. (2019)

International Academy, Research, and Industry Association (IARIA)
412 Derby Way
Wilmington, DE 19810

Phone: (408) 893-6407
Fax: (408) 527-6351

petre@iaria.org

Additional copies of this publication are available from:

Curran Associates, Inc.
57 Morehouse Lane
Red Hook, NY 12571 USA
Phone: 845-758-0400
Fax: 845-758-2633
Email: curran@proceedings.com
Web: www.proceedings.com

Table of Contents

INTERNET 2019

Foreword

The Eleventh International Conference on Evolving Internet (INTERNET 2019), held between June 30 – July 4, 2019 - Rome, Italy, dealt with challenges raised by evolving Internet making use of the progress in different advanced mechanisms and theoretical foundations. The gap analysis aimed at mechanisms and features concerning the Internet itself, as well as special applications for software defined radio networks, wireless networks, sensor networks, or Internet data streaming and mining.

Originally designed in the spirit of interchange between scientists, the Internet reached a status where large-scale technical limitations impose rethinking its fundamentals. This refers to design aspects (flexibility, scalability, etc.), technical aspects (networking, routing, traffic, address limitation, etc), as well as economics (new business models, cost sharing, ownership, etc.). Evolving Internet poses architectural, design, and deployment challenges in terms of performance prediction, monitoring and control, admission control, extendibility, stability, resilience, delay-tolerance, and interworking with the existing infrastructures or with specialized networks.

We take here the opportunity to warmly thank all the members of the INTERNET 2019 Technical Program Committee, as well as the numerous reviewers. The creation of such a high quality conference program would not have been possible without their involvement. We also kindly thank all the authors who dedicated much of their time and efforts to contribute to INTERNET 2019. We truly believe that, thanks to all these efforts, the final conference program consisted of top quality contributions.

Also, this event could not have been a reality without the support of many individuals, organizations, and sponsors. We are grateful to the members of the INTERNET 2019 organizing committee for their help in handling the logistics and for their work to make this professional meeting a success.

We hope that INTERNET 2019 was a successful international forum for the exchange of ideas and results between academia and industry and for the promotion of progress in the field of the evolving internet.

We are convinced that the participants found the event useful and communications very open. We also hope that Rome provided a pleasant environment during the conference and everyone saved some time for exploring this beautiful city.

INTERNET 2019 Chairs

INTERNET Steering Committee

Eugen Borcoci, University "Politehnica" of Bucharest (UPB), Romania
Dirceu Cavendish, Kyushu Institute of Technology, Japan
Steffen Fries, Siemens AG, Germany
Terje Jensen, Telenor, Norway

Cristina Alcaraz, University of Malaga, Spain
Parimala Thulasiraman, University of Manitoba - Winnipeg, Canada
Wladyslaw Homenda, Warsaw University of Technology, Poland
Onur Alparslan, Osaka University, Japan

INTERNET Industry/Research Advisory Committee

Michael Bahr, Siemens AG Corporate Technology, Munich, Germany
Marcin Markowski, Wroclaw University of Science and Technology, Poland
Hanmin Jung, KISTI, Korea
Paolo Barattini, Kontor 46, Italy
Yung Ryn (Elisha) Choe, Sandia National Laboratories, Livermore, USA

INTERNET 2019

Committee

INTERNET Steering Committee

Eugen Borcoci, University "Politehnica" of Bucharest (UPB), Romania
Dirceu Cavendish, Kyushu Institute of Technology, Japan
Steffen Fries, Siemens AG, Germany
Terje Jensen, Telenor, Norway
Cristina Alcaraz, University of Malaga, Spain
Parimala Thulasiraman, University of Manitoba - Winnipeg, Canada
Wladyslaw Homenda, Warsaw University of Technology, Poland
Onur Alparslan, Osaka University, Japan

INTERNET Industry/Research Advisory Committee

Michael Bahr, Siemens AG Corporate Technology, Munich, Germany
Marcin Markowski, Wroclaw University of Science and Technology, Poland
Hanmin Jung, KISTI, Korea
Paolo Barattini, Kontor 46, Italy
Yung Ryn (Elisha) Choe, Sandia National Laboratories, Livermore, USA

INTERNET 2019 Technical Program Committee

Alex Afanasyev, Florida International University, USA
Ala Al-Fuqaha, Western Michigan University, USA
Cristina Alcaraz, University of Malaga, Spain
Onur Alparslan, Osaka University, Japan
Ioannis Anagnostopoulos, University of Thessaly, Greece
Mário Antunes, Polytechnic of Leiria & INESC-TEC | University of Porto, Portugal
Liz Bacon, University of Greenwich, UK
Mohamad Badra, Zayed University, Dubai, UAE
Michael Bahr, Siemens AG Corporate Technology, Munich, Germany
Zubair Baig, Edith Cowan University, Western Australia
Marcin Bajer, ABB Corporate Research Center Krakow, Poland
Arijit Banerjee, Federated Wireless Inc., USA
Deepak Bansal, Microsoft, USA
Paolo Barattini, Kontor 46, Italy
Andrzej Beben, Warsaw University of Technology, Poland
Nik Bessis, Edge Hill University, UK
Maumita Bhattacharya, Charles Sturt University, Australia
Eugen Borcoci, University "Politehnica" of Bucharest (UPB), Romania
Fernando Boronat, Universidad Politécnica De Valencia-Campus De Gandia, Spain

Stefan Bosse, University of Bremen, Germany
Christos J. Bouras, University of Patras, Greece
Alina Buzachis, University of Messina, Italy
Dirceu Cavendish, Kyushu Institute of Technology, Japan
Lianjie Cao, Hewlett Packard Labs, Palo Alto, USA
Hao Che, University of Texas at Arlington, USA
Kang Chen, Southern Illinois University, USA
Albert M. K. Cheng, University of Houston, USA
Hongmei Chi, Florida A&M University, USA
Yung Ryn (Elisha) Choe, Sandia National Laboratories, Livermore, USA
Andrzej Chydzinski, Institute of Informatics | Silesian University of Technology, Poland
Angel P. del Pobil, Jaume I University, Spain
Said El Kafhali, Hassan 1st University, Settat, Morocco
Nicola Fabiano, Studio Legale Fabiano, Italy
Maria Fazio, Università degli Studi di Messina, Italy
Zongming Fei, University of Kentucky, USA
Elena Fersman, KTH Royal Institute of Technology, Sweden
Steffen Fries, Siemens AG, Germany
Marco Furini, University of Modena and Reggio Emilia, Italy
Antonino Galletta, University of Messina, Italy
Filippo Gandino, Politecnico di Torino, Italy
Victor Govindaswamy, Concordia University Chicago, USA
Wladyslaw Homenda, Warsaw University of Technology, Poland
Pao-Ann Hsiung, National Chung Cheng University, Taiwan
Fu-Hau Hsu, National Central University, Taiwan
Chao Huang, University of Notre Dame, USA
Takeshi Ikenaga, Kyushu Institute of Technology, Japan
Sergio Ilarri, University of Zaragoza, Spain
Marc Jansen, University of Applied Sciences Ruhr West, Germany
Ivan Jelinek, Czech Technical University in Prague, Czech Republic
Terje Jensen, Telenor, Norway
Hanmin Jung, KISTI, Korea
Sokratis K. Katsikas, Center for Cyber & Information Security | Norwegian University of Science & Technology (NTNU), Norway
Rasool Kiani, University of Isfahan, Iran
Lucianna Kiffer, Northeastern University Khoury College of Computer and Information Sciences, USA
Wojciech Kmiecik, Wroclaw University of Technology, Poland
Raj Kosaraju, Maxil Technologies Solutions Inc, USA
Igor Kotenko, SPIIRAS, Russia
Mariano Lamarca i Lorente, Barcelona City Council, Spain
Mikel Larrea, University of the Basque Country UPV/EHU, Spain
Jörg Lässig, Fraunhofer IOSB | Institutsteil Angewandte Systemtechnik (AST), Germany
Gyu Myoung Lee, Liverpool John Moores University, UK
Kevin Lee, Deakin University, Australia
Pierre Leone, University of Geneva, Switzerland
Zhijing Li, UC Santa Barbara, USA
Jinwei Liu, Clemson University, USA
Olaf Manuel Maennel, TalTech University, Estonia

Imad Mahgoub, Florida Atlantic University, USA
Abdelhamid Mammeri, University of Ottawa, Canada
Zoubir Mammeri, IRIT - Université Paul Sabatier, France
Marcin Markowski, Wroclaw University of Science and Technology, Poland
Kais Mekki, CRAN - University of Lorraine, France
Philippe Merle, Inria, France
Ivan Mezei, University of Novi Sad, Serbia
Sangman Moh, Chosun University, South Korea
Augusto Morales, Check Point Software Technologies, Spain
Ahmad M. Nagib, Cairo University, Egypt
Algirdas Pakštas, London Metropolitan University, UK
Fidel Paniagua Diez, Universidad Internacional de La Rioja - UNIR, Spain
Luigi Patrono, University of Salento, Italy
Muni Prabaharan, Independent Researcher - Mexico City, Mexico
Danda B. Rawat, Georgia Southern University, USA
Marek Reformat, University of Alberta, Canada
Domenico Rotondi, FINCONS SpA (ICT solution provider), Italy
Abdel-Badeeh M. Salem, Ain Shams University, Cairo, Egypt
Ignacio Sanchez, University of the West of Scotland, UK
Paul Sant, University of Bedfordshire, UK
José Santa Lozano, University of Murcia, Spain
Jason Sawin, University of St. Thomas, USA
Peter Schartner, Alpen-Adria-Universität Klagenfurt, Austria
Wentao Shang, University of California Los Angeles, USA
Piyush Kumar Sharma, IIIT DELHI, India
Xiufang Shi, Zhejiang University, China
Kuei-Ping Shih, Tamkang University, Taiwan
Roman Y. Shtykh, CyberAgent, Inc., Japan
Pedro Sousa, University of Minho, Portugal
Álvaro Suárez Sarmiento, Universidad de Las Palmas de Gran Canaria, Spain
Diego Suárez Touceda, Universidad Internacional de La Rioja - UNIR, Spain
Yuzo Taenaka, Nara Institute of Science and Technology, Japan
Bedir Tekinerdogan, Wageningen University, Netherlands
Geraldine Texier, IMT Atlantique, France
Sabu M. Thampi, Indian Institute of Information Technology and Management - Kerala (IIITM-K), India
Parimala Thulasiraman, University of Manitoba - Winnipeg, Canada
Homero Toral Cruz, University of Quintana Roo (UQROO), Mexico
Herwig Unger, FenUniversitaet in Hagen, Germany
Neven Vrček, University of Zagreb, Croatia
Armin Wasicek, Technical University Vienna, Austria
Mudasser F. Wyne, National University, USA
Habib Zaidi, Geneva University Hospital, Switzerland

Copyright Information

On Orchestration Interactions for Preparation of Slice Creation in Multi-domain 5G Networking Environment

Eugen Borcoci, Serban Georgica Obreja
University POLITEHNICA of Bucharest
Bucharest, Romania
eugen.borcoci@elcom.pub.ro, serban@radio.pub.ro

Abstract— **Network slicing is a major concept in 5G networking technology, offering multi-tenant, multi-domain, multi-operator and end-to-end (E2E) capabilities. 5G slicing allows tenants to share resources while customizing their own services via slice isolation. Integrated management and control based on ETSI Management and Orchestration (MANO) is applied, but enriched, in order to cope with multi-domain slicing. Several architectures have been proposed in the literature, with different views on the complex orchestration functions. This paper is oriented to some open architectural issues. It presents a short analysis of the orchestration interactions, focusing to some aspects of initial slice design and preparation, in a multi-domain and multi-operator environment. A specific paper contribution is on inter-domain topology discovery and collection of information by a multi-domain capable slice orchestrator, especially on specifying the design and preparation phase of a slice construction.**

Keywords-5G slicing; Multi-domain; Multi-tenant; Management and orchestration; Software Defined Networking; Network Function Virtualization

I. INTRODUCTION

The emergent 5G mobile network technologies aim to answer the increasing demand and challenges addressed to communication systems and Internet [1]. 5G can support dedicated use-cases and provide specific types of services to satisfy simultaneously various customer/tenant demands in a multi-tenant fashion [2]-[4].

The 5G network slicing concept (based on virtualization and softwarization) enables programmability and modularity for network resources provisioning, adapted to different vertical service requirements (in terms of bandwidth, latency, etc.) [2]-[9]. A *Network Slice* (NSL) is a managed logical group of subsets of resources, Physical/Virtual network functions (PNFs/VNFs) in the architectural Data Plane (DPl), Control Plane (CPl) and Management Plane (MPl). The slice is programmable and has the ability to expose its capabilities to the users.

The NSL behavior is realized via *Network Slice* Instance(s) (NSLI), which are created (based on NSL templates) at request of a tenant or at Slice Provider initiative (the word "tenant" defines a user or group of users with specific access rights and privileges over a shared set of resources). A *blueprint/template* is a logical representation of network function(s) and the associated resource requirements. It describes the structure, configuration and work flows for instantiating and controlling an NSLI; it includes certain network characteristics (e.g., bandwidth, latency, reliability) and refers to the required physical and logical resources, and the sub-networks. An NSLI may be dedicated or shared across multiple *Service Instances*.

The verticals may use a common infrastructure, with appropriate levels of isolation and Quality of Services (QoS) provisioning. The slicing allows 5G to create an eco-system, multi-tenant, multi-domain, multi-operator and end-to-end (E2E) - capable.

Software Defined Networks (SDN) and Network Function Virtualization (NFV) technologies, combined with cloud/edge computing are used in 5G slicing architectures and implementations [10]-[13].

In a multi-domain, multi-tenant, multi-operator, and E2E context, the slice construction includes a design and preparation phase. This phase requires a lot of orchestration/inter-domain interactions in order to construct the network services (NS) and NSL catalogues to be used later for actual slice creation in the subsequent phases. Information on available resources (network, compute, storage) in several domains should be collected by an orchestration entity charged with the task of creation of a multi-domain slice.

The specific contribution of this paper is to propose a mechanism for multi-domain interconnection topology information collection, by the highest-level orchestration entity. The mechanism is essentially usable in the design and preparation phase of an NSLI. This work is still preliminary, limited for the time being, to architectural and high level interactions solutions.

The structure of the paper is described here. Section II recalls some major features of the 5G management and orchestration framework. Section III provides few relevant examples of related architectural work on orchestration. Then, based on a generic relevant architecture, Section IV details the design and preparation phase interactions, providing inputs to the Section V. The latter is focused on collection of topological information in a multi-domain context. Section VI presents conclusions and a future work outline.

II. NETWORK SLICE MANAGEMENT AND ORCHESTRATION

The objective of this section is to shortly introduce the slice management and orchestration framework, in order to help the identification of the work area for Section V

The 5G networks need efficient services and resource *orchestration* and programmable management systems. It is necessary to model the E2E services and to abstract and automate the control of physical and virtual resources. Orchestration extends the traditional management: it consists in a coordinated set of activities to automatically select and control multiple resources, services and systems, aiming to meet certain objectives (e.g., serve a tenant requesting a specific network service) [14].

At services level, the term *Network Service Orchestration* (NSO) can be defined, [15]-[17], as an automated management and control (M&C) process for services deployment and operations, performed mainly by telecommunication operators and service providers. The NSO involves different types of resources and potentially multiple providers; it can decouple the high-level service layer from the underlying management and resources layers (e.g., NFV functional components like Virtualized Infrastructure Manager (VIM), Element Management Systems (EMS), SDN controllers, etc.). The NSO defines the interaction with (chains of) network functions (NFs) of the underlying technologies and infrastructures through adequate abstractions. In a multi-domain (technological or administrative) context, the NSO should have an overall high-level view of all domains, *including topology information*, in order to be able to orchestrate E2E slices and associated services, independently of geographical location. The NSO cooperates with NFV MANO functional blocks.

The orchestration activities can appear at several architectural levels (e.g., slice, resources and NFV MANO - levels). An orchestration entity interacts, vertically and horizontally, with other M&C entities in the same or peer domains. Currently, there is not yet a standard for information exchange process in multi-domain technological/administrative environments. There are many multi-domain orchestration architecture variants and candidates, proposed (see [2]-[6] for examples). This paper is working in the information exchange area.

The *life-cycle management* (LCM) of an NSLI comprises several phases performed by the Slice Provider: (1) *instantiation, configuration*, and *activation*, (2) *run-time* and (3) *decommissioning* [6]. The phase (1) is split into the instantiation/ configuration sub-phase (the necessary shared/dedicated resources, including NFs, are configured and instantiated, but not yet used) and the activation sub-phase (the NSLI becomes active for handling network traffic). The run-time phase focuses on data traffic transport, reporting the network service performance and possible NSLI re-configurations or scaling, if dynamic conditions impose that. The phase (3) includes the deactivation and termination of the NSLI and release of the allocated resources.

The LCM is preceded by a *design and preparation phase* (0) for the future instantiation and support of an NSLI. The functional architecture, steps and interactions within this preliminary phase are still open research issues. The paper is focused on design and preparation phase, treated in Section V.

III. EXAMPLES OF RELEVANT ARCHITECTURES

This section presents few examples of relevant 5G slicing architectures in order to emphasize the orchestration entities roles.

A. *ETSI slicing architecture (high level)*

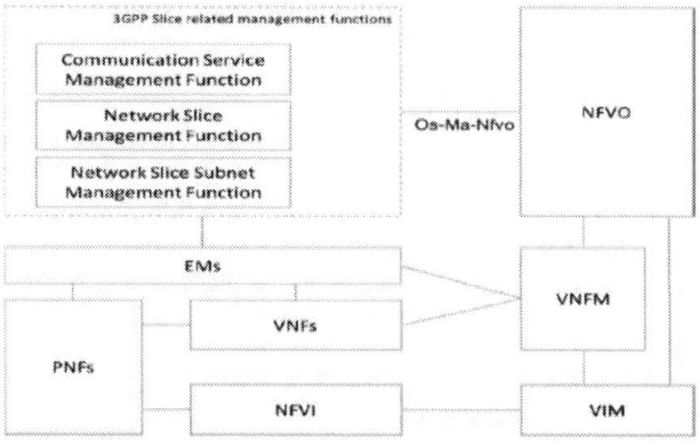

Figure 1. Network slice management in an NFV framework (ETSI GR NFV-EVE 012 V3.1.1, [6])

NFV -Network Function Virtualization; EM - Element Manager; MANO - Management and Orchestration (NFVO – NFV Orchestration; VNFM – VNF Manager; VIM Virtual Infrastructure Manager); VNF/PNF – Virtual/Physical Network Function; NFVI -NFV Infrastructure; NS-Network Service; OSS-Operations Support System.

Figure 1 shows the ETSI NFV architecture [10], to which several new functional blocks are added in order to support the network slicing (ETSI-NFV EVE 012 [6]).

The 3GPP TR 28.801 document [7] identifies three new management functions: *Communication Service Management Function* (CSMF) – it translates the communication service requirements to NSL requirements; *Network Slice Management Function* (NSMF) - responsible for the management (including lifecycle) of NSLIs (it derives network slice subnet requirements from the network slice related requirements); *orchestration* system.

Network Slice Subnet Management Function (NSSMF) - responsible for the management (including lifecycle) of *Network Slice Subnet Instances* (NSSIs). The Os-Ma-NFVO Reference Point (RP) is the interface with ETSI NFV-MANO. To interface properly with NFV-MANO, the NSMF and/or NSSMF need to determine the type of NS or set of NSs, VNF and PNF that can support the resource requirements for a NSLI or NSSI, and whether new instances of these NSs, VNFs, and the connectivity to the PNFs, need to be created, or existing instances can be re-used.

B. *5GPPP slicing architecture*

The 5GPPP Working Group proposes in [1] a slicing architecture having four planes: *Service, Management and Orchestration, Control and Data plane*. The Service plane comprises the *Business Support Systems* (BSSs) and business-level Policy and Decision functions, as well as applications and services operated by the tenant. Note that this plane includes an *end-to-end orchestration* system.

The *Management* and *Orchestration plane* includes several functional blocks: *Service Management*, *Software-Defined Mobile Network Orchestrator* (SDMO), and *NFV managers* like VIM and VNFM.

The SDMO is composed of a *domain specific application management*, an *Inter-slice Resource Broker*, and *NFV-NFVO*. The SDMO performs the E2E management of network services; it can set up slices by using the network slice templates and merge them properly at the described multiplexing point. The Service Management intermediates between the service layer and the Inter-slice Broker; it transforms consumer-facing service descriptions into resource-facing service descriptions and vice versa. The Inter-slice Broker handles cross-slice resource allocation. The domain-specific application management functions could be, e.g., for 3GPP: Element Managers (EM) and Network Management (NM) functions, including Network (Sub-) Slice Management Function.

The *Control plane* includes two types of SDN –type controllers: *Software-Defined Mobile Network Coordinator* (SDM-X) and *Software-Defined Mobile Network Controller* (SDM-C), as well as other control applications. The SDM-C and SDM-X take care of dedicated and shared NFs respectively. Following the SDN principles, they translate decisions of the control applications into commands to VNFs and PNFs. Note that SDM-X and SDM-C, as well as other control applications, can be implemented as VNFs or PNFs.

The *Data plane* comprises the VNFs and PNFs needed to carry and process the user data traffic.

The architecture also includes a *Multi-Domain Network Operating System* containing different adaptors and network abstractions above the networks and clouds heterogeneous fabrics. It is responsible for allocation of (virtual) network resources and maintains network state to ensure network reliability in a multi domain environment.

C. *ETSI Multi-domain Multi-tenant slicing architecture – example 1*

Figure 2 shows (adapted from ETSI GR NFV-EVE 012 [6] and J.Ordonez-Lucena et. al. [3][18]) a multi-domain slicing architecture, viewed at run-time phase. A given slice instance can span several *Infrastructure Providers* (InP) and/or administrative domains.

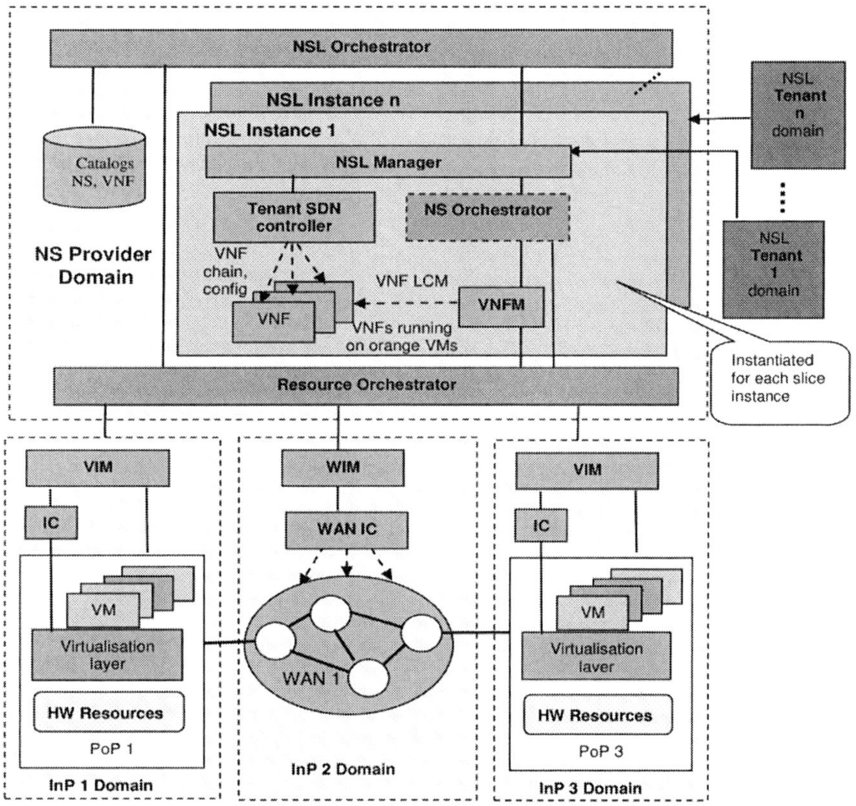

Figure 2. Run-time image of a multi-domain slicing architecture - example 1 (adapted from ETSI GR NFV-EVE 012 [6] and Ordonez-Lucena [3][18])

NS – Network Service; NSL - Network Slice; VNF – Virtualized Network Function; VNFM – VNF Manager; SDN Software Defined Networking; LCM –Life Cycle Management; VIM – Virtual Infrastructure Manager; WIM – WAN Infrastructure Manager; IC- Infrastructure SDN controller; HW- Hardware; WAN – Wide Area Network

The architecture is still high–level depicted, e.g., the NSL orchestrator and Resource Orchestrator are multi-domain capable, but not detailed. Note also that (for simplicity sake), this architectural picture focuses on the transport and core network domains, omitting the RAN (Radio Access Network) domain.

The NSL provider can simultaneously operate multiple NSLIs, which run on top of a common infrastructure, spanning across multiple administrative domains and each belonging to a different infrastructure provider. The NSL provider, taking the role of an infrastructure tenant, rents the infrastructure resources owned by the underlying InPs and uses them to provision the NSLIs.

The NSL provider has a *Resource Orchestration* (RO) functional block. The (RO) uses the finite set of resources that are at its disposal (the resources are supplied by the underlying VIMs/WIMs) and dispatches them to the NSLIs in an optimal way. All the NSLIs receive the resources needed to satisfy their (potentially different) requirements, while preserving their performance isolation. Note that RO should have information on resource availability in each domain, and this supposes a set of inter-domain interactions. The work [18] does not specify the implementation of the RO (distributed or centralized).

Each NSLI has its own management plane, (to assure isolation across NSLIs), consisting of four functional blocks: *NSL Manager, NS Orchestrator (NSO), Tenant SDN Controller*, and *VNF Manager (VNFM).* The VNFM(s) and the NSO perform the required life cycle operations (e.g., instantiation, scaling, termination, etc.) over the instances of the VNFs and NS(s), respectively. Interactions between these functional blocks and the RO are necessary.

The NSL Manager coordinates the operations and management data from Tenant SDN Controller and the NS Orchestrator, performing the fault, configuration, accounting, performance, and security management within the NSLI. Each tenant consumes its NSLI and operates it at its convenience (within the limits agreed with the NSL provider) through the NSL Manager.

The *NSL Orchestrator* (NSLO) is the highest layer of the architecture, *having a key role in the creation phase* and in the run-time phase. In the creation phase, NSLO receives the order to deploy an NSL instance for a tenant (or the Slice Provider decides to construct a slice). The NSLO has enough information (including on multi-domain) as to check the order feasibility and, if feasible, then triggers the instantiation of the NSL. To accomplish this, it interacts with RO, and accesses the VNF and NS Catalogues. These catalogues contain VNF and NS descriptors, exposing the capabilities of all the VNFs and services that an NSL provider can select for the NSLs.

At run-time, the NSLO performs policy-based inter-slice operations, e.g., it analyses the performance and fault management data, received from the operative NSL instances, to manage their Service Level Agreements (SLAs). In case of SLA violations, the NSLO decides which NSL instances need to be modified, and sends corrective management actions (e.g., scaling, healing, etc.) to their NSL Managers.

D. Multi-domain Multi-tenant Architecture -example 2

Creation of slices across a federated environment is a complex task, in terms of slice decomposition (per-domain), both in the construction phase and (to assure the performance maintenance) in running phase. T.Taleb, I.Afolabi et.al., recently proposed in [17] a hierarchical multi-domain orchestration architecture (see adapted Figure 3). They introduced a *Multi-domain Service Conductor* (MSC) stratum, to perform service management across federated domains. The MSC analyses and maps the service requirements of incoming slice requests onto appropriate administrative domains and maintains the desired service performance during service lifecycle. Below MSC, a *Cross-domain Slice Coordinator* is defined for each slice, which aligns cloud and networking resources across federated domains and carries out the (LCM) operations of a multi-domain slice. It also establishes and controls inter-domain transport layer connectivity, assuring the desired performance.

In [17], a multi-domain NSLI can combine several *Fully-Fledged NSIs* that belong to distinct administrative domains, to get an E2E multi-domain (i.e., federated) NSLI. The constituent Fully-Fledged NSIs, instantiated in different administrative domains, can be called NSSI of the multi-domain NSLI.

When a slice request is received from a 3rd party, a sequence of actions will be performed [17]: 1) mapping of the service requirements onto capability requirements; 2) translating the capability requirements into: a. NSLI resource requirements (compute, storage, networking); b. NSLI topology and connectivity type, policy, isolation and security requirements; 3) identifying the infrastructure-domains with the required resources, able to assure the E2E NSLI functional and operational requirements; 4) instantiating NSSIs in each infrastructure domain and then "stitching" them to create the federated NSLI; 5) run-time coordination management operations across different domains for maintaining the E2E NSLI service integrity.

The architecture introduces (at top level) a novel plane - *Service Broker* (SB) to handle incoming slice requests from verticals, *Mobile Virtual Network Operators* (MVNO), and application providers.

The main SB operation are: NS *admission control* and negotiation, considering service aspects; management of slice user/owner relationship enabling a direct tenant interface with the MSC plane; billing and charging; NSLI scheduling, i.e., start and termination time related with slice composition and decommission.

The SB collects abstracted service capability information regarding different administrative domains, creating a global service support repository. The SB interacts with the Operating/Business Support System (OSS/BSS) in order to collect business, policy, and administrative information, when handling slice requests. Each domain will have a dedicated Orchestration plane, involving the NFV style architecture for the management and control.

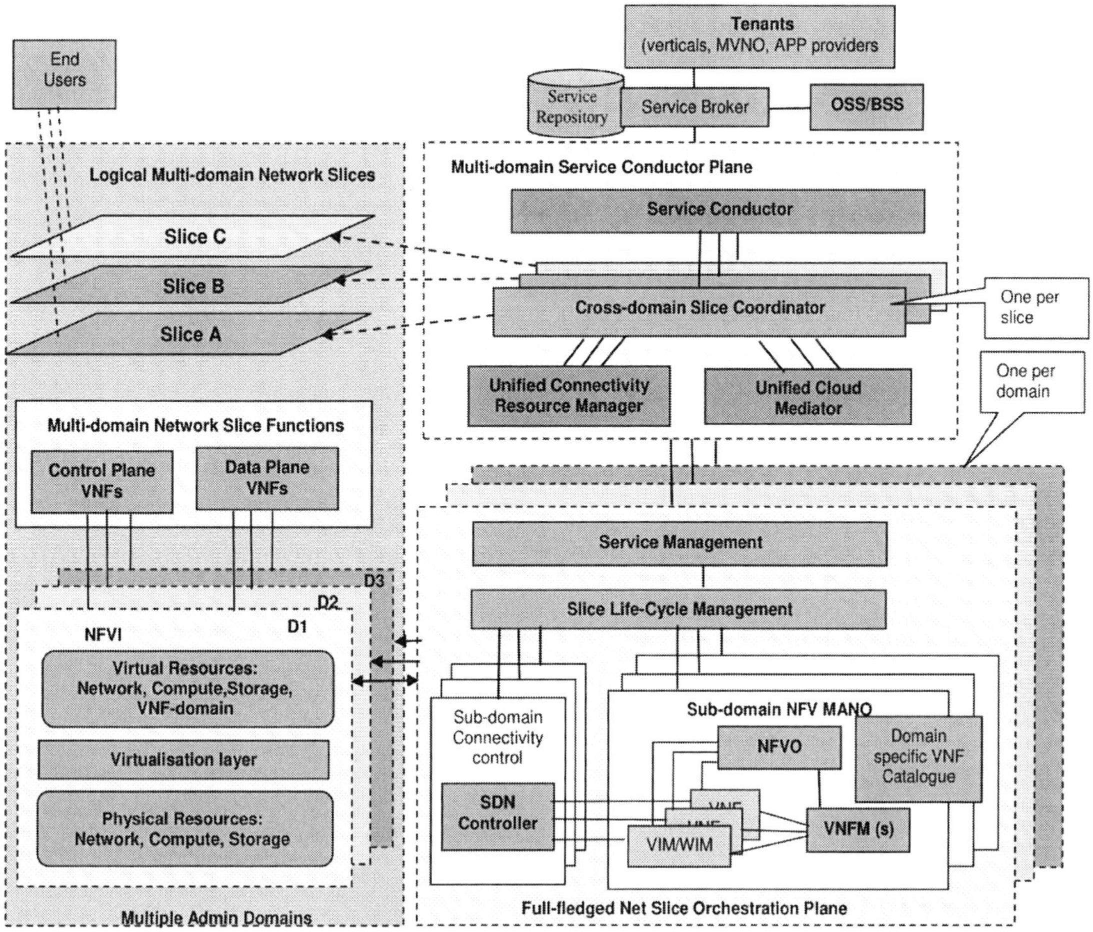

Figure 3. Multi-domain Multi-tenant slicing architecture example 2 (adapted from [17])

IV. NETWORK SLICING DESIGN AND PREPARATION

The design and preparation activities are very important in slicing technology. Among others, catalogues of available services and resources must be constructed in advance to slice instantiation, usable by the tenants in order to select a slice model fitted to their needs.

The general steps performed by the management and orchestration (i.e., higher layers in the architecture examples 1 and 2: NSLO and RO in Example 1; Service Broker and Service Conductor in Example 2) for a slice instance creation are [18]: a. Service ordering; b. Network slice resource description; c. Admission control; d. Optimization and Resource Reservation; e. Network slice preparation.

Service ordering: the NSL provider should construct a *Service Catalogue* (business-driven), containing for each service a *service template*, i.e., a framework to specify the service offering. The Catalogue contains NSLs specifications optimized for different usage scenarios: general 5G services like enhanced Mobile Broadband (eMBB), massive Machine Type Communications (mMTC), and ultra Reliable Low Latency Communications (uRLLC), or vertical-specific applications. A service template includes all information required to drive the deployment of an NSL, e.g.: the NSL (technology-agnostic) *topology*, NSL network requirements (functional, performance, security), temporal, *geolocation* and other operational requirements [18]. The NSL provider offers APIs to tenants, to express their needs and giving them access to the Service Catalogue, where the tenant can select the service template that best matches its requirements. Some parameters and attributes can be customized by the tenant. The result of this dialogue is a catalogue driven NSL *service order* containing information to be mapped on RAN, transport, and core network domains). The Slice Orchestrator entity of the system should process such information.

Network Slice Resource Description: this step creates a resource-centric view of the ordered NSL. Different levels of implementations (NSL-IL) can be defined (for a higher flexibility and better adaptation to the tenant needs) [18]. The NSLO extracts the relevant content from a resource viewpoint (e.g., the *NSL topology*, NSL network requirements) and constructs an NSL-IL for the NSL instance, i.e.: the NSL topology serves to identify which NS(s) need to be deployed for the NSL, retrieving the corresponding NS descriptor(s) from the NS Catalogue; the deployment option is selected for each descriptor (*NS descriptor ID, NS FlavorID, NS-IL ID*), that best matches the features and the performance level required for the NSL; a NSL-IL is constructed by referencing the selected triplet(s).

Admission Control: the target NSL-IL specifies the resources needed for the tenant's demands. Now, an *admission control* (AC) will be enforced on the ordered NSL-IL, from a resource viewpoint, to decide acceptance /rejection for deployment. Several types of information are needed [18] in this process: (1) the NSL instance resource requirements (resources to be allocated for each VNF instance and virtual link, affinity/anti-affinity rules applicable between VNF instances, reliability requirements for each VNF instance and virtual link; (2) the geographical region(s) where each VNF is needed; (3) the time intervals for activation of the NSL instance; (4) information of the PoPs (Points of Presence) (and the WAN network(s) connecting them) to which the NSL provider is subscribed. Such information is available partially at the NSL orchestrator and partially at RO; therefore, these two functional blocks need to cooperate within the AC acting.

Optimization and *Resource Reservation*: if several variants of NSL-ILs are found feasible by the AC, then RO can run an algorithm to select an optimal solution (note that this is a multi-criteria optimization problem). Afterwards, RO may proceed with resource reservation; it sends resource reservation requests to the underlying VIM(s)/WIM(s). The hard and soft nature of this reservation depends on the use case and NSL provider's policies.

Network Slice Preparation: this is the last step prior to get an operational NSL. It consists of setting up all that is required to manage the NSLI throughout its life cycle, i.e., from commissioning (instantiation, configuration, and activation) to decommissioning (de-activation and termination) (see 3GPP TS 28.801 V.15.1.0 [7]). It comprises preparation of the network environment; designing and on-boarding the NSL descriptor.

For the preparation of the network environment, the NSL Orchestrator performs (see Figure 2) the following tasks:

- negotiation with RO a priority level for the NSLI this allows the RO to manage the cases when the NSL instances compete for the same resources, or the case of lack of enough resources.
- instantiation of the management plane of the NSLI (NSL Manager, Tenant SDN Controller, NS Orchestrator, VNFM(s)); it configures these functional blocks, making them ready for the run-time phase.

In parallel to the network environment preparation, the NSL Orchestrator builds up the NSL descriptor, which is a deployment template used by the NSL Manager to operate the NSLI during its life cycle. This descriptor includes the following parts: a set of policy-based workflows; the set of NSL-ILs available for use, constructed in the Network Slice Resource Description phase; VNF configuration primitives at application level and VNF chaining management instructions; information about management data, used for performance management.

V. Collecting Topology Information in a Multi-domain Environment

The focus and contribution of this section is on inter-domain topology discovery and collection of information by a multi-domain capable slice orchestrator (MDSO), in the design and preparation phase of a slice. Given the large number of variants of multi-domain slicing architecture, we consider, in this section, a generic MDSO; it could be equivalent to the NSL Orchestrator in Figure 2 or Multi-domain Service Conductor in Figure 3. The MDSO could belong to a separate third-party business entity (call it Slice Provider), or each administrative domain can be a slice-provider capable (i.e., each domain owns a MDSO). In the last case, peering relationships may exist between the different orchestrators.

The (MDSO) needs to obtain (among others) topological inter-domain information, in order to be able to perform all steps of the design and preparation phase, including the admission control and split of the multi-domain NSL among the respective participating domains.

Usually, the administrative independent domains are not willing to disclose their detailed topology and resource information to third parties. Therefore, a solution based on an abstract summary *overlay network topology* (ONT) [19] could solve the problem. Inside MDSO, a functional *Inter-domain Peering* block can be defined, to provide an *ONT-service* (ONTS), i.e., deliver information on inter-domain topology graph, inter-domain link capacities, etc.

It is supposed here that a given MDSO is the initiator, which plans a new target NSL template (at a specific tenant request or following the Slice Provider initiative). The initiator MDSO obtains (from ONTS) the ONT information. The ONT should be sufficiently rich to span the geographical area of the required NSL.

The objectives of the MDSO, with respect to network topology, are: to get ONT; determine the domains candidates to participate to the required NSL; get information on inter-domain (links) resources; possibly - apply a constrained inter-domain routing algorithm (upon the ONT acquired from ONTS), with an appropriate metric depending on the target NSL characteristics. Using this information, the MDSO can split the multi-domain NSL among the domains.

Figure 4 shows a generic example of a tentative multi-domain NSL (for simplicity the NSL covers only the core network and not the access networks (AN). The required NSL-0 should contain some domains, e.g., D1, D2, D7, D8. The identities of these domains result from the edge specification of the NSL wanted. However, to get a contiguous topology, possible some other transit domains should be involved (e.g., D4, D5), so the final slice will be NSL-1.

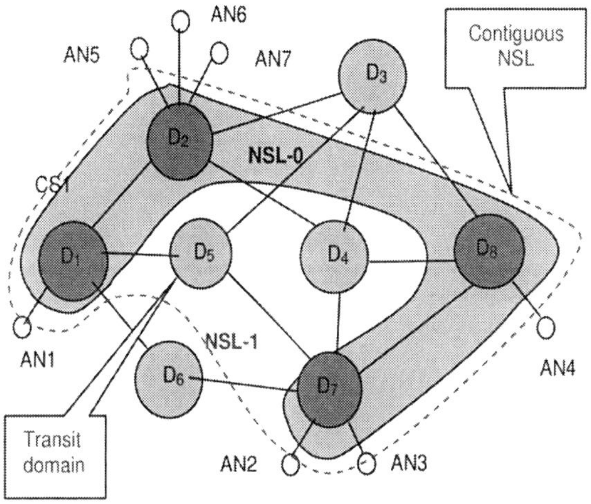

Figure 4. Multi-domain topology of a tentative slice

Depending on the characteristics of the tentative NSL, appropriate routes can be computed (with a specific metric on inter-domain links). For instance, between AN1and AN4, one may have the paths D1, D2, D4, D8 or D1, D5, D7, D8.

If some QoS requirements are imposed in this slice, then resource reservation (see section III) can be done on the inter-domain links.

The sequence of MDSO actions related to collection of information on topology is shortly described below.

The tenant/Slice Provider issues to an initiator MDSO an *NSL_request* (this could be mapped onto a given QoS class) for a target NSL-0.

The initiator MDSO:

1. obtains from ONTS the inter-domain level ONT (topology graph, inter-domain link capacities, etc.). The ONT is sufficiently rich to cover the required NSL.
2. Determines the involved domains in NSL-0 by using the border ingress-egress points knowledge (actually border routers addresses) indicated in the *NSL_request.*
3. Determines a contiguous inter-domain connectivity graph (each domain is abstracted as a node) resulting in an extended NSL-1 (represented by dotted line in Figure 4). In NSL-1 graph, some additional transit core network domains need to be included, e.g., D_4, D_5. Therefore, a contiguous new NSL-1 is defined. Optimization techniques can be applied in this phase.
4. Can run a constrained routing algorithm to determine inter-domain best paths.
5. Can make the first split of the initial NSL among core network domains. This means to produce a set of NSL parameters valid to be requested to each individual domain.
6. Negotiates with each MSDO of a domain, concerning the availability for that part of slice.
7. Run admission control for the overall multi-domain slice.
8. Prepare the networking environment and on–boards the slice template in the catalogue.

VI. Conclusions and Future Work

This paper analyzed several relevant 5G slicing architectures, from the point of view of the management and orchestration functions. It is observed that no unique vision about the scope of orchestration and its hierarchical spilt onto architectural layer exist today.

The second part of the paper has been dedicated to the design and preparation phase of slices. A solution is proposed by this paper related to the problem of inter-domain topology information acquisition and associated actions in a multi-domain context. Note that the solution discussed here only cover a part of information needed by the MDSO initiator in order to split the multi-domain NSL. More complete set of information should be considered (see Section II and III) in order to construct the NSL catalogues. A negotiation dialogue between the initiator MDSO and other MDSOs of peering domain must be performed to provide more information on resources of each domain involved. This will be for future study.

References

[1] 5GPPP Architecture Working Group, "View on 5G Architecture", Version 2.0, December 2017.

[2] NGMN Alliance, "Description of Network Slicing Concept, NGMN 5G P1 Requirements & Architecture, Work Stream End-to-End Architecture", Version 1.0, Jan. 2016.

[3] J. Ordonez-Lucena, et al., "Network Slicing for 5G with SDN/NFV: Concepts, Architectures and Challenges", IEEE Communications Magazine, 2017, Citation information: DOI 10.1109/MCOM.2017.1600935.

[4] X. Foukas, G. Patounas, A. Elmokashfi, and M. K. Marina, "Network Slicing in 5G: Survey and Challenges", IEEE Communications Magazine, May 2017, pp.94-100

[5] P. Rost, et al., "Network Slicing to Enable Scalability and Flexibility in 5G Mobile Networks", IEEE Communications Magazine, Vol.55, May 2017, pp.72-79.

[6] ETSI GR NFV-EVE 012 V3.1.1 (2017-12), Release 3 "NFV Evolution and Ecosystem; Report on Network Slicing Support with ETSI NFV Architecture Framework".

[7] 3GPP TR 28.801 (V15.0.0) (09-2017): "Telecommunication management; Study on management and orchestration of network slicing for next generation network".

[8] 3GPP TS 28.530, "Management of 5G networks and network slicing; Concepts, use cases and requirements", Rel.15, April2018.

[9] A. Galis "Network Slicing- A holistic architectural approach, orchestration and management with applicability in mobile and fixed networks and clouds", http://discovery.ucl.ac.uk/10051374/ [retrieved: April, 2019].

[10] ETSI GS NFV 002 v1.2.1 2014-12, "NFV Architectural Framework".

[11] ETSI GS NFV-IFA 009 V1.1.1 (2016-07) "Network Functions Virtualisation (NFV); Management and Orchestration; Report on Architectural Options". Technical Report.

[12] ETSI GR NFV-IFA 028 V3.1.1 (2018-01): "Network Functions Virtualisation (NFV) Release 3; Management and

Orchestration; Report on architecture options to support multiple administrative domains" Technical Report.

[13] ONF TR-526, "Applying SDN Architecture to 5G Slicing", April 2016.

[14] K.Katsalis, N.Nikaein, and A.Edmonds, "Multi-Domain Orchestration for NFV: Challenges and Research Directions", 2016 15th Int'l Conf. on Ubiquitous Computing and Communications and International Symposium on Cyberspace and Security (IUCC-CSS), DOI: 10.1109/IUCC-CSS.2016.034, ttps://ieeexplore.ieee.org/document/7828601

[15] N. F. Saraiva de Sousa, D. A. Lachos Perez, R. V. Rosa, M. A. S. Santos, and C. E. Rothenberg, "Network Service Orchestration: A Survey", 2018, https://arxiv.org/abs/1803.06596 [retrieved: April, 2019].

[16] I. Afolabi, T. Taleb, K. Samdanis, A. Ksentini, and H. Flinck, "Network Slicing & Softwarization: A Survey on Principles, Enabling Technologies & Solutions", IEEE Communications Surveys & Tutorials, Mar. 2018.

[17] T. Taleb, I. Afolabi, K. Samdanis, and F. Z. Yousaf, "On Multi-domain Network Slicing Orchestration Architecture & Federated Resource Control", http://mosaic-lab.org/uploads/papers/3f772f2d-9e0f-4329-9298-aae4ef8ded65.pdf [retrieved: April, 2019]

[18] J. Ordonez-Lucena, et al., "The Creation Phase in Network Slicing: From a Service Order to an Operative Network Slice", European Conference on Networks and Communications (EuCNC), 2018, https://arxiv.org/abs/1804.09642 [retrieved: April, 2019]

[19] F. Verdi, M. F. Magalhaes, "Using Virtualization to Provide Interdomain QoS-enabled Routing", Journal of Networks, April 2007, pp. 23-32.

Privacy Risk in the IoT Environment: the Need for a Multiple Approach According to the GDPR Principles

Giovanni De Marco

Freelance Engineer - Data Protection Consultant
UNIDPO associate
Napoli, Italy
Email: gdemarco@demarcoconsulting.it

Abstract—**The Internet of Things environment poses many problems of technological, socio-technical and legal nature. Many efforts have been made to solve the several technical challenges and issues arising from the peculiar characteristics of IoT devices, but none of them seems to be decisive at present. Moreover, the user's behaviour is almost always excluded from the premises of these approaches, causing them to be systematically weak towards non-proactive attitudes of end users. In particular, the relationship between risk awareness and the attitude towards privacy preserving behaviours seems to be undervalued. Outside of that, the centralized system on which common Internet devices work is not suitable in the IoT environment, asking for decentralized methods. Referring to the principles of the General Data Protection Regulation UE/679/2016 may be the key to a global approach to both the technical and non-technical challenges that the IoT environment presents. The objective of the paper is to delimit the problem's contours, as they emerge from the analysed technical, legal and sociological contributions, and therefore to propose an optimization of the management strategies for the protection of personal data in the Internet of Things ecosystem.**

Keywords–IoT; GDPR; Privacy by Design; Data Protection by Design and by Default; Privacy Risk Awareness

I. INTRODUCTION

Under the acronym IoT -standing for *Internet of Things*- are grouped several technologies from a vast variety of contexts and an ultimate definition of the ecosystem going under this term is not easy. An effective logical synthesis is given in [1]: *"an IoT system can be depicted as a collection of smart devices that interact on a collaborative basis to fulfil a common goal."*. These devices are smart in the sense that they have (at least) one sensor and are capable of interacting with other devices, IoT or not IoT, connected to them via a network. IoT technologies have already started flooding our daily life, but their endemic diffusion is yet to come; should there be as much as 20 billions or 47 billions [2] connected devices in 2020, it will make no difference: the set of problems to be faced will be the same. This new kind of technology has distinct peculiarities translating into completely new sets of problems, related to their huge multiplicity, their pervasiveness and ubiquity and their primary function, i.e., gathering (personal) data from the physical environment. Consequently, the potential harm that the spreading of IoT devices can cause in terms of privacy and data protection is really high. Many efforts have been made to solve the several technical challenges and issues arising from the peculiar characteristics of IoT devices, but none of them seems to be decisive at present (see, for instance, [1]). Moreover, approaching these issues only from a technical point of view may be not effective, both because these problems are not only technical problems, and because the intrinsic dynamism of these technologies requires a structured strategy covering socio-technical and legal aspects alongside the technical ones. In particular, the relationship between risk awareness and the attitude towards privacy preserving behaviours should be taken into account. The paper is structured as follows: in section II the technical issues proper of the IoT environment are enumerated and legal requirements for data protection are analysed. In section III the focus is on the interaction between these new technologies and user's behaviour. In section IV a synthesis of the various aspects of the problem is presented and a proposal of management strategy compliant to the principles of the European Union *General Data Protection Regulation EU/679/2016* (GDPR) is suggested, as the key to a global approach to both the technical and non-technical challenges that the IoT environment poses. Finally, in section V, the critical points of the suggested strategy are underlined and the path to the future needed work is indicated.

II. TECHNICAL AND LEGAL ASPECTS

The peculiarities of IoT devices result in specific arguments to be addressed in order to keep this technological blossoming under control, in terms of practical usability, security and privacy protection; even if an exhaustive catalogue cannot be determined, due to the intrinsic dynamical and very varied nature of devices falling under the IoT category, the following can reasonably be the list of principal topics (see [3]-[5] for detailed analysis):

A. *Physical and resource restraints*

Particular types of IoT technologies, such as wearable devices or equipment designed to carry out tasks in contexts of high mobility and lack of sources of supply, are characterized by very limited physical resources [3][4]; reduced form factors implying small or no user interface and limited processing and/or supply power are very common features to many IoT products [6][7]. These limitations have immediate repercussions on the security aspects, since many consolidated strategies and techniques prove to be inapplicable due to lack of resources.

B. *Heterogeneity and scale*

IoT products are extremely various, in terms of field of application, conditions of use, physical and technical properties

[3], and their number will be unprecedented [6]. These peculiarities mean big challenges to be faced, such as an adequate network infrastructure able to manage an enormous number of connections and a robust frame to permit the correct interaction between very different IoT devices and between these devices and the infrastructure itself [4][5][8].

C. Authentication and confidentiality

The IoT ecosystem will be an overpopulated world blurring physical and virtual reality. In such a context the usual techniques of authentication lose any effectiveness and, in relation to the heterogeneity aspect, multiple solutions have been and will be implemented; thus, authentication and consequently confidentiality become a much bigger problem to manage compared to the usual Internet context [3][4][9].

D. Updating and accountability

Even though these two points can appear as fringe issues, their impact can be devastating, considering the huge number of devices and, hence, of manufacturers [10]. In the daily usage of the "common" connected devices, like desktop and laptop computers, tablets and smartphones, we take for granted the surveying of basic and application software and the consequent releases of patches and updates [11]. This is going to be even more true in the IoT environment, exactly because of the big heterogeneity of manufacturers and of products. In this scenario, accountability conflicts are an obvious side effect [3][12].

In various percentages, all these aspects contribute to give rise to threats for the personal data processed in the IoT environment; hence, one of the main goals to be achieved in the IoT ecosystem is to provide adequate *trust* strategies and practical solutions. As everything else in the IoT world, this question is very complex, too. For sake of simplicity, we will detect two macro-areas of relationships occurring in the IoT world: the trust of the end user towards the IoT system itself and the trust between different devices collaborating and exchanging data in the network. Both areas have been thoroughly examined in several researches, and many solutions have been proposed (see surveys [1][3]-[5][13]); the central point is that many of these works start from existing technologies and try their best to adapt them to the context of IoT.

The negative side effect of this approach is dual: first, many solutions developed for the "traditional" Internet security scenario, such as encryption protocols [3][4] or IP (Internet Protocol) standard addressing [8] are literally not suitable in the IoT context; second, and even more important, adapting some existing technique or paradigm in an effort to manage unprecedented challenges, as those posed by the IoT environment are, is in conflict with the principles of *Data Protection by Design and by Default*, prescribed in the *General Data Protection Regulation EU/679/2016* (GDPR, [14]) – Article 25.

As explained in [15], these principles are slightly different from the *Privacy by Design* (PbD) principle [16], since the approach adopted in the GDPR focuses on the data protection rather than on privacy. Nevertheless, without any prejudice towards this important distinction, the two concepts are strictly related; so to say, the prescriptions in Article 25 of the GDPR are in a child-parent relationship with the PbD, and, in this context, it's much more useful to focus on the common idea that connects them. In other words, any technical or organisational measure to be undertaken must have as a cornerstone the privacy protection itself. To be even more clear, and referring to the last of the 7 foundational principles of PbD [16], the *mantra* is ***keep it user-centric***.

GDPR compliant solutions should consequently consider, for instance, data preprocessing, i.e., data minimisation, data anonymisation and data pseudonymisation, as told in Recital n. 26, 28 and in Articles 25 and 32 of the Regulation, to reduce the risks *at source*. In any case, the cited countermeasures are not the only possible ones, since the Regulation describes them simply as some amongst many remedies. An important suggestion about further countermeasures to be undertaken comes from the *European Data Protection Supervisor* (EDPS) opinion on online manipulation [17], in which one of the biggest current problems in the context of cybersecurity is identified in the centralisation of personal data in few private hands: *"[...] Big data analytics and artificial intelligence systems have made it possible to gather, combine, analyse and indefinitely store massive volumes of data. Over the past two decades, a dominant business model for most web-based services has emerged which relies on tracking people online and gathering data on their character, health, relationships and thoughts and opinions with a view to generating digital advertising revenue. These digital markets have become concentrated around a few companies that act as effective gatekeepers to the internet and command higher inflation-adjusted market capitalisation values than any companies in recorded history."*. The endemic diffusion of IoT products is an obvious aggravating circumstance to these worries; hence, in a *proactive* approach [16], the decentralisation of databases is a fundamental criterion for data protection, in addition to the aforementioned countermeasures. Moreover, strictly related to the issues emerging from this EDPS opinion, there is another very important and challenging novelty introduced with the GDPR, i.e., the *right to be forgotten*, as per article 17 of the Regulation. The practical implementation of this new right of the data subject, i.e., the right to ask for (and to obtain) a complete and definitive cancellation of her/his data held by a specific data controller, would be largely facilitated and better granted by the use of decentralised databases in addition with anonymisation techniques, since a large part of personal data would be, in this scheme, stored locally rather than in a remote server managed by the data controller.

Nevertheless, it is very important to underline that the *ex ante* approach required by the PbD and embedded in the GDPR, is of crucial importance also when the trust problem in IoT is addressed in innovative ways, and thus the proposed solution is the effect of a fresh start. Starting from scratch does not lead, by itself, to achieve the goal: for instance an authentication system relying on the blockchain is *per se* compliant with the decentralization idea, being the blockchain an intrinsically decentralized technology; furthermore the example of the blockchain sounds particularly striking to address the trust management, given the capability of blockchains to ensure trust between participants without relying on a supervising authority. Nevertheless, a blockchain solution could reveal itself to be non-compliant with the PbD principles. For instance, in [18] a very interesting trust system for IoT is developed exploiting the blockchain technology; the system hinges on "promises to be honored" between a *service provider* and a *service consumer*, and the "reputation" of each participant to the chain is brilliantly built up not only from the previous history already stored in the chain, but it is also linked to other trust indicators coming from external environment, so that a new participant to the chain is not obliged to start from "zero trust", but can inherit his (good) reputation from other contexts. All the transactions are encrypted *"[...] to provide confidentiality between the parties [...]"*, but the side effect of this *ex post* privacy countermeasure is that the encryption could also be exploited by malicious consumers to keep their bad reputation hidden; the problem is solved *"[...] publishing the obligations that were not fulfilled in an unencrypted form [...] and linking them to the previous encrypted ones."*. The result is that *"[...] all the non-fulfilled obligations are public."*, and this solution, since the non-fulfilled obligations have immediate negative impact on the reputation of the participant, is hardly acceptable, being the blockchain records immutable and not subject to any impartial trust agency, making it impossible to erase a potential *perp walk* effect caused by the disclosure of non-fulfilled obligations to all other participants.

Moreover, as explained again in [15], not all blockchain systems are compatible with the GDPR (only *private*, i.e. *permissioned*, blockchains and *combined* blockchains can be GDPR compatible) and this means that any measure developed without accounting these legal constraints will be almost useless in a global interconnected virtual market in which the GDPR becomes day by day the main normative reference. This one is far from being a secondary detail: there have been several works addressing the trust issue in IoT through the blockchain technology [19] but, unfortunately, those adopting *public*, i.e., *permissionless* blockchains are intrinsically non-compliant with the GDPR. The risk can be that some technically effective solutions may be implemented and spread, and possibly become established as reference solutions, while they cause in the approach itself a compliance problem.

III. Socio-Technical aspects

As we have seen, the security and trust challenges presented by the growing IoT ecosystem are really arduous; but there are even more problems to be taken into account. Let us refer to another concept expressed in [15], i.e., the fundamental relation:

$$security \neq privacy.$$

This inequality summarizes the real possibility of scenarios in which, despite the computer security countermeasures, no effective privacy protection has been achieved. From this point of view, the aforementioned examples are perfectly suitable.

Another remarkable and extremely concrete example of this kind is the so called *privacy paradox*; this expression refers to a recurring finding of several researchers: very often individuals who claim to be really concerned about their privacy, actually behave in strong contradiction with their statements [3][6][20][21].

As it is clearly understandable, such a phenomenon cannot be easily limited by standard security countermeasures of any kind, being it a disrupting attitude, capable of undermining the system from the inside. An end user who would correctly fulfil all the established security and trust criteria though behaving according to the privacy paradox, could however put her/his personal data under threat, considering that she/he acts with full privileges and authorizations: a perfect example of security without privacy. Furthermore, as stated in [6], the limited resources typical of many IoT devices, in combination with the huge scale of data exchange that we expect with the further diffusion of these technologies, can only worsen this gap between intentions and actual behaviour [22].

These socio-technical aspects seem to be at least as important as the strictly technical ones; in any case, it must be pointed out once more that the consideration of the behaviour of individuals when facing these new technologies is far from being totally clear. In [20], the complexity of these problems is well documented, and the intrinsic difficulty to identify the cause of the phenomenon is underlined. Some studies even question the actual existence of the privacy paradox [23], however, further and more recent evidence, and more strongly related to the IoT blossoming, suggests the contrary [22].

In any case, notwithstanding the fact that the privacy paradox phenomenon must always be estimated while taking into account all the biasing parameters, such as age [22], digital literacy and skills [6], convenience and context [20][24][25], a robust privacy protection strategy cannot afford to ignore it.

Moreover, these behavioural issues interact and intertwine themselves with other aspects of individual's behaviour in articulated technological environments, such as the *herding effect* [26][27], where, in a nutshell, individual's decisions are strongly biased by decisions previously taken by other subjects in a closed social group or category. As underlined in [6], the interaction between these two attitudes of the end users represents a serious threat to any security frame, being these weaknesses *outside* the security system.

As already said, in order to understand the nature of these phenomena, several works have addressed the problem; amongst various interesting aspects emerging from these works, three of them seem particularly relevant in the IoT context: the correlation between individual's digital skills and risk awareness [6][28], the correlation between individual's risk awareness and how coherent are her/his attitude and behaviour in terms of privacy [28] and the "privacy for convenience" mechanism [20][25]. In short, in the sociological literature a direct proportionality relation is detected between digital skills and privacy risks awareness [6]; furthermore, in [29]-[31] the relation between risk awareness and choices in terms of privacy is outlined. Even if no definitive results come out of these researches, the aforementioned aspects are very interesting clues to try to understand which the parameters favouring proactive user's behaviours are.

In addition, in [28], a further interesting assumption is made, i.e., that the incoherence of some behaviours can be explained with the concept of *privacy cynicism*: *"[...] an attitude of uncertainty, powerlessness and mistrust towards the handling of personal data by online services, rendering privacy protection behavior subjectively futile."*. The results of the study seem to confirm the hypothesis, and this sheds even more worries in view of the definitive diffusion of the IoT technologies. This research is also directly linked to other works, like [32][33], in which the tendency to ignore terms and condition of online services is underlined, and it results to be the standard behaviour; moreover the common experience of the average user do aims to a substantial feeling of impotence, being the so called EULA (*End User License Agreement*) perceived as pretty mocking for their length and complexity [34]-[37]. On the Internet, it is even possible to listen for hours and hours to a guy reading some appliance's terms and conditions [38].

Last but not least, the trading of privacy for convenience must be considered in relation to the two previously remarked aspects. This mechanism, analysed in [39], is summarized by the authors stating: "*[...] small incentives, costs or misdirection can lead people to safeguard their data less [...]. Moreover, whenever privacy requires additional effort or comes at the cost of a less smooth user experience, participants are quick to abandon technology that would offer them greater protection. This suggests that privacy policy and regulation has to be careful about regulations that inadvertently lead consumers to be faced with additional effort or a less smooth experience in order to make a privacy-protective choice.*".

IV. Discussion

The scenario described in the previous sections is really complex and challenging, as well as worrying. The unprecedented number of devices that will more and more permeate our daily experience, their multiplicity and the consequent variety of ways of interaction pose very big issues to be solved, in order to have concrete benefits from the IoT ecosystem, rather than achieving an ungovernable myriad of devices collecting, transmitting, comparing and processing personal data without control.

In many cases, the problems are mostly technical [40], and it comes out that much better could have been done by simply applying basic security countermeasures, such as, for instance, data encryption. Nevertheless, the complex relations between new hyper-connected technologies and human behaviour pose even bigger problems. Many researches reveal disconcerting attitude towards the possible use and misuse of personal data widespread on the Internet, to the point where individual's behaviours become really difficult to understand and explain [41][42], but these events cannot be regarded as totally conscious and aware behaviours.

Once again, it is appropriate to refer to the GDPR principles and prescriptions in order to correctly address the whole set of problems. Besides the already mentioned principles of Data Protection by Design and by Default, we should consider another fundamental prescription of the GDPR, i.e., the necessity of a risk assessment for any potential harmful data processing in order to support the central concept of accountability of the data controller, on which the whole regulation hinges.

Indeed, the Data Protection Impact Assessment (DPIA) is a legal obligation under Article 35 of the regulation. This obligation, together with the Data Protection by Design and by Default principle, can be taken as a jumping-off point to imagine a solution, which may be seen as a natural application of the GDPR prescriptions.

- *Data management model in relation to privacy risks intrinsic to IoT technologies and compliance criteria to the privacy by design and privacy by default principles*
  Article 35, paragraph 1 of the GDPR prescribes: "*Where a type of processing in particular using new technologies, and taking into account the nature, scope, context and purposes of the processing, is likely to result in a high risk to the rights and freedoms of natural persons, the controller shall, prior to the processing, carry out an assessment of the impact of the envisaged processing operations on the protection of personal data. A single assessment may address a set of similar processing operations that present similar high risks.*". It looks pretty clear that this prescription does apply to IoT technologies; this means that any data controller dealing with IoT devices is obliged to undergo a DPIA process and to evaluate its results in order to comply with the EU/679/2016 Regulation. Moreover, in article 35, paragraph 7, is told that: "*The assessment shall contain at least:*
  (a) *a systematic description of the envisaged processing operations and the purposes of the processing, including, where applicable, the legitimate interest pursued by the controller;*
  (b) *an assessment of the necessity and proportionality of the processing operations in relation to the purposes;*
  (c) *an assessment of the risks to the rights and freedoms of data subjects referred to in paragraph 1; and*
  (d) *the measures envisaged to address the risks, including safeguards, security measures and mechanisms to ensure the protection of personal data and to demonstrate compliance with this Regulation taking into account the rights and legitimate interests of data subjects and other persons concerned.*".
  In other words, an evaluation of the risk inherent in personal data processing intrinsic to the usage of an IoT device is necessarily included into any compliance process to the GDPR; the evaluation must detail and specify the techniques adopted in order to ensure personal data protection during the operation of the device. In this sense, amongst the DPIA results, the countermeasures put in place to respond to the basic principles of *privacy by design and by default* must also appear. All these DPIA outcomes can be stored in a database managed by a third party Authority (it could be, for instance, the EDPS, or a further Authority related to the EDPS). In this way, any (new) IoT device would be automatically classified and archived in this public database, and, alongside the device, the database would register the details of the risk level for each processing and of the countermeasures implemented to mitigate those risks; the crucial task of the managing Authority would be the harmonisation of each device's DPIA results, so to have an evaluation scale as homogeneous as possible. Something similar already happens with many privacy-friendly services, such as, for instance, the *DuckDuckGo* browsing service [43]; however, in order to ensure real impartiality, the involvement of a supervisory Authority appears necessary, as was the case, for example, with the *Privacy Flag* project [44]. The harmonization process is for sure a critical point of the whole management strategy; nevertheless, in accordance with Articles 40 et seq. of the GDPR, the diffusion of common *codes*

of conduct could be the shared background on which to build a widely supported reference frame for the comparison of different services and devices in terms of privacy risk. Indeed, respecting determined codes of conduct approved by the EDPS, would mean, by itself, ensuring the compliance to well known, shared and detailed data protection criteria.
For how much it concerns, instead, possible cases of unreliable or untruthful DPIAs, they come under the more general casuistry of infringements of the GDPR, and they must be treated as breaches of the accountability principle; in the same way, here is not considered the extreme case in which the use of a prior consultation is needed (article 36 of the GDPR).

- *Basic risk mitigation criteria*
Given that a detailed description of each specific situation would be unachievable, precisely because of the already examined extreme heterogeneity of the IoT ecosystem, it is, in any case, possible to identify two macro-categories: indoor devices and outdoor devices. For devices belonging to the first category, they will, in almost all cases, be connected to a trusted Local Area Network (LAN); thus, for these equipments, the basic criterion for risk reduction must include the implementation of strict anonymisation and/or pseudonymisation procedures which, together with the use of a local database for data storage, must lead to a standard for the transmission of data outside the LAN on the basis of which only data rendered appropriately anonymous must be able to reach the central management server of the device. In other words, inside of the trusted LAN the user's personal data are normally processed in order to safeguard the quality of the service provided through the device and its customization by means of the progressive learning of user's tastes and preferences, so that the appeal and the convenience of the specific IoT device are not compromised. On the other hand, only data made anonymous according to the techniques indicated above will be sent to the main external server of the considered equipment, thus safeguarding the possibility, for the manufacturer, to carry out statistical processing on the data processed by his own devices, but in anonymous form. For the second category, namely that of outdoor devices, the problems are greater, as they cannot rely on the support of a trusted LAN. However, there is nothing to prevent from reproducing the previous scheme by sending user's personal data to a private server, that is to say inside of the user's trusted LAN; at this point an application related to the device and operating locally in the trusted LAN, provides for the anonymization and/or pseudonymisation of the data and the subsequent sending of the data made anonymous to the central server of the device. Alternatively, a second personal device could play the role of the trusted LAN and of the local storage space, for instance taking advantage of a smartphone generated Personal Area Network (PAN) or through some other sort of short range connection between the IoT device and the user's smartphone. In addition, for such equipment, the default setting should provide for the deletion of all data whose sharing with the central server of the device is indispensable for the use of the service itself (e.g., geolocation data in the navigation devices) at the end of every single usage. This kind of data processing policy would be of great help also to fulfil the obligations in terms of *right to be forgotten*. These countermeasures obviously have nothing to do with the security issues of data transmission, which must be addressed and resolved beforehand, so that this granular privacy management system can be based on a solid foundation of computer security, avoiding incurring cases like that illustrated in [40]. For instance, symmetric cryptography could be the right choice due to cost and power restraints [7], and an OTP (One Time Password) second security level may be the solution to improve security by pairing the IoT device with the user's smartphone. However, this aspect has no trivial solution, given that, as already mentioned, IoT devices are almost never suitable for the application of standardized security methods due to their limited resources; therefore this aspect must certainly be deepened, although this deepening goes beyond the scope of this contribution.

- *Real time signalling of the risk level based on the settings in terms of protection of personal data of the device*
As already seen, to obtain adequate levels of protection of personal data it is absolutely essential to take into due account the behavioural aspects of the end user. From what we have seen in section III, it appears necessary to implement a mechanism that, with immediacy and without interfering with the functions of the device, is able to signal in real time to the user the level of risk to which the user is exposed. Furthermore, this indicator must take into account all the possible modifications to the device settings that impact on data protection, so that the signalling changes instantaneously and consistently according to the specific settings chosen, so to allow the user an effective, rapid and conscious balancing between practicality of use and risk for personal data. In consideration of the scheme illustrated in the previous two points, this can be achieved through a chromatic signalling system on board the device, or shown through an application specifically related to the device, by correlating to each different setting of the personal data management parameters (which is normally a possibility already included in almost all network devices or applications) a different colour signal. For example, imagining a scale on five levels, you would have:
(1) Bright green: high personal data protection level and privacy safeguarding.
(2) Yellow-green: medium-high personal data protection level. Good privacy safeguarding.
(3) Yellow: medium personal data protection level. Privacy safeguarding acceptable: some risks.
(4) Orange: medium-low personal data protection level. Privacy safeguarding weak: significant risk.
(5) Red: low personal data protection level. Bad privacy safeguarding: high risk.

The scale can obviously be deepened by adding more levels and the corresponding colour nuances beyond these five sample levels. This dynamic signalling system would allow the user to choose the balance point between practicality of use and data protection that best suits her/his needs. In other words, with reference to the previous point, the level of protection chosen may or may not include anonymisation as well as automatic deletion of navigation data, but these choices, accompanied by the corresponding signal indicating the level of risk, would certainly be more aware, even in the case of "unscrupulous" users who, knowingly, choose the most dangerous settings for the protection of their personal data.

In this way, associating in real time with each change in the settings a signal of the corresponding level of protection of personal data, it is possible to actively oppose the tendency of users to yield to the dynamics of *privacy for convenience*, which, as the literature on this topic shows, are often not very conscious dynamics because of the lack of perception of the risks to which the users are exposing themselves. Such a privacy risk management frame, explicitly thought to maximize the protection of user's data, could nevertheless be of great convenience for the manufacturers too, since any choice made in a context of maximum understandability of the privacy risk could hardly leave room for litigations seizing on the lack of awareness. In other words, an increase in user's privacy risk awareness can be the most effective strategy not only to let individuals make their choices in the most conscious way, but also to build up a proactive environment involving users and manufacturers, in order to reduce the sense of impotence in front of personal data violations and misuses that, in the long term, could ultimately bring to a "lose-lose" situation, into which, obviously, no one would be glad to get.

Nevertheless, the obvious premise to all these considerations is the compliance to the GDPR and the fair play of all manufacturers and players in the cyber-market.

V. CONCLUSION AND FUTURE WORK

The IoT technologies are expected to become a pervasive aspect of the life of us all in the very near future. Its special characteristics, such as the unprecedented number of devices, their ubiquitous nature and the capability of making virtual and physical world blur together, outline an intrinsic duplicity in this incoming revolution: it promises to drastically transform our way of living, but it also poses threats to the privacy of us all end users as never before. The profound interaction, almost a symbiosis, between IoT devices and the surrounding world, including human beings, forces a multiple approach in order to frame the problem and then have chances of solving it; in this regard, the principles stated in the GDPR appear even more as the correct guidance to lead the way. Waiting for ambitious, visionary and fascinating projects of self-protecting personal data to come true [45], we need to develop right now an effective strategy to manage this paradigm shift.

This contribution proposes a general strategy of approach to these problems which puts the respect of norms on the protection of personal data, first of all the GDPR, above the identification of technical solutions. Moreover, the strict interaction between IoT technologies and human beings also means a strict interaction between user's behaviour and personal data protection, this reflecting itself in the need of integrating, into the technical solution, practical and effective signalling of the risks to which the user is exposed when using a specific IoT device or equipment. The proposed strategy tries to solve these problems by means of rearrangement and optimisation of already existing technologies and solutions. The legal obligation to undergo a DPIA is a very important starting point, since, at least in markets in which the data protection regulation is the GDPR or a *GDPR like* regulation, it can be the starting point on which to build the crucial component of the strategy proposed, i.e., the existence of a common standard for the evaluation of risk levels between different IoT devices. As already underlined, this task should include the involvement of a supervisory Authority to ensure the necessary level of impartiality for all parties involved; nevertheless, the current panorama already offers systems that compare various services in terms of privacy protection, and these examples can act as a reference point for a comparison platform as broad and shared as possible. Hence, amongst many possible and needed next steps to be made, two appear more urgent: the development of a prototype application which implements the signalling system taking into account any possible configuration of the data parameters of a significant selection of IoT device, and the testing of this prototype application in therms of usability and risk awareness increase on a sample of users.

ACKNOWLEDGMENT

The author would like to sincerely thank the reviewers for the great help given. Their ability in highlighting critical points and in indicating all necessary modifications has been decisive to improve this contribution.

REFERENCES

[1] S. Sicari, A. Rizzardi, L. A. Grieco, and A. Coen-Porosini, "Security, privacy and trust in Internet of Things: The road ahead," Computer Networks, vol. 76, 2015, pp. 146–164.

[2] "IoT numbers vary drastically: devices and spending in 2020," 2017, URL: https://www.wespeakiot.com/iot-numbers-devices-spendings-2020/ [retrieved: may, 2019].

[3] C. Maple, "Security and privacy in the internet of things," Journal of Cyber Policy, vol. 2, no. 2, 2017, pp. 155–184.

[4] Z. Yan, P. Zhang, and A. V. Vasilakos, "A survey on trust management for Internet of Things," Journal of network and computer applications, vol. 42, 2015, pp. 120–134.

[5] A. Al-Fuqaha, M. Guizani, M. Mohammadi, M. Aledhari, and M. Ayyash, "Internet of things: A survey on enabling technologies, protocols, and applications," IEEE Communications Surveys & Tutorials, vol. 17, no. 4, 2015, pp. 2347–2376.

[6] M. Williams, J. R. C. Nurse, and S. Creese, "The Perfect Storm: The Privacy Paradox and the Internet-of-Things," in 2016 11th International Conference on Availability, Reliability and Security (ARES), 2016, pp. 644–652.

[7] K. A. RafidhaRehiman and S. Veni, "Security, Privacy and Trust for Smart Mobile devices in Internet of Things – A Literature Study," IJARCET, vol. 4, no. 5, 2015, pp. 1775–1779.

[8] H. Ma, "Internet of Things: Objectives and Scientific Challenges," Journal of Computer Science and Technology, vol. 26, no. 6, 2011, pp. 919–924.

[9] "Internet of Things Security and Privacy Challenges," 2018, URL: https://reolink.com/internet-of-things-security-privacy-challenges/ [retrieved: may, 2019].

[10] "The Internet of Things will be vulnerable for years, and no one is incentivized to fix it," 2014, URL: https://venturebeat.com/2014/08/23/the-internet-of-things-will-be-vulnerable-for-years-and-no-one-is-incentivized-to-fix-it/ [retrieved: may, 2019].

[11] "IoT Security Upgradability and Patching," 2016, URL: https://www.ntia.doc.gov/files/ntia/publications/ota_ntia.pdf [retrieved: may, 2019].

[12] "IoT and Blockchain Convergence: Benefits and Challenges - IEEE Internet of Things," 2017, URL: https://iot.ieee.org/newsletter/january-2017/iot-and-blockchain-convergence-benefits-and-challenges.html retrieved: may, 2019].

[13] A. S. Neeraj and A. Singh, "Internet of Things and Trust Management in IoT - Review," IRJET, vol. 03, no. 6, 2016, pp. 761–767.

[14] "Regulation (EU) 2016/679 of the European Parliament and of the Council of 27 April 2016 on the protection of natural persons with regard to the processing of personal data and on the free movement of such data, and repealing Directive 95/46/EC (General Data Protection Regulation) ," 2016, URL: https://eur-lex.europa.eu/legal-content/EN/TXT/PDF/?uri=CELEX:32016R0679&from=EN [retrieved: may, 2019].

[15] N. Fabiano, "Internet of things and blockchain: Legal issues and privacy. the challenge for a privacy standard," in 2017 IEEE International Conference on Internet of Things (iThings) and IEEE Green Computing and Communications (GreenCom) and IEEE Cyber, Physical and Social Computing (CPSCom) and IEEE Smart Data (SmartData). IEEE, Jun. 2017, pp. 727–734.

[16] A. Cavoukian, "Privacy by Design The 7 Foundational Principles," 2016, URL: https://www.ipc.on.ca/wp-content/uploads/resources/7foundationalprinciples.pdf [retrieved: may, 2019].

[17] "Opinion3/2018EDPS Opinion on online manipulation and personal data," 2018, URL: https://edps.europa.eu/sites/edp/files/publication/18-03-19_online_manipulation_en.pdf [retrieved: may, 2019].

[18] R. Di Pietro, X. Salleras, M. Signorini, and E. Waisbard, "A blockchain-based trust system for the internet of things," in Proceedings of the 23Nd ACM on Symposium on Access Control Models and Technologies. ACM, Jun. 2018, pp. 77–83. [Online]. Available: http://doi.acm.org/10.1145/3205977.3205993

[19] X. Zhu and Y. Badr, "Identity Management Systems fot the Internet of Things: A Survey Towards Blockchain Solutions," Sensors, vol. 18, no. 12, 2018. [Online]. Available: http://www.mdpi.com/1424-8220/18/12/4215

[20] S. Barth and M. D. T. de Jong, "The privacy paradox: Investigating discrepancies between expressed privacy concerns and actual online behavior - A systematic literature review," Telematics and Informatics, vol. 34, no. 7, 2017, pp. 1038–1058.

[21] "The EMC Privacy Index," 2014, URL: https://www.emc.com/collateral/brochure/privacy-index-global-in-depth-results.pdf [retrieved: may, 2019].

[22] M. Williams, J. R. C. Nurse, and S. Creese, " *"Privacy is the boring bit"*: User Perceptions and Behaviour in the Internet-of-Things," in Proceedings of the 15th Annual Conference on Privacy, Security and Trust (PST) Aug. 28–30, 2017, Calgary, AB, Canada. IEEE Computer Society, Aug. 2017, pp. 181–190, ISBN: 978-1-5386-2487-6.

[23] T. Dienlin and S. Trepte, "Is the privacy paradox a relic of the past? an in-depth analysis of privacy attitudes and privacy behaviors," European Journal of Social Psychology, vol. 45, no. 3, 2015, pp. 285–297.

[24] A. Gambino, J. Kim, S. S. Sundar, J. Ge, and M. B. Rosson, "User disbelief in privacy paradox: Heuristics that determine disclosure," in Proceeding of the 2016 CHI Conference Extended Abstracts. ACM, May 2016, pp. 2837–2843.

[25] S. Kokolakis, "Privacy attitudes and privacy behaviour: A review of current research on the privacy paradox phenomenon," Computers & Security, vol. 34, Jan. 2015, pp. 122–134.

[26] H. Sun, "A longitudinal study of herd behavior in the adoption and continued use of technology," MIS Quarterly: Management Information Systems, vol. 37, 12 2013, pp. 1013–1041.

[27] Y. E. Huh, J. Vosgerau, and C. K. Morewedge, "Social defaults: Observed choices become choice defaults," Journal of Consumer Research, vol. 41, Oct. 2014, pp. 746–760.

[28] C. P. Hoffmann, C. Lutz, and G. Ranzini, "Privacy cynicism: A new approach to the privacy paradox," Cyberpsychology: Journal of Psychosocial Research on Cyberspace, vol. 10, no. 4, 2016.

[29] L. M. Coventry, D. Jeske, and P. Briggs., "Perceptions and actions : Combining privacy and risk perceptions to better understand user behaviour," in Symposium on Usable Privacy and Security (SOUPS) 2014. USENIX Association, Jul. 2014, pp. 443–457.

[30] I. Oomen and R. Leenes, Privacy Risk Perceptions and Privacy Protection Strategies. Springer, 05 2008, vol. 261, pp. 121–138.

[31] L. Shepherd, J. Archibald, and I. Ferguson, "Perception of risky security behaviour by users: Survey of current approaches," in Human Aspects of Information Security, Privacy, and Trust: First International Conference, HAS 2013, Held as Part of HCI International 2013, Las Vegas, NV, USA, July 21-26, 2013. Proceedings, vol. 8030. 0302-9743, 07 2013, pp. 176–185.

[32] Y. Bakos, F. Marotta-Wurgler, and D. R. Trossen, "Does anyone read the fine print? consumer attention to standard-form contracts," The Journal of Legal Studies, vol. 43, no. 1, 2014, pp. 1–35.

[33] J. A. Obar and A. Oeldorf-Hirsch, "The biggest lie on the internet: ignoring the privacy policies and terms of service policies of social networking services," Information, Communication & Society, vol. 0, no. 0, 2018, pp. 1–20.

[34] "How Silicon Valley Puts the 'Con' in Consent," 2019, URL: https://www.nytimes.com/2019/02/02/opinion/internet-facebook-google-consent.html [retrieved: may, 2019].

[35] A. M. McDonald and L. F. Cranor, "The cost of reading privacy policies," A Journal of Law and Policy for the Information Society, vol. 4, no. 3, 2008, pp. 543–568.

[36] "You're not alone, no one reads terms of service agreements," 2017, URL: https://www.businessinsider.com/deloitte-study-91-percent-agree-terms-of-service-without-reading-2017-11 [retrieved: may, 2019].

[37] "Reading the Privacy Policies You Encounter in a Year Would Take 76 Work Days," 2012, URL: https://www.theatlantic.com/technology/archive/2012/03/reading-the-privacy-policies-you-encounter-in-a-year-would-take-76-work-days/253851/ [accessed: 2019-03-04].

[38] "Here's nine hours of a guy reading the entire terms and conditions for the Amazon Kindle," 2017, URL: https://news.avclub.com/here-s-nine-hours-of-a-guy-reading-the-entire-terms-and-1798259191 [retrieved: may, 2019].

[39] S. Athey, C. Catalini, and C. Tucker, "The digital privacy paradox: Small money, small costs, small talk," National Bureau of Economic Research, Working Paper w23488, Jun. 2017.

[40] "European Commission orders mass recall of creepy, leaky child-tracking smartwatch," 2019, URL: https://cyware.com/news/european-commission-orders-mass-recall-of-creepy-leaky-child-tracking-smartwatch-e61468b3 [retrieved: may, 2019].

[41] J. P. Carrascal, C. Riederer, V. Erramilli, M. Cherubini, and R. de Oliveira, "Your browsing behavior for a big mac: Economics of personal information online," in Proceedings of the 22Nd International Conference on World Wide Web. ACM, May 2013, pp. 189–200. [Online]. Available: http://doi.acm.org/10.1145/2488388.2488406

[42] "Amazon Key asks users to trade privacy for convenience," 2017, URL: https://money.cnn.com/2017/10/26/technology/business/amazon-key-privacy-issue/index.html [retrieved: may, 2019].

[43] "DuckDuckGo," 2019, URL: https://duckduckgo.com/ [retrieved: may, 2019].

[44] "The Privacy Flag Project," 2019, URL: https://privacyflag.eu/ [retrieved: may, 2019].

[45] G. J. Tomko, D. S. Borrett, H. C. Kwan, and G. Steffan, "Smartdata: Make the data "think" for itself," Identity in the Information Society, vol. 3, no. 2, 2010, pp. 343–362.

BeamMaP: Beamforming-based Machine Learning for Positioning in Massive MIMO Systems

Chong Liu, Hermann J. Helgert

School of Engineering and Applied Science, The George Washington University,
Washington, DC 20052
Email: cliu15@gwu.edu, hhelgert@gwu.edu

***Abstract*—Existing positioning techniques can mostly overcome problems caused by path loss, background noise and Doppler effects, but multiple paths in complex indoor or outdoor environments present additional challenges. In this paper, we propose *BeamMaP* that can instantaneously locate users after training input data and steer the beams efficiently in a distributed massive Multiple-Input Multiple-Output (MIMO) system. To simulate a realistic environment, we evaluate the positioning accuracy with channel fingerprints collected from uplink Received Signal Strength (RSS) data, including Line-of-Sight (LoS) and Non-Line-of-Sight (NLoS), in the training data sets. Based on the adaptive beamforming, we employ the Rice distribution to sample the current mobile users locations in the testing data sets. Our simulation results achieve Reduced Root-Mean-Squared Estimation Error (RMSE) performance with increasing volume of training data. We prove our proposed model is more efficiency and steady in the positioning system compared with kNN and SVM. The results also demonstrate the effectiveness of the adaptive beamforming model in the testing process.**

Keywords–outdoor localization; machine learning; data training; beamforming.

I. Introduction

The future developing technologies, such as autonomous vehicles, Virtual Reality (VR) and the Internet of Things (IoT), are relying on more efficient bandwidth distribution and higher speed transmission [1] [2] [3] [4]. The next generation of wireless networks 5G should provide more accurate localization of the connected mobile devices and distribute the limited bandwidth in a more efficient way. Some new technologies employed in localization, especially including the massive Multiple-Input Multiple-Output (MIMO) and beamforming technologies, are explored in the 5G system [5]. The innovative design of massive MIMO disclosed in some publications utilizes a large number of upgraded array antennas (more than one hundred) to multiplex messages for several devices simultaneously. This component, implemented in future Base Stations (BSs), has been shown to play an essential role in positioning of Mobile Users (MUs) in cellular networks, including increased spectral efficiency, improved spatial diversity, and low complexity [6]. More importantly, a distributed design for massive MIMO is beneficial for positioning due to the better spatial diversity, which will be employed in this paper. Some proposed solutions applying the MIMO positioning techniques are mainly focused on the received signal information from the users, such as the Angle-of-Arrival (AoA), Time-of-Arrival (ToA), and Received Signal Strength (RSS) [7] [8] [9]. These features, singly or in combination, can be used in the localization of mobile users in indoor or outdoor environments.

Even though positioning in cellular networks widely uses the Global Positioning System (GPS) in urban or rural areas, the method becomes unreliable when the Line-of-Sight (LoS) and Non-Line-of-Sight (NLoS) are difficult to distinguish, such as in highly cluttered multipath scenarios (tens meters error) [10]. In some conventional method using the two-step localization techniques, the received LoS signals are processed at different base stations and AoA and/or ToA of each user can be obtained. Then the position of the user can be found by triangulation calculation [8]. However, the LoS path may be damped or obstructed, leading to large positioning errors, as is often the case in complex scenarios. Also, [8] is exploiting channel properties to distinguish LoS from NLoS signal paths, resulting in an improvement of performance. However, a large data gain with a combination of LoS and NLoS signal paths will require high computational complexity.

A. Related work

Big data collections combined with machine learning methods have been mentioned in solving the MUs localization in some of the literature [9] [11] [12]. For example, through collecting RSS, AoA and/or ToA, we typically provide efficient supervised or unsupervised techniques to estimate the coordinates of MUs. Some unsupervised methods, such as k-Nearest Neighbors (kNN), assume that there are many reference users at which vectors of RSS are obtained, and the target MU can be located as a weighted average of the closest k reference positions [11]. Although kNN is able to provide good performance in uniformly distributed references, we have to choose a better regression under the different k dimension, which will generate the large number of input training data and cause higher computational complexity. Additionally, supported machine learning methods, such as Support Vector Machines (SVM) [12] and deep learning methods [9], are explored to predict the coordinates of MUs after collecting amounts of RSSs and/or AoAs through different base stations. However, the method in [9] [12] will cause the estimation to be degraded when the number of MUs increases and interference between cells in the cellular networks becomes dramatically higher.

Based on the features of raw data sets, such as RSS mentioned below in the system, we employ a Gaussian Process Regression (GPR) model to estimate the locations of MUs, discussed in [7]. GPR is a generic supervised learning method designed to solve regression and probabilistic classification problems. Under this method, an unknown nonlinear function is assumed to be random, and to follow a Gaussian Process (GP). In contrast to kNN and SVM, GPR is able to provide probabilistic output, for example, the posterior distribution of the MU position, after given an online measurement and a set of fingerprints with RSS vectors. Besides, without LoS and NLoS identification, this machine learning approximation method can efficiently identify MUs positions after training with limited reference users, and it significantly decreases the computational complexity as well.

B. Our Approach and Contributions

In this paper, we propose a novel positioning technique, called Beamforming-based Machine Learning for Positioning (*BeamMaP*) to meet the above challenges. *BeamMaP* employs a machine learning regression technique based on the efficient beamforming transmission patterns in order to estimate the location of MUs. *BeamMaP* can instantaneously predict the locations of MUs after generating the Machine Learning (ML) regression network model and help the base stations to distribute beams in an efficient way. Moreover, *BeamMaP* can implement the real-time detection to update the input data sets including LoS and NLoS multipath channels.

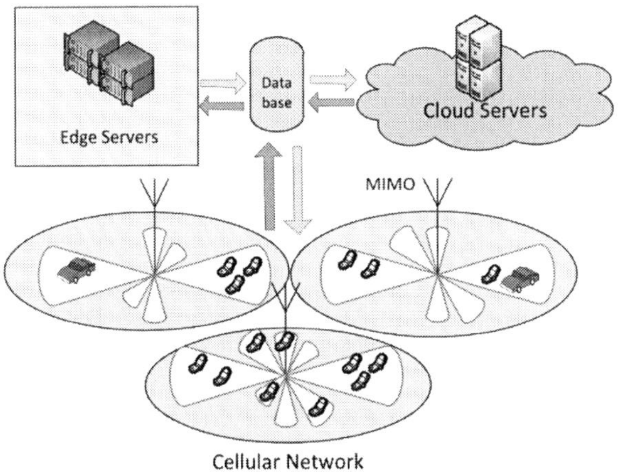

Figure 1. BeamMap positioning system in cellular networks.

The *BeamMaP* design is illustrated in Figure 1. The beamforming system in each BS installed massive MIMO antennas serves more than one MU. When a MU transmits on the uplink, we can obtain a vector of RSS (or a fingerprint) comprising LoS and NLoS multipaths measured by the massive antennas array in the BS. The detected uplink signals or RSS information are collected and submitted to the edge servers or cloud servers for calculation. Then the adaptive array systems can formulate a single or more beams with different weights to different directions according to the demands of MUs. Furthermore, MUs can process signals from a single MIMO base station, provided the BS and users were synchronized, which can be easily implemented by a two-way protocol by adding some additional overheads [13]. Besides, in order to avoid the pilot contamination occurred in massive MIMO system between cells, some reuse pilot schemes and particular modulation technology, such as Orthogonal Frequency-Division Multiplexing (OFDM) or Code-Division Multiple Access (CDMA) should be applied in our system [14]. Furthermore, massive MIMO systems combined with beamforming antenna technologies are considered to play a key role in the next generation wireless communication systems [15]. Optimal beamforming techniques, such as adaptive beamforming, are mentioned to be employed in localization and provide energy saving of the MIMO systems. *BeamMaP* employs adaptive beamforming as a candidate in building the testing process. Compared with switched beamforming, adaptive beamforming can cover a larger area of MUs when the number of beams and bandwidths range shared are the same, and it also offers more comprehensive interference rejection [15]. Therefore, *BeamMaP* not only can improve the efficiency of coverage for users, but can also result in significant reduction in energy consumption of base stations.

The following contributions are made in this paper:

- We employ a supervised machine learning regression approach to accurately locate the MUs in a single cellular system.
- We present extensive performance results from simulations exploring the effects of various componential parameters.
- We prove our proposed machine learning method is more efficiency and steady in the positioning system compared with kNN and SVM.
- We use an adaptive beamforming method to build the testing users model to increase the efficiency of the ML model.

The rest of this paper is organized as follows: Section II presents the *BeamMaP* positioning system design, including the input data sets collected for training, the machine learning model and testing process. In Section III, we present performance evaluation results to analyze the impact factors. Section IV presents our conclusions.

II. BeamMaP Positioning System Design

Driven by the above motivations, the *BeamMaP* framework is illustrated in Figure 2.

We firstly need to collect the fingerprints (RSS vectors) to generate the training data sets. Due to the unknown directions of MUs, we assume the beams weights in a uniform distribution trying to cover more MUs in comparison with the random distribution in the beginning status. Then, *BeamMaP* starts to explore the GPR method to train the collected raw data arrays, which include the RSSs of LoS and NLoS in the scenario. Some parameters set up in the ML regression model are able to be estimated in the training process. Furthermore, in order to avoid the overfitting in the training process, we follow the K^*-fold cross-validation to partition a sample of input data sets into complementary subsets, performing one subset as the training set (the orange blocks in the figure), and validating the analysis on the other subset as the testing set (the blue blocks in the figure). Multiple rounds of cross-validation are performed using different partitions, and the validation results are combined (e.g., averaged) over the rounds to give an estimate of the model's predictive performance. Moreover, we choose the Root-Mean-Square Estimation Error (RMSE) as the metric, which will be introduced in the experiment section. We set up a threshold σ to analyze the training process of the ML model. If the RMSE in the model is larger than σ, it will back up to the beginning of the ML process, requiring that

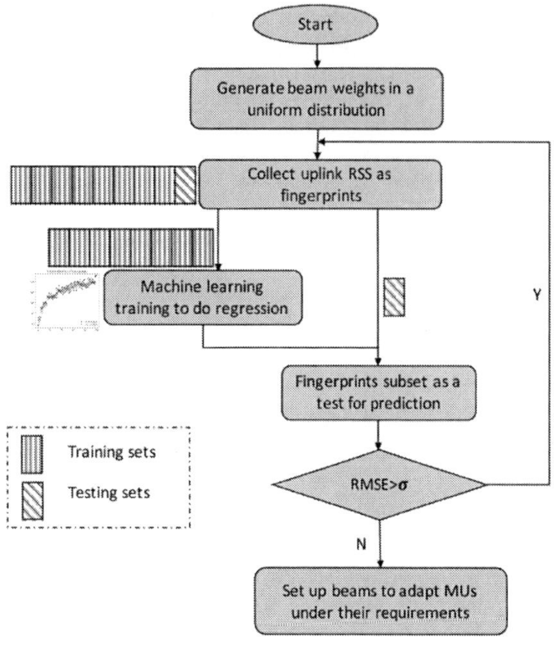

Figure 2. BeamMap's positioning system framework (adaptive σ chosen)

TABLE I. BASIC NOTATIONS REPRESENTATIVE.

Notation	Corresponding meaning
K, k	the number of antennas in BS, antenna index
M, m	the number of MUs, MU index
ρ	the transmission power of each mobile user
S	the number of training reference MUs
s_m $\mathbf{s}$	the symbol vector transmitted by the mth mobile user, the sum symbol vectors transmitted by all MUs
r_k $\mathbf{r}$	the received symbol vector at the kth antenna in BS, the sum signal strength vectors in BS
$h_{k,m}$ $\mathbf{H}$	fading uplink channel between mth MU and kth antenna , the uplink channel matrix between all MUs and BS antennas
$\alpha_{k,m}$ $q_{k,m}$	small-scale fading coefficient between mth MU and kth antenna , large-scale fading coefficient between mth MU and kth antenna
n_k $\mathbf{n}$	the additive white Gaussian noise vector received in the antenna k the sum additive white Gaussian noise vectors in the BS
$p_{k,m}$ $\mathbf{p}_m$	RSS of mth MU at kth antenna in BS uplink RSS vectors of MU in all antennas of BS
n	the Path Loss Exponent (PLE) for LoS or NLoS channel
σ_s	the shadow fading in dB
$\widetilde{\mathbf{p}}_a$ $\widetilde{\mathbf{P}}$	the uplink RSS vector for the ath training MU the training data matrix for S coordinates of MUs chosen
$\widehat{\mathbf{p}}_m$	the uplink RSS vector of the mth testing MU
$(\widehat{\mathbf{x}}_m, \widehat{\mathbf{y}}_m)$ $(\widetilde{\mathbf{x}}_m, \widetilde{\mathbf{y}}_m)$	the coordinate of the mth testing user in vector $(\widehat{\mathbf{x}}, \widehat{\mathbf{y}})$ the coordinate of the mth training user in vector $(\widetilde{\mathbf{x}}, \widetilde{\mathbf{y}})$
$[\mu^x]_m$ $[\sigma^x]_m$	the estimation value of the mth testing user $\widehat{\mathbf{x}}_m$-coordinate the variance for errors of user $\widehat{\mathbf{x}}_m$-coordinate

the ML process continue the training process. If the RMSE is less than or equal to σ, the parameters in the model have been generated successfully in the estimation, and we should adjust the system to set up beams to cover the mobile users under their requirements. The detailed model is designed in the following part.

A. *Input Data Sets for Training – Uplink Transmission in 5G MIMO Model*

In this section, we build a wireless network model to locate Mobile Users (MUs) in a single cellular 5G network system. We assume one Base Station (BS) with K ($K \geqslant M$) antennas to serve M single-antenna MUs in the cell. We consider MUs simultaneously transmit M symbols, $\mathbf{s} = (s_1, ..., s_M)^T$, the massive MIMO antennas array in the base station can receive the sum signal strength vectors $\mathbf{r} = (r_1, ..., r_K)^T$:

$$\mathbf{r} = \sqrt{\rho}\mathbf{H}\mathbf{s} + \mathbf{n} \tag{1}$$

Here ρ is a constant denoting the transmission power of each mobile user; $\mathbf{H}$ is the $K \times M$ channel matrix, with $h_{k,m} = \alpha_{k,m}\sqrt{q_{k,m}}, \forall k = 1, ..., K$ and $m = 1, ..., M$ as the transmission channel element for mth mobile user uplink to the kth antenna in the base station. $\alpha_{k,m}$ and $q_{k,m}$ are respectively the small-scale and large-scale fading coefficients. The large-scale fading $q_{k,m}$ (related to shadowing noise variance) is assumed to be a constant in the urban or suburban environment, and the small-scale fading $\alpha_{k,m}$ is considered to be an independent and identically distributed complex Gaussian distribution (Rayleigh distribution), with $\alpha_{k,m} \sim \mathcal{CN}(0, 1)$. In addition, $\mathbf{n} = (n_1, ..., n_K)^T$ represents the additive white Gaussian noise vector given by $n_k \sim \mathcal{N}(0, 1)$. We list the basic notations in Table I.

From (1), we are considering the sum signal strength vectors from all users to antennas. In order to separate the multiple users RSS in $\mathbf{r}$, we have different schemes to extract the kth user RSS r_k. In order to capture the effective signals, the pilot signal vector s_k should be modulated as mutually orthogonal during transmission so that it can satisfy $s_i^H \cdot s_j = 0$ $(i \neq j)$ [14]. Particular modulation techniques, such as OFDM or orthogonal CDMA employed as the coded schemes in the transmission systems. Minimum Mean Square Error (MMSE) being an appropriate solution, we can simply extract each user signal strength from the combination signals of all MUs and then distinguish the signals and noise by setting a threshold in the receiving part.

$$\mathbf{s}^H\mathbf{r} = \sqrt{\rho}\mathbf{H} + \mathbf{s}^H\mathbf{n} \tag{2}$$

Taken all assumptions into account, we can acquire the single user's RSS as $p_{k,m}$ in:

$$p_{k,m} = \left\|s_m^H r_k\right\|^2 = \rho \left|h_{k,m}\right|^2 = \rho\alpha_{k,m}^2 \left|q_{k,m}\right| \tag{3}$$

Also, we accumulate all MU uplink power vectors from all antennas in BS: $\mathbf{p}_m = [p_{1,m}^{\mathrm{dB}}, p_{2,m}^{\mathrm{dB}}, ..., p_{K,m}^{\mathrm{dB}}]$. Established on the received power model, we can acquire the power data sets by converting (3) to the log distance path-loss model but they are limited in the lower frequency and small cellular environment [16]. Additionally, through our experiment, we observe the COST Hata model (COST is a radio propagation model that extends the urban Hata model to cover a more elaborate range of frequencies, which is developed by a European Union Forum for cooperative scientific research) also cannot adapt the different higher frequency 5G network system, even though it is popularly employed in the urban cellular network [17]. Also, the path loss models currently employed in the 3GPP 3D model is the ABG model form but without a frequency dependent parameter and additional dependencies on base station or terminal height, and only used in LoS scenario [18]. Therefore, we are considering to employ the Close-in (CI) free space reference distance Path Loss (PL) model, which is noted multi-frequency and covers the 0.5-100 GHz band [18]. The CI-PL model is also transferred from (3) to adapt LoS and NLoS realistic scenarios through adding the free space path loss and optimizing the parameters:

$$P_{loss}(f_c, d)[\text{dB}] = \text{FS}(f_c, 1\text{m}) + 10n\log_{10}(\frac{d}{1\text{m}}) + \sigma_s \quad (4)$$

Here f_c is the carrier frequency in Hz, n is the Path Loss Exponent (PLE) describing the attenuation of a signal passing through a channel, d is the distance between MU and each antenna in BS and σ_s is the shadow fading in dB. The Free Space Path Loss (FS) in (4) is standardized to a reference distance of 1 m. FS with frequency f_c is given by:

$$\text{FS}(f_c, 1\text{m}) = 20\log_{10}(\frac{4\pi f_c}{\nu}) \quad (5)$$

In (5), ν denotes the speed of light. The CI-PL model is represented as the relationship between propagation path loss and TX-RX distance based on a straight line drawn on a two-Dimensional (2D) map, passing through obstructions, and used in both LoS and NLoS environment. While we are considering CI-PL in the urban cellular network of 5G system model, the parameters are measured as $n = 2.0, \sigma_s = 4.1$dB in LoS and $n = 3.0, \sigma_s = 6.8$dB in NLoS using omnidirectional antennas [18]. Due to the same transmission power assumed for each MU, we can use the CI-PL model as the RSS parameters to acquire the training data sets.

Additionally, for each MU's uplink transmission, multi-paths signals can be received by multiple antennas, some of them are LoS and the others are NLoS responses. So we consider the LoS probability model in the current 3GPP/ITU model in the MIMO receiving part when setting up the training data. It means the uplink response array of MIMO antenna includes LoS and NLoS components for each MU. From [18], in terms of Mean Squared Error (MSE) between the LoS probability from the data and the models, we choose the d_1/d_2 model as follows:

$$p(d) = \min(\frac{d_1}{d_2}, 1)(1 - e^{-\frac{d}{d_2}}) + e^{-\frac{d}{d_2}} \quad (6)$$

where d is the 2D distance between MU and antennas in meters and d_1, d_2 can be optimized to fit a scenario of parameters (we choose $d_1 = 20$, $d_2 = 39$ because it acquires minimum MSE in adapting the urban scenario).

B. Machine Learning Model

Given the RSS vector $\mathbf{p}_m = [p^{\text{dB}}_{1,m}, p^{\text{dB}}_{2,m}, ..., p^{\text{dB}}_{K,m}]$, our goal is to find the position of the mth MU in the two dimensional plane, denoted by (x_m, y_m). We build the functions $f_x(.)$ and $f_y(.)$ which take the uplink RSS vector $\mathbf{p}_m$ of a given user m as input and provide the user's location coordinates (x_m, y_m) as output, and try to learn as follows:

$$x_m = f_x(\mathbf{p}_m) \quad \text{and} \quad y_m = f_y(\mathbf{p}_m), \forall x_m, y_m \quad (7)$$

Derived from CI-PL model for the input training model, the learning functions can be classified as a nonlinear regression problem. We follow GPR as a supervised machine learning approach, with a training phase and a test phase, to learn $f_x(\mathbf{p}_m)$ and $f_y(\mathbf{p}_m)$. In the training level, we consider RSS vector $\mathbf{p}_m$ derived from the CI-PL model in both LoS and NLoS conditions. Prior to it, we need to acquire the antennas coordinates, the training users coordinates, and some other parameters. In the testing phase, the RSS vectors of the testing users will be chosen distributed according to a Rice distribution to satisfy the adaptive beamforming pattern, whose location coordinates are unknown.

C. Training and Beamforming-based Prediction Phase

GPR uses the kernel function to define the covariance over the objective functions and uses the observed training data to define a likelihood function. Gaussian processes are parameterized by a mean function μ_x and covariance function $\mathbf{K}(\mathbf{p}_i, \mathbf{p}_j)$, which means $f_x(.), f_y(.) \sim \mathcal{N}(\mu, \sigma^2)$. Usually the mean matrix function is equal to 0, and the covariance matrix function, also known as kernel matrix function, is used to model the correlation between output samples as a function of the input samples. The kernel matrix function $\mathbf{K}(.,.)$ contains $k(\mathbf{p}_i, \mathbf{p}_j), \forall i, j = 1, ..., M$ as the entries to define the relationship between the RSS of the users. We usually use a weighted-sum of squared exponential and linear functions, which servers the stationary component and non-stationary component respectively, to generate the regression function:

$$k(\mathbf{p}_i, \mathbf{p}_j) = \upsilon_0 e^{-\frac{1}{2}\mathbf{A}\|\mathbf{p}_i - \mathbf{p}_j\|^2} + \nu_1 \mathbf{p}_i^T \mathbf{p}_j \quad (8)$$

Here $\mathbf{A} = \textbf{diag}(\eta_k), \forall k = 1, ...K$. It will cover the LoS and NLoS matching with each MU. So the parameters vector $\Lambda = [\upsilon_0, \mathbf{A}, \upsilon_1] = [\upsilon_0, \eta_1 ..., \eta_K, \upsilon_1]$ can be estimated from the training data. In order to learn the target vector $\overline{\Lambda}$, we choose S coordinates of MUs as the training data matrix $\widetilde{\mathbf{P}}$ denoted $\widetilde{\mathbf{P}} = [\widetilde{\mathbf{p}_1}, \widetilde{\mathbf{p}_2} ... \widetilde{\mathbf{p}_S}]$ and use the maximum-likelihood method to predict the $(\widetilde{x}, \widetilde{y})$-coordinates. According to the property of a Gaussian process, we can acquire the learned vector $\overline{\Lambda}$ by employing the maximum-likelihood of the $S \times 1$ training $\widetilde{\mathbf{x}}$-coordinate vector:

$$\overline{\Lambda} = \underset{\Lambda}{\text{argmax}} \log(p(\widetilde{\mathbf{x}}|\widetilde{\mathbf{P}}, \Lambda)) \sim N(\widetilde{\mathbf{x}}; 0, \widetilde{\mathbf{K}}) \quad (9)$$

The parameter vector follows as GP, which is a non-convex function as shown in the [7], and can not be solved well in the training process. Several methods introduced in [19], such as stochastic gradient descent, mini-batching or momentum, can help to solve the non-convex problem. Established on the ML method in the training problem, we decided to employ stochastic gradient descent method [19] to obtain the optimum vector $\overline{\Lambda}$ in convergence to a local maximum.

In the prediction phase, the predictive distribution $p(\widehat{\mathbf{x}}_m|\widetilde{\mathbf{P}}, \widetilde{\mathbf{x}}, \widehat{\mathbf{p}}_m)$ in terms of posteriori density function, is applied as estimation of the testing user $\widehat{\mathbf{x}}_m$-coordinate, which also follows the Gaussian distribution with mean $[\mu^x]_m$ and variance $[\sigma^x]_m$, $\widehat{\mathbf{x}}_m|\widetilde{\mathbf{P}}, \widetilde{\mathbf{x}}, \widehat{\mathbf{p}}_m \sim \mathcal{N}([\mu^x]_m, [\sigma^x]_m)$:

$$[\mu^x]_m = \sum_{a=1}^{S} k(\widehat{\mathbf{p}}_m, \widetilde{\mathbf{p}}_a)[\widetilde{\mathbf{K}}^{-1}\widetilde{\mathbf{x}}]_a,$$

$$[\sigma^x]_m = k(\widehat{\mathbf{p}}_m, \widehat{\mathbf{p}}_m) - \sum_{a=1}^{S}\sum_{b=1}^{S} k(\widehat{\mathbf{p}}_m, \widetilde{\mathbf{p}}_a)[\widetilde{\mathbf{K}}^{-1}]_{ab} \cdot k(\widetilde{\mathbf{p}}_b, \widehat{\mathbf{p}}_m) \quad (10)$$

where the mean $[\mu^x]_m$ indicates the estimation value of test user $\widehat{\mathrm{x}}_m$-coordinate and the variance $[\sigma^x]_m$ represents the variance for errors of user $\widehat{\mathrm{x}}_m$-coordinate. $\widehat{\mathbf{p}}_m$ denotes the received power vector of the mth testing MU, and $\widetilde{\mathbf{p}}_a$ denotes the ath power vector in the received training power matrix $\widetilde{\mathbf{P}}$. For the computational complexity of GPR, we observe from (10), $[\mu^x]_m$ needs to sum up S operations for $\widetilde{\mathbf{K}}^{-1}\widetilde{\mathrm{x}}$, which requires $\mathcal{O}(S^2)$. In total, $[\mu^x]_m$ incurs a time complexity of $\mathcal{O}(S^3)$.

Subsequently, we choose the locations of test MUs based on the beamforming pattern. Beams can be optimized to distribute and spread with the demand users. In the real scenarios, some hot spot areas need large bandwidth and some other areas only need small bandwidth to satisfy with few mobile users. The locations of MUs always follow a Rice distribution. Therefore, the coordinates of test users in positions prediction can be chosen from input fingerprints following a Rice distribution, which will satisfy with the beams distribution in an adaptive way. *BeamMaP* being as a prediction assistant, it will cooperate with a better beamforming scheme to distribute the bandwidths in efficiency. During the experiments, we will compare with switched beamforming patterns which beams are distributed uniformly in the system. Furthermore, we employ the same proposed regression method to estimate the $\widehat{\mathrm{y}}_m$-coordinate of test user. Also, we can acquire the mean $[\mu^y]_m$ and variance $[\sigma^y]_m$ as the predictive parameters.

III. PERFORMANCE EVALUATION

In this section, we conduct simulations to evaluate the performance of *BeamMaP* as the machine learning method in estimating the locations of testing MUs. In order to simulate a realistic environment, we set up the parameters of path loss model based on the 5G 3GPP/ITU Micro-Urban model [18].

TABLE II. PARAMETERS FOR SIMULATION.

Description	Value
Path loss parameters (5G 3GPP/ITU Micro-Urban model [18])	$n = 2.0, \sigma_s = 4.1$dB for LoS, $n = 3.0, \sigma_s = 6.8$dB for NLoS, $d_1 = 20$, $d_2 = 39$
Modulation Scheme	OFDM (Orthogonal CDMA)
MU transmit power	23 dBm (200 mW)
Minimum SNR for channel estimation	1 dBm
Number of antennas in BS	64(8×8),100(10×10),144 (12×12)
Maximum number of training fingerprints	90000
Number of testing MUs	100
The space between antennas	0.12, 0.3, 0.48 m
The space between training MUs	1 m
Threshold to control the training process (σ)	[5, 35] m

A. *Parameters Set Up*

The parameters used in the simulation are shown in Table II. According to the analysis of different environment in Section II-A, the path loss parameters n and σ_s are chosen for adapting the crowded urban area. The MU transmit power is chosen as per LTE standards to be 23 dBm [20]. In practice testing, the minimum SNR required is determined by the normalized mean squared error of the channel estimates [18]. For our simulations, we set the minimum required SNR to 1 dB. Considering that currently the number of MIMO antennas of the BS can be designed from 64 to 156, we assume $K = 64, 100, 144$ antennas uniformly distributed as a 8×8, 10×10 and 12×12 squares. We assume that the MIMO antennas are installed at the center of a cellular network which can distribute the beams in each direction with the same maximum reach. Figure 3 shows an example of the deployment of the base station antennas and the surrounding reference MUs consisting of a squared antennas array with 16 antennas covering $x \in [5, 30]$ and $y \in [10, 70]$ area (meters in unit). The fingerprints for MUs are distributed in a grid covering dimensions $x \in [50, 130]$ and $y \in [20, 140]$. We split the fingerprints into a training part and a testing part, then follow the K^*-fold cross-validation method (i.e., $K^* = 10$) to do the regression and average the result over several runs.

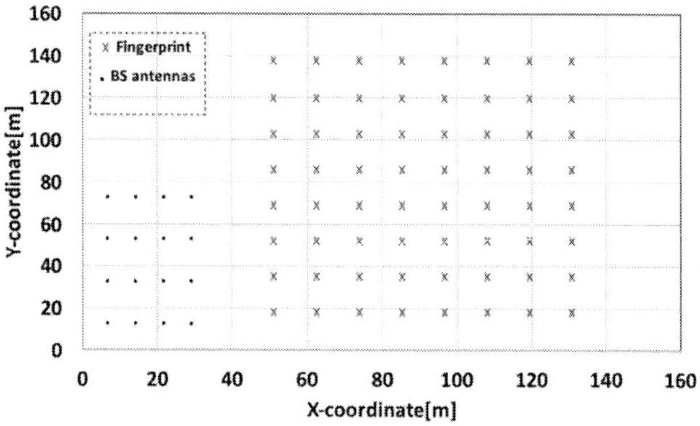

Figure 3. The deployment example of MIMO antennas (BS antennas) and reference MUs (Fingerprint)

The coordinates of MUs and antennas are selected as positive values in the simulation. In order to reduce the interference between the uplink received signals in the massive MIMO, the spacing between antennas can be selected from 0.12 to 0.5 m, which is based on the function of the OFDM signal wavelength [21]. If without considering the influence of the other parameters, we assume the space between antennas be 0.5 m to better differentiate the RSS vectors in the simulation. In addition, we choose $S = 90000$ as the maximum number of fingerprints with 1 meter spacing between MUs in a grid covering about 300 m $\times$ 300 m, which covers 95% of LoS components in the single cellular system. In practice, for example, we can install a cellular BS with a 12×12 square antennas on the top roof of our engineering building located in Washington DC of United States. Each antenna equipped with one transceiver can receive and/or send the signals from and/or to each MU. The coordinates of references MUs will be chosen in a grid around the building, the spaces between MUs are set up as 1 meter. We can use a moving MU in each chosen locations to send the signals to all the receivers in BS each time. The computers as a RSS reader in BS will calculate each RSS vector from the signals of the reference MUs and accumulate all the uplink RSSs as the training data sets. Due to lack of hardware support, the RSS vector $\mathbf{p}_m$ for each MU in antennas is generated from the CI-PL model in (4) and (5), which is proved in the Aalborg, Denmark environment [18].

Meanwhile, each antenna in MIMO can receive LoS or NLoS from the different direction. In order to model the real-life scenario including LoS and NLoS, the RSS matrix $\widetilde{\mathbf{P}}$ as the fingerprints collected from all antennas follows the

LoS and NLoS distribution in (6). We calculate them through generating a probability function in the simulation. During the training phase, while we are learning the parameter vector $\overline{\Lambda}$, we run the training locations on randomly choosing the start points, so as to avoid the convergence to a bad optimal solution. We assume the threshold $\sigma \in [5, 35]$ m, which needs to be feasibly chosen depending on the different training data sets to fit in the experiment. In the testing phase, we choose the Rice distribution of 100 testing users from RSS vectors in fingerprints to efficiently steer beams in a flexible way. The Rice distribution is selected as $R \sim \text{Rice}(50, 1)$ through experiments because of the maximum coverage of a single cell network and variance of spacing in 1 m.

B. *Performance on Metrics*

After RMSE is reaching less than σ, we test the accuracy of the simulation model in using the linear sampling coordinates, which are convenient to observe. For example, we use a 12 $\times$ 12 antenna array located in $x \in [40, 46]$ and $y \in [100, 106]$ area as reference locations. In order to observe the tracking locations in a 'linear' status, we initialize to employ a linear log-function ($y = 50\log x$) to sample the positions of 100 testing mobile users from fingerprints. We can then track the MUs and compare with their true positions, as shown in Figure 4. It is simple to find the estimated position of testing users not far from the linear true positions 'line', where the interval between them can not exceed 8.5 m. Due to the limitation of test users and sampling, we are not able to decide other impact factors for the accuracy of estimation.

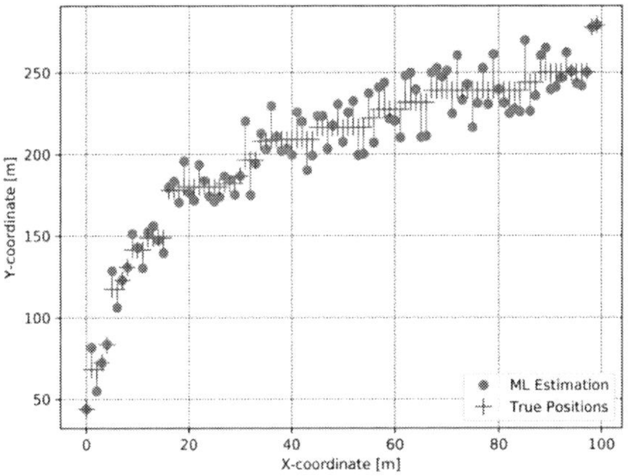

Figure 4. Position estimation in a linear distribution of Testing MUs

Furthermore, we use the Root-Mean-Squared Estimation Error (RMSE) as the metric to analyze the performance of the estimation methods. RMSE is formulated as:

$$\text{RMSE} = \sqrt{\frac{\sum_{m=1}^{\widehat{M}} (\widehat{\mathrm{x}}_m - [\mu^x]_m)^2 + (\widehat{\mathrm{y}}_m - [\mu^y]_m)^2}{\widehat{M}}} \quad (11)$$

where $[\mu^x]_m$ and $[\mu^y]_m$ are the estimation of test user's coordinates $\widehat{\mathrm{x}}_m$ and $\widehat{\mathrm{y}}_m$, respectively. $\widehat{M}$ is the number of testing MUs. We limit the analysis to the RMSE metric.

In Figure 5, we are trying to determine the influence of training samples for different number of antennas in the base station. As the antennas are installed in a fixed space, some of them will receive the LoS signals and others will receive the NLoS signals. The distribution between LoS and NLoS follows the probability function of LoS in (6), as assumed previously. We show 95% confidence intervals from 30 trials for each data point. As observed from Figure 5, we know when the sampling in training locations increases, the RMSE keeps decreasing with fixed antennas size, which means acquiring the higher the accuracy of estimation. When the sampling is the same, more LoS signals will be received in the large size antenna array, which will help to decrease the interference, while fewer NLoS signals will be identified as LoS in the receiver. For example, RMSE in 12×12 antennas is almost half of 8 $\times$ 8 in the same sampling condition. Also, the higher dimension of fingerprints for training will acquire more accuracy estimation in the terms of the increase number of antennas.

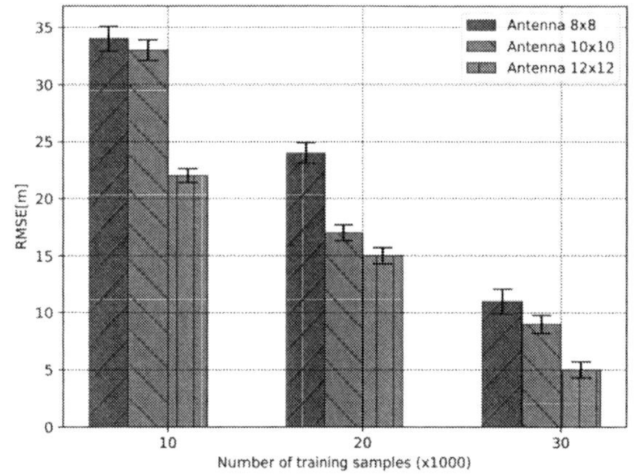

Figure 5. RMSE vs. number of training samples for different size of antennas array

In order to know the effect of antenna size in a MIMO system, we change the spacing between antennas as in Figure 6. The RMSE for different spacing but the same number of antennas shows no significant change. When the space is changed from 0.12 m to 0.30 m, the differential in RMSE for 8 $\times$ 8, 10 $\times$ 10 and 12 $\times$ 12 antennas is 5 m on average. However, comparing the spacing in 0.12 m and 0.48 m, the RMSE is dramatically decreased, caused by the ability of identification between LoS and NLoS, and the size of sampling.

We compare the running time performance and RMSE metric of different machine learning approaches (*BeamMaP*, kNN and SVM) in the dynamic environments. The shadowing noises for LoS and NLoS are set up to change from 1 dB to 4 dB, which can be regarded as different scenarios in practice. The same training data sets are generated through CI-PI model. We run the simulations simultaneously on the three same workstations (Ubuntu 16.04 LTS system on 3.6GHZ Intel Core i7-4790 CPU with eight cores). The results are shown in Table III. In general, with the increase of shadowing noise, the RMSE (in meters) for all approaches gradually becomes larger. Compared with kNN and SVM, RMSE for the proposed *BeamMaP* is obviously smaller. Although the training time for kNN is much less than *BeamMaP* and SVM, the testing time for our proposed is averaged as 0.35 s which is far less than the

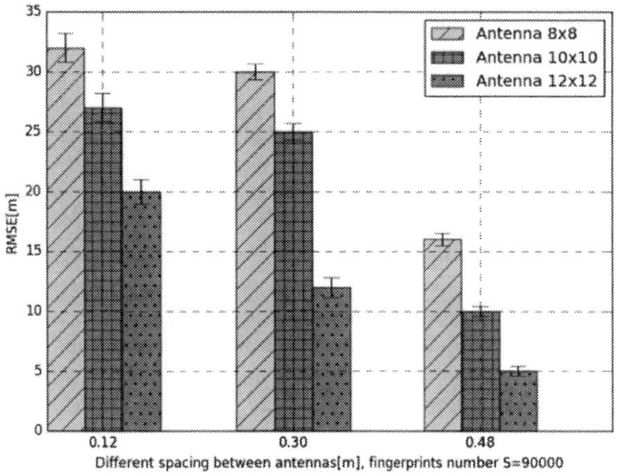

Figure 6. RMSE vs. different spacing between antennas for different size of antennas array

others. The testing time is calculated from 100 testing samples in average.

TABLE III. COMPARISON BETWEEN DIFFERENT APPROACHES.

Shadowing Noise	BeamMap	kNN	SVM
	RMSE[m]		
1 dB	3.5	8.5	10.2
2 dB	8.4	13.2	15.5
3 dB	15.6	20.2	20.4
4 dB	22.3	27.4	30.8
Phase	**Running time**		
Training	20.30 hours	8 hours	21 hours
Testing	0.35 s	1.20 s	0.874 s

kNN being as a unsupervised method, is served as positioning the target MU through collecting and analyzing the closest k reference neighbors. The time complexity known as $\mathcal{O}(KS + kS)$ is depended on the S cardinality of the training data set and the K (the number of antennas) dimension of each sample [11]. Despite SVM is mostly used in the linear condition, our nonlinear problem needs to be transferred into the quadratic problem directly, which involves inverting the kernel matrix. It has complexity on the order of $\mathcal{O}(S^3)$ same with our proposed model. The estimation of this method is based on a subset of the training samples (known as support vectors). However, these two models can only choose LoS signals in the RSS vector of training data sets, the NLoS elements have to be removed and become 0. The imbalance of the training data sets (no distinguishment between LoS and NLoS in the vectors) will degrade the performance of kNN and SVM. The original data sets can influence the RMSE which reaches two times larger than recent simulation. For example, while the shadowing noise is 2 dB, the RMSE for kNN and SVM will become 25 and 30 m. Therefore, the shortest testing time spent and smallest RMSE in the simulation will prove that our proposed model is steadier and better optimized in the much noisy or highly cluttered multipath scenarios; also the gap of the training time between them can be shortened in the future advanced hardware.

Furthermore, even though we choose the testing users from fingerprints in Rice distribution for the estimation process, the adaptive beamforming pattern in BS appears not to be necessary in the machine learning localization. In order to compare adaptive beamforming with switched beamforming, we assume the number of antennas as 12×12 to maximize the sampling ratio. During the testing phase, we model the switched beamforming as a uniform distribution with the same mean and variance as the Rice distribution in adaptive beamforming. In Figure 7, we conclude that adaptive beamforming or Rice distribution in the regression system plays a better role, it only can reach the half of RMSE compared with uniform distribution with the same sampling training index.

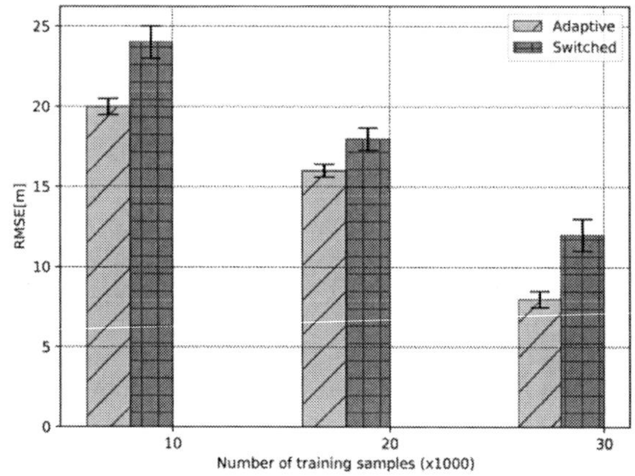

Figure 7. RMSE vs. number of samples for different beamforming patterns

More efficiency for adaptive beamforming is achieved by randomly selecting the testing users similar to Monte-Carlo sampling. The reason is that more testing users are gathered together in one direction for the adaptive pattern, but testing users in uniform distribution (switched pattern) are separately localized, which will accumulate the estimation errors and lead to the increase of RMSE. In addition, the slow offline machine learning process can help to speed up the distribution of bandwidth in adaptive beamforming after employing the faster online testing system. The testing process only needs less than 0.35 s.

IV. CONCLUSION AND FUTURE WORKS

In this paper, we present a *BeamMaP* positioning method, combined with a supervised machine learning approach and an online adaptive beamforming testing process, to estimate the position of mobile users. *BeamMaP* can estimate the location of the MUs within 5 meters deviation, which is much better than some conventional methods like GPS and also is sufficient for beam signals to cover the channels between MU and BS. Numerical results show the accuracy of positioning, as determined by the size of sampling, the dimension of antennas, their quantity and distance, and the number of received LoS and NLoS signals. In comparison with kNN and SVM, our proposed machine learning method is proved more efficiency and steadier for positioning in highly cluttered multipath system. Furthermore, we conclude that the adaptive beamforming pattern can increase the accuracy and efficiency of position estimation in comparison with switched beamforming. However, the RSS fingerprinting methods may fail in changeable environments (e.g., rainy or windy weather) due to the long online training time, and more training data sets in different dimensions should be collected to increase the adaption of positioning system. Moreover, some deep learning or hybrid machine learning methods can be explored and make some improvements in the future research.

REFERENCES

[1] C. Liu, M. Xu, and S. Subramaniam, "A reconfigurable high-performance optical data center architecture," in 2016 IEEE Global Communications Conference (GLOBECOM). IEEE, 2016, pp. 1–6.

[2] M. Xu, C. Liu, and S. Subramaniam, "Podca: A passive optical data center network architecture," Journal of Optical Communications and Networking, vol. 10, no. 4, 2018, pp. 409–420.

[3] M. S. Leeson, "Introductory chapter: The future of mobile communications," in The Fifth Generation (5G) of Wireless Communication. IntechOpen, 2019.

[4] S. K. Routray, P. Mishra, S. Sarkar, A. Javali, and S. Ramnath, "Communication bandwidth for emerging networks: Trends and prospects," arXiv preprint arXiv:1903.04811, 2019.

[5] F. Boccardi, R. W. Heath, A. Lozano, T. L. Marzetta, and P. Popovski, "Five disruptive technology directions for 5G," IEEE Communications Magazine, vol. 52, no. 2, 2014, pp. 74–80.

[6] L. Lu, G. Y. Li, A. L. Swindlehurst, A. Ashikhmin, and R. Zhang, "An overview of massive MIMO: Benefits and challenges," IEEE journal of selected topics in signal processing, vol. 8, no. 5, 2014, pp. 742–758.

[7] S. Kumar, R. M. Hegde, and N. Trigoni, "Gaussian process regression for fingerprinting based localization," Ad Hoc Networks, vol. 51, 2016, pp. 1–10.

[8] N. Garcia, H. Wymeersch, E. G. Larsson, A. M. Haimovich, and M. Coulon, "Direct localization for massive MIMO," IEEE Transactions on Signal Processing, vol. 65, no. 10, 2017, pp. 2475–2487.

[9] J. Vieira, E. Leitinger, M. Sarajlic, X. Li, and F. Tufvesson, "Deep convolutional neural networks for massive MIMO fingerprint-based positioning," arXiv preprint arXiv:1708.06235, 2017.

[10] B. Hofmann-Wellenhof, H. Lichtenegger, and J. Collins, Global positioning system: theory and practice. Springer Science & Business Media, 2012.

[11] L. M. Ni, Y. Liu, Y. C. Lau, and A. P. Patil, "LANDMARC: indoor location sensing using active RFID," Wireless networks, vol. 10, no. 6, 2004, pp. 701–710.

[12] M. Brunato and R. Battiti, "Statistical learning theory for location fingerprinting in wireless LANs," Computer Networks, vol. 47, no. 6, 2005, pp. 825–845.

[13] H. Wymeersch et al., "5G mm wave downlink vehicular positioning," in 2018 IEEE Global Communications Conference (GLOBECOM), 2018, pp. 206–212.

[14] A. Gorokhov, A. F. Naguib, A. Sutivong, D. A. Gore, and J. Tingfang, "Pilot signal transmission for an orthogonal frequency division wireless communication system," Oct. 4 2016, US Patent 9,461,859.

[15] E. Ali, M. Ismail, R. Nordin, and N. F. Abdulah, "Beamforming techniques for massive MIMO systems in 5G: overview, classification, and trends for future research," Frontiers of Information Technology & Electronic Engineering, vol. 18, no. 6, 2017, pp. 753–772.

[16] S. Jung, C. Lee, and D. Han, "Wi-Fi fingerprint-based approaches following log-distance path loss model for indoor positioning," in Intelligent Radio for Future Personal Terminals (IMWS-IRFPT), 2011 IEEE MTT-S International Microwave Workshop Series on. IEEE, 2011, pp. 1–2.

[17] M. Hata, "Empirical formula for propagation loss in land mobile radio services," IEEE transactions on Vehicular Technology, vol. 29, no. 3, 1980, pp. 317–325.

[18] K. Haneda et al., "5G 3GPP-like channel models for outdoor urban microcellular and macrocellular environments," in Vehicular Technology Conference (VTC Spring), 2016 IEEE 83rd. IEEE, 2016, pp. 1–7.

[19] P. Jain and P. Kar, "Non-convex optimization for machine learning," Foundations and Trends® in Machine Learning, vol. 10, no. 3-4, 2017, pp. 142–336.

[20] P. Joshi, D. Colombi, B. Thors, L.-E. Larsson, and C. Törnevik, "Output power levels of 4g user equipment and implications on realistic rf emf exposure assessments," IEEE Access, vol. 5, 2017, pp. 4545–4550.

[21] "Cisco 1250 dipole antenna spacing," 2019, available online: https://community.cisco.com/t5/other-wireless-mobility-subjects/specs-on-distance-between-antennas/td-p/1030478 [retrieved: May, 2019].

Legitimate E-mail Forwarding Server Detection Method by X-means Clustering Utilizing DMARC Reports

Kanako Konno
Department of Computer and Information Sciences,
Graduate School of Engineering,
Tokyo University of Agriculture and Technology
Tokyo, Japan
Email: k_konno@net.cs.tuat.ac.jp

Naoya Kitagawa
Division of Advanced Information Technology
and Computer Science,
Institute of Engineering,
Tokyo University of Agriculture and Technology
Tokyo, Japan
Email: nakit@cc.tuat.ac.jp

Shuji Sakuraba
Application Service Department,
Network Division,
Internet Initiative Japan Inc.
Tokyo, Japan
Email: saku@iij.ad.jp

Nariyoshi Yamai
Division of Advanced Information Technology
and Computer Science,
Institute of Engineering,
Tokyo University of Agriculture and Technology
Tokyo, Japan
Email: nyamai@cc.tuat.ac.jp

***Abstract*—There are several effective spoofed e-mail countermeasures, such as Sender Policy Framework (SPF), DomainKeys Identified Mail (DKIM), and Domain-based Message Authentication, Reporting and Conformance (DMARC). However, these verification methods have an issue of erroneously determining many forwarded e-mails as malicious spoofing e-mails. When an e-mail is forwarded, the sender's IP address is changed to the forwarder's, thus the receiver cannot verify whether the e-mail is legitimate or not. On the other hand, DMARC has a function, which e-mail senders can receive DMARC aggregate reports that include information about e-mails, such as the authentication results of SPF and DKIM. In this paper, we propose a method to classify legitimate forwarding servers by X-means clustering analysis using a large number of summarized DMARC aggregate reports data. In addition, we apply our method to 5,366 e-mail sending servers that send 207,193,987 e-mails in total. As a result of the clustering, our method detects 451 servers as legitimate forwarders' server. As a result of verification of these servers by utilizing the IP blacklists and the spam filter results, we confirmed that 451 servers are legitimate e-mail sending server. On the other hand, 50.17% in median of the e-mails delivered from these 451 servers are erroneously failed in DMARC authentication. Thus, our method can significantly reduce DMARC verification's False Positives, and e-mail server administrators can detect many legitimate forwarded messages.**

***Keywords*–Spoofed e-mail; SPF; DKIM; DMARC; Clustering.**

I. INTRODUCTION

E-mail is one of the most convenient communication services all over the world. However, especially in business, e-mail has a serious problem that spoofed e-mails are increasing rapidly. According to the statistics report of FBI, the total financial damage is 12.5 billion US dollar from October 2013 to May 2018 [1]. Spoofing e-mails are abused by spammers to steal sensitive information or send malicious programs, such as computer virus.

Sender domain authentication has been proposed as an effective method to measure the spoofed e-mails. SPF [2] and DKIM [3] are widely used in the world. In SPF mechanism, the receivers check the sender's SPF record include IP addresses which the senders use to send e-mails, and confirm whether the e-mails senders are legitimate or not. However, SPF cannot verify forwarded messages correctly, because the sender's IP address is changed to the forwarder's IP address which is not included in the sender's SPF record when the e-mails are forwarded. In DKIM, the receivers verify the digital signatures generated from e-mails header and body and confirm whether the e-mail has not been rewritten by spammers. DKIM allows third parties to sign e-mails, thus DKIM has a problem that spoofed e-mails signed by a spammer's own malicious domain pass the verification incorrectly.

DMARC [4] is one of the most effective frameworks which has reporting and policy controlling mechanism in sender domain authentication. DMARC utilizes SPF and DKIM authentication mechanisms. In addition, DMARC has a concept called "alignment" which does not allowed third party's signature. Thus, DMARC is effective method to measure spoofed e-mail, however, DMARC cannot solve the issue that SPF cannot properly verify forwarded messages. For example, when an e-mail which is forwarded and signed by third party's domain, SPF verification is failed and DKIM verification is also failed with DMARC alignment.

DMARC has reporting function that allows a sender to receive "DMARC aggregate report" (hereinafter, this is called DMARC report). This report indicates information, such as e-mails header and the authentication results. In general, DMARC reports are utilized to confirm the effectiveness of sender domain authentications by the e-mail senders. On the other hand, we can observe the transmission behaviors for each e-mail sending servers by analyzing the information of DMARC reports. Moreover, we consider that forwarding servers have similarity in trends of e-mail transmission behaviors.

In this paper, we propose a method to detect legitimate forwarding servers by X-means clustering analysis utilizing massive DMARC reports data. Our approach divides the sender's IP addresses into some clusters. In addition, we identify the forwarder's cluster based on several already-known forwarders' IP addresses. We compare our clustering results and Spamhaus blocklist and results of Internet Service Provider (ISP)'s spam filter in order to evaluate our approach. As a result, our approach detects 451 legitimate forwarding servers that may verified as malicious servers by the conventional verification methods. Thus, e-mail administrators can detect many legitimate forwarding servers by utilizing our method when they know a few forwarding servers, such as ther own organization's servers beforehand.

This paper organized as follows. In Section II, we explain some anti-spam methods as related works. In Section III, we describe the design of our mechanism. Then we show the dataset which we utilize the experiment in Section IV. Section V shows results of our method applying and evaluate the validity of the servers classified as forwarding servers by our method. Finally, we present the concluding remarks in Section VI.

II. Related Work

A large number of anti-spam methods have been proposed over the years. Contents filtering is an effective and widely used anti-spam method. For example, Bayesian Filter [5] [6] is a famous contents filtering method utilizing Bayes theorem. In addition, Natural Language Processing [7], support vector machines [8] [9], and machine learning [10] [11] are widely utilized. In actual operation, therefore contents filtering is high calculation cost, it is used after reducing the number of e-mails to be inspected by other anti-spam methods in advance.

SpamAssassin [12] [13] scores e-mails based on keyword, public database, and Bayesian Filter, etc., in order to detect spam e-mails. This method utilizes several anti-spam methods, such as Blacklist [14] [15] and sender domain authentication methods when the e-mails are received before Bayesian Filter.

Blacklist detects spammers utilizing a list including attackers' IP addresses and domains. Sender domain authentication methods can verify whether the e-mails are spoofed or not based on the information of e-mail senders.

SPF, DKIM, and DMARC are popular methods among sender domain authentication. We explain these three methods in the following subsections, II-A and II-B.

A. SPF & DKIM

SPF and DKIM are widely utilized methods as sender domain authentication.

SPF uses a SPF record to check whether IP address of sender's SMTP server is legitimate or not. SPF record indicates a list of server's IP addresses that the senders may use to send e-mails. The sender domain's administrator should publish an SPF record on their own authoritative DNS server beforehand. The receiver asks the SPF record of the sender's DNS server using sender's Envelope-From domain, then verifies whether the IP address of the sender's SMTP sever is included in the SPF record. However, SPF has a problem that SPF verification cannot authenticate forwarded messages properly, because the IP address of the original SMTP server changes to the IP address of the forwarding server, which is not included in the SPF record.

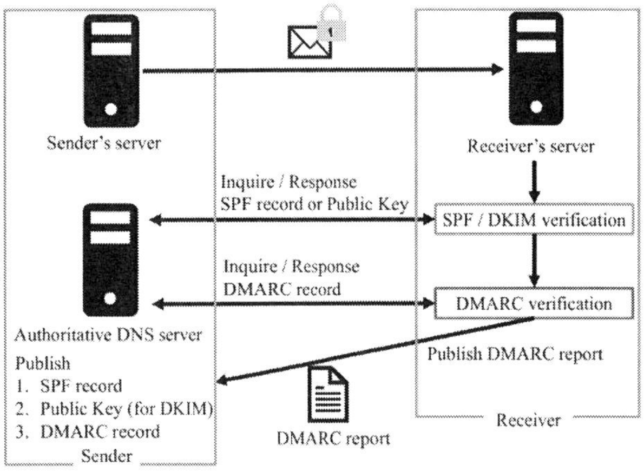

Figure 1. Flow of DMARC verification.

DKIM is an authentication method using digital signature (hereinafter, this is called "DKIM signature") generated from e-mail header and body. In order to use DKIM mechanism, the sender domain should prepare a pair of a private key and public key in advance and publish the public key on their authoritative DNS server. The sender domain generates a DKIM signature from the e-mail body and header using private key, and attaches it to "b=" tag of the e-mail header as the DKIM signature. Next, the receiver inquires the public key to the authoritative DNS server of sender's domain that is obtained in "d=" tag of the e-mail header. The receiver compares the hash value obtained from DKIM signature using the public key with the value of "bh=" tag. When these values are the same, the e-mail is passed the DKIM verification. With this mechanism, DKIM can verify forwarded messages correctly unlike SPF. Although DKIM allows third party domains to sign e-mails, it has an issue which the spoofed e-mails signed with spammers' own malicious domain will be passed the verification.

B. DMARC

DMARC is a reporting and policy controlling framework utilizing SPF and DKIM mechanism to authenticate e-mails.

Figure 1 shows the flow of DMARC verification. In order to use DMARC, the sender domain administrator must publish SPF record for SPF verification and public key for DKIM verification on the authoritative DNS server beforehand to utilize SPF and DKIM mechanism. Moreover, the sender domain needs to publish the DMARC record on their DNS server. For example, when the sender domain is "example.com", DMARC record is published as TXT record of "_dmarc.example.com" in the following rules.

v=DMARC1; p=reject; rua=mailto:rua@example.com

In policy controlling function, DMARC provides a mechanism for the sender domain's administrator to declare the policy how the receiver handles the e-mail, which fails sender domain authentication in the "p=" tag of the DMARC record. The value of "p=" tag has three variations, "none (do not anything even if authentication failure)", "quarantine (quarantine the authentication failure e-mail)", and "reject (reject the authentication failure e-mail)".

In reporting function, an e-mail receiver sends DMARC reports to e-mail address of sender domain's administrator shown in "rua=" tag of DMARC record.

DMARC report provides information, such as e-mail domains, authentication results, and effectiveness of DMARC policy. The examples of information included in DMARC reports are as follows.

- DMARC reporter's name
- Strictness of DMARC alignment
- Handling policy published by sender for failure e-mails (shown in "p=" tag of DMARC record)
- The IP address of the sender's server
- Disposition of e-mails based on DMARC policy
- DKIM authentication result when DMARC alignment is applied
- SPF authentication result when DMARC alignment is applied
- Header-From domain
- Envelope-From domain
- DKIM signature domain
- DKIM authentication result
- SPF authentication result

Thus, the sender domain's administrator can obtain the performance of DMARC authentication from DMARC reports, and they can take measures to prevent spoofed e-mails abusing their domain.

With the concept of "alignment", DMARC verification will be failed when domains for SPF and DKIM verification are different from the sender's Header-From domain. The sender's Header-From domain need not be the same as the Envelope-From domain or the DKIM signature domain. On the other hand, spammers can fraud the Header-From domain easily. As a countermeasure against this issue, by utilizing alignment, the receiver can check whether the Header-From domain is correct or not. The sender domain can choose from two strictness of alignment, "strict" and "relaxed", using DMARC record. When the sender domain's administrator uses "strict" mode, DMARC verification passes only when Header-From address and domain for SPF or DKIM verification match completely. On the other hand, when the alignment mode is "relaxed", DMARC verification will success if subdomains of Header-From address and subdomains of domain for SPF or DKIM verification match.

DMARC is one of the effective countermeasure to spoofed e-mail. However, DMARC cannot solve the issues that SPF cannot properly verify forwarded messages. As mentioned above, DMARC utilizes SPF and DKIM mechanism to authenticate e-mail. SPF cannot authenticate forwarded messages because the sender's IP address changes to forwarder's IP address when the e-mails are forwarded. Moreover, although DKIM allows third party's signature, which utilized widely over the world, the e-mails signed by third party's signer will be failed the DMARC verification due to alignment. Therefore, there are cases that legitimate forwarded messages will be failed the DMARC authentication, for example, when the e-mails utilize third party's signature or the e-mail's domains are not compatible with DKIM.

III. DESIGN OF OUR METHOD

As described in subsection II-B, DMARC cannot solve the problem of SPF about forwarded messages. To overcome this issue, we propose a method adopting X-means clustering analysis to massive DMARC report data.

X-means clustering is K-means extended algorithm proposed by D.Pelleg and A. Moore [16]. K-means has been utilized as one of the most popular clustering methods. However, K-means has shortcoming which the number of clusters K has to be provided by users in advance. On the other hand, X-means can determine the number of clusters X by iterations of k-means and splitting decision based on Bayesian Information Criterion (BIC). Our method utilizes X-means clustering analysis in order to classify the sender's IP address.

Figure 2 shows the flow of our method. At first, in order to adapt X-means clustering analysis to DMARC reports, our approach summarizes the DMARC reports focus on the sender domain authentication results and the e-mail domains.

As the summarization of sender domain authentication results, we calculate the acceptance rate of SPF, DKIM, and DMARC for each sender's IP addresses. SPF, DKIM, and DMARC have several types of results as shown in Figure 2. Thus, our approach calculates not only the percentage of the authentications pass e-mails but also the percentage of other authentication results e-mails, such as "fail", "none", and so on.

In summarization the domain agreement rate part in in Figure 2, our approach calculates the percentage of e-mails which combinations of domains 1), 2), and 3) in Figure 2 are same or different for each combinaitons.

As described in subsection II-B, DMARC mechanism compares the combinations of Envelope-From domain and Header-From domain (combination 1) in Figure 2) for SPF alignment of DMARC. In addition, the combinations of Header-From domain and DKIM signature domain (combination 2) in Figure 2) are compared for DKIM alignment of DMARC. Although Envelope-From domain, Header-From domain, and DKIM signature domain are not necessarily the same because SPF and DKIM allows using third party domains to verify the e-mails, the domains combinations 1) and 2) have relations in DMARC authentication mechanism.

On the other hand, there is no need to compare the combinations of Envelope-From domain and DKIM signature domain (combination 3) in Figure 2) in SPF, DKIM, and DMARC verification processes. However, since the combinations 1) and 2) has relationships in sender domain authentications, we can considered that the combination 3) also has a relationship, such as rules of domain naming. Thus, we utilize domains combination 3) in order to improve accuracy of our method.

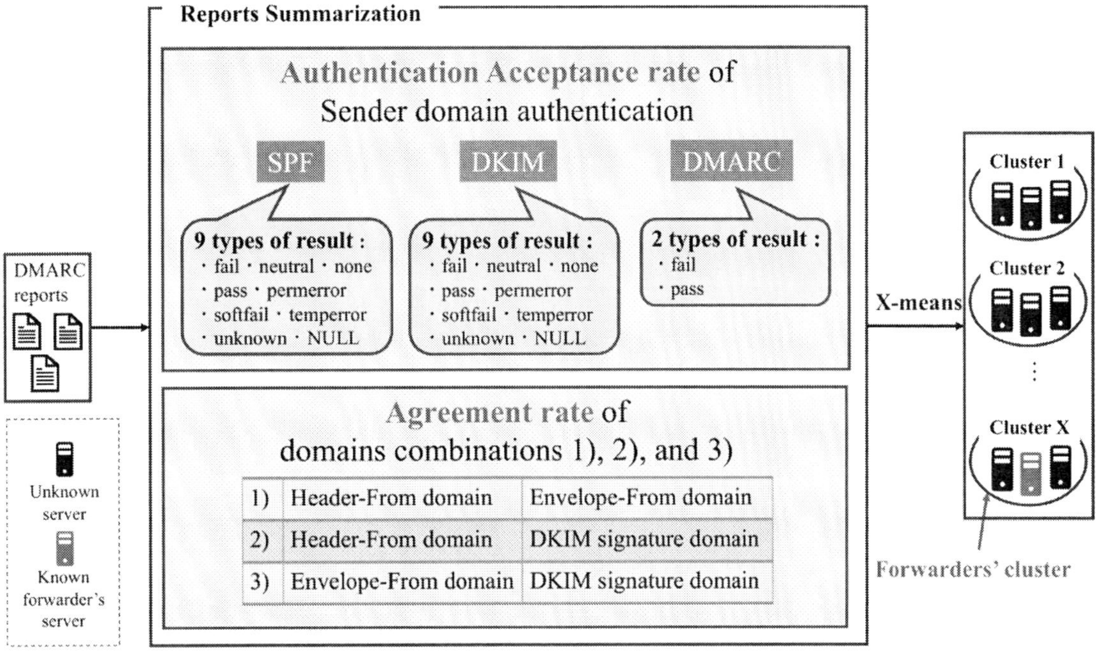

Figure 2. Design of our method.

Then, we classify the sender's IP addresses by X-means clustering analysis utilizing summarized DMARC reports information. As the result of X-means clustering analysis, the sender's IP addresses are divided into some clusters according to their e-mail transmission behavior trends, such as similarities of sender domain authentication results and e-mail domains' naming rules.

Finally, we specify clusters which are considered as forwarding servers' clusters. We already know several white forwarders' IP addresses (hereinafter, they are called "known forwarders"). When the cluster has known forwarders, the servers included in this cluster have similarly transmission situation with legitimate known forwarders. Thus, we determine these servers of the cluster as forwarding servers.

IV. Dataset

In this section, we explain the dataset that applies to our method. We utilize DMARC reports that received 31st December 2018 in one of the most famous ISPs' domains in Japan. The number of DMARC reports is 22,305,844, and the number of e-mails including DMARC reports is 232,492,822. In addition, the number of sender's IP address is 536,657.

Figure 3 shows the number of e-mails for each sender's IP address. As shown in Figure 3, top 1% of senders (5,366 IP addresses) based on the total number of e-mails cover about 89.1% of total e-mails in our DMARC reports, which is enough large data to analyze. On the other hand, 99% of senders (531,291 IP addresses) send only a few e-mails in our DMARC reports. In this experiment, we use the DMARC reports from 5,366 (top 1%) servers, excluding the reports from servers with low deliveries. Additionally, these 5,366 servers contain five known forwarders. Thus, we summarize these 5,366 senders'

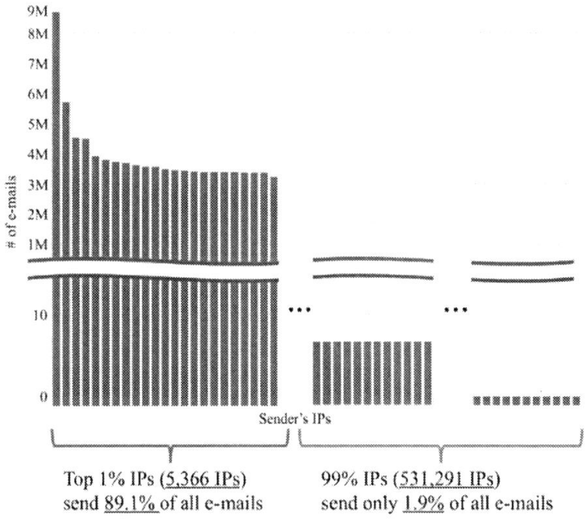

Figure 3. The number of E-mails for each sender's IP address.

DMARC reports and adapt X-means clustering analysis in our approach.

TABLE I shows the number of spammer's IP addresses included in our dataset by checking famous IP blacklists ("spamhaus blocklists" [17]) and spam filter results. Spamhaus blocklists are provided by the Spamhaus Project, which is international nonprofit organization tracking spam and related cyber threats. Spam filter results are provided by Japanese famous ISP which is different from DMARC reports provider.

As shown in TABLE I, some spammer's servers are in-

TABLE I. SPAMHAUS AND SPAM FILTER RESULTS OF THE 5,366 IP ADDRESSES.

		Listed	Not Listed
Spamhaus		293 (5.46%)	5,073 (94.5%)
Spam filter	Spam	630 (11.74%)	4,736 (88.26%)
	Ham	1810 (33.73%)	3,566 (66.46%)

TABLE II. THE RESULTS OF APPLYING OUR METHOD TO THE 5,366 IP ADDRESSES.

Clustering Results	#
Clusters	20
Known forwarders	5
Forwarder cluster	1
IP addresses in Forwarder cluster	451

TABLE III. EVALUATION OF FORWARDER CLUSTER IP ADDRESSES UTILIZING SPAMHAUS AND SPAM FILTER RESULTS

	Spamhaus Blocklisted	Spam Filter		# of IPs
		Listed as Spam	Listed as Ham	
1)	True	True	True	0
2)	True	True	False	0
3)	True	False	True	0
4)	True	False	False	0
5)	False	True	True	159
6)	False	True	False	1
7)	False	False	True	196
8)	False	False	False	95

cluded in our dataset applying our method.

V. RESULTS AND EVALUATIONS

In this section, we describe the results of applying our method to our dataset in subsection V-A, and evaluate our approach in subsection V-B.

A. Results of applying our method to DMARC reports

TABLE II shows the results of the clustering. As shown in TABLE II, our method divides 5,366 IP addresses into 20 clusters by X-means clustering analysis. We confirmed that five known forwarders are classified into the same cluster of 20 clusters. Forwarder cluster contains 451 servers, five known forwarders and 446 forwarding server candidates detected by the clustering. Our method determines these 451 servers as e-mail forwarding servers.

B. Evaluation of the clustering results focusing on the forwarder cluster

We evaluate the validity of our approach by analyzing 451 IP addresses. First of all, in order to check whether 451 IP addresses included in forwarder cluster are spammers or not, we compare 451 IP addresses with the spamhaus blocklists and the spam filter results.

As the comparison, we check whether 451 IP addresses are listed in the spamhaus blocklists or not. In addition, we confirm whether 451 IP addresses are listed as spam e-mails sender or ham e-mails sender by using the spam filter results.

TABLE III shows all combinations of the evaluation results. For example, the combination 1) in TABLE III shows that no IP address is listed in spamhaus blocklists, listed as spam e-mail, and listed as ham e-mail.

As shown in results 1), 2), 3), and 4) in TABLE III, all 451 IP addresses are not listed in the spamhaus blocklists. This result means that 100% of forwarder cluster's IP addresses are not included in the blocklists.

Then, we describe the comparison results 5), 6), 7), and 8) in TABLE III. 159 IP addresses of 5) in TABLE III send both ham e-mails and spam e-mails in the observation. We can consider that there are two types of transmission behaviors.

The first assumed behavior is that owners of IP addresses are famous E-mail Service Providers (ESPs), ISPs and famous free e-mail services. The spammers often abuse these kinds of IP addresses in order to send malicious e-mails. Therefore, it is obvious that the IP addresses of these providers and services are not spammers' IP addresses. The e-mail accounts hacking is also considered as IP addresses of 5). When the spammers compromise e-mail accounts, the spammers can send spam e-mails utilizing legitimate sender's IP addresses. From these reasons, 159 IP addresses are not spammers' IP addresses although spam e-mails sent from these 159 IP addresses are observed. In addition, 159 IP addresses of 5) are not listed in spamhaus blocklists, therefore these IP addresses are considered as white IP address.

The IP address of 6) sends spam e-mails. This is Japanese application service provider's IP address. This IP address is not spammer's IP address according to spamhaus blocklists, therefore we considered that this IP address is abused by spammers.

196 IP addresses of 7) does not send any spam e-mails. In addition, these IP addresses are not listed in spamhaus blocklists. Thus, we can determine these IP addresses as legitimate senders obviously.

95 IP addresses of 8) does not send both ham e-mails and spam e-mails. In other words, ISP providing spam filter results cannot observe any e-mails from 95 IP addresses of 8). Thus, we cannot determine whether 95 IP addresses are spammers or not by using spam filter results. However, we can consider that these 95 IP addresses are not spammers according to the results of spmahaus blocklists.

To summarize, according to the confirmation results of spam filter results, our approach detected legitimate forwarding server with the accuracy of $\frac{(451-95)-1}{451-95} * 100 \approx 99.72\%$ in the observation of the ISP providing spam filter results.

Next, we show the False Positives that can be reduced by our method. Figure 4 shows the DMARC authentication failure rate of 451 servers classified as legitimate forwarding servers by our method. As shown in Figure 4, amoung the e-mails delivered from each 451 IP addresses, the e-mails with a minimum of 7.9%, a maximum of 74.94%, and a median of 50.17% are failed DMARC authentication. On the other hand, as mentioned above in this section, none of these 451 IP addresses were included in the spamhaus blocklist. Also, from the comparison with the spam filtering result, we confirmed that our method can classify the legitimate forwarding servers with 99.72% accuracy.

From these results, by utilizing the proposed method, e-mail receiving servers can detect 7.9% to 74.94% (median

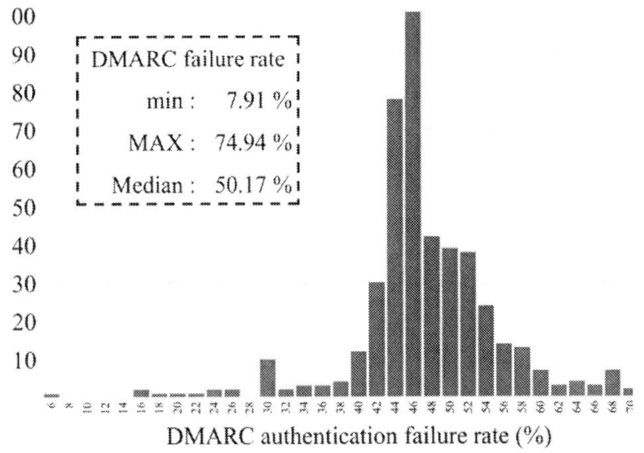

Figure 4. Distribution of DMARC authentication failure rate of 451 IP addresses.

of 50.17%) of legitimate e-mails from each 451 servers that have become False Positives in the conventional DMARC authentication without using heavy loaded spam filter.

VI. CONCLUSION

In this paper, we proposed a method to detect legitimate forwarding servers by X-means clustering analysis utilizing a large number of DMARC reports data.

In order to classify the legitimate forwarded messages correctly, our approach summarizes DMARC reports focusing on the sender domain authentication results and the e-mail domains at first. In addition, our method classifies the senders' IP addresses by X-means clustering analysis. As a result, we confirmed that the proposed method can classify transfer servers with high accuracy. Thus, when e-mail server administrators know a few forwarding servers, such as the servers in their own organization beforehand, they can detect many other legitimate forwarders by utilizing our method.

In our approach, the sender's IP addresses are classified based on their transmission behavior. Although we focus on one forwarding IP addresses cluster, we consider that other clusters have similarity of transmission behavior each other. Thus, in order to detect forwarding server or spammer's server in higher accuracy, analyzing other clusters' e-mail sending behavior is future subject.

In addition, we consider that our clustering results can utilize the model of forwarding servers' transmission behavior. By modeling forwarders' transmission behaviors, we can improve the accuracy to detect legitimate forwarding servers. Therefore, modeling our clustering results is also future subject.

ACKNOWLEDGMENT

This study was supported by TwoFive Inc. through a collaborative research project.

REFERENCES

[1] FBI (Federal Bureau of Investigation), "Public Service Announcement, Business E-mail Compromise The 12 billion dollar scam," 2018, URL: https://www.ic3.gov/media/2018/180712.aspx [Accessed: 15th May. 2019].

[2] M. Wong and W. Schlitt, "Sender Policy Framework (SPF) for authorizing use of domains in e-mail," RFC4408, Tech. Rep., 2006.

[3] D. Crocker, T. Hansen, and M. Kucherawy, "DomainKeys Identified Mail (DKIM) signatures," STD76, Tech. Rep., sep 2011.

[4] M. Kucherawy and E. Zwicky, "Domain-based message authentication, reporting, and conformance (DMARC)," RFC 7489, Tech. Rep., 2015.

[5] I. Androutsopoulos, J. Koutsias, K. V. Chandrinos, G. Paliouras, and C. D. Spyropoulos, "An evaluation of Naive Bayesian anti-spam filtering," Proceedings of the workshop on Machine Learning in the New Information, 2000, pp. 9–17.

[6] I. Androutsopoulos, J. Koutsias, K. V. Chandrinos, and C. D. Spyropoulos, "An experimental comparison of naive Bayesian and keyword-based anti-spam filtering with personal e-mail messages," Proceedings of the 23rd annual international ACM SIGIR conference on Research and development in information retrieval, 2000, pp. 160–167.

[7] S. Aggarwal, V. Kumar, and S. D. Sudarsan, "Identification and detection of phishing emails using natural language processing techniques," in Proceedings of the 7th International Conference on Security of Information and Networks. ACM, 2014, p. 217.

[8] H. Ducker, D. Wy, and V. N. Vapnik, "Support vector machines for spam categorization," IEEE Transactions on Neural networks, vol. 10, no. 5, 1999, pp. 1048–1054.

[9] W. Feng, J. Sun, L. Zhang, C. Cao, and Q. Yang, "A support vector machine based naive Bayes algorithm for spam filtering," in Performance Computing and Communications Conference (IPCCC), 2016 IEEE 35th International. IEEE, 2016, pp. 1–8.

[10] T. S. Guzella and W. M. Caminhas, "A review of machine learning approaches to spam filtering," Expert Systems with Applications, vol. 36, no. 7, 2009, pp. 10 206–10 222.

[11] M. Crawford, T. M. Khoshgoftaar, J. D. Prusa, A. N. Richter, and H. A. Najada, "Survey of review spam detection using machine learning techniques," Journal of Big Data, vol. 2, no. 1, 2015, p. 23.

[12] "The Apache SpamAssassin Project." URL: http://spamassassin.apache.org/ [Accessed: 15th May. 2019].

[13] J. Mason, "Filtering spam with spamassassin," In HEANet Annual Conference, 2002.

[14] S. Sinha, M. Bailey, and F. Jahanian, "Shades of Grey: On the effectiveness of reputation-based "blacklists"," in 3rd International Conference on Malicious and Unwanted Software (MALWARE). IEEE, 2008, pp. 57–64.

[15] C. J. Dietrich and C. Rossow, Empirical research of ip blacklists. Springer, 2009, pp. 163–171.

[16] D. Pelleg and A. Moore, "X-means: Extending K-means with Efficient Estimation of the Number of Clusters," in Proceedings of the 17th International Conference on Machine Learning. Morgan Kaufmann, 2000, pp. 727–734.

[17] The Spamhaus Project Ltd., "Spamhaus ZEN," URL: https://www.spamhaus.org/zen/ [Accessed: 15th May. 2019].

Consideration of a Countermeasure Model against Self-Evolving Botnets

Kouji Hirata*, Koki Hongyo*, Takanori Kudo†, Yoshiaki Inoue‡, and Tomotaka Kimura§,
* Faculty of Engineering, Kansai University, Osaka 564-8680, Japan, Email: {hirata, k896955}@kansai-u.ac.jp
† Faculty of Science and Engineering, Setsunan University, Osaka 572-8508, Japan, Email: t-kudo@ele.setsunan.ac.jp
‡ Graduate School of Engineering, Osaka University, Osaka 565-0871, Japan, Email: yoshiaki@comm.eng.osaka-u.ac.jp
§ Faculty of Science and Engineering, Doshisha University, Kyoto 610-0321, Japan, Email: tomkimur@mail.doshisha.ac.jp

***Abstract*—The literature has suggested the appearance of self-evolving botnets, which autonomously discover vulnerabilities by performing machine learning with computing resources of zombie computers and evolve accordingly. The infectablity of the self-evolving botnets is too strong compared with conventional botnets. This paper introduces a countermeasure model against the self-evolving botnets. This model aims at preventing the self-evolving botnets from spreading by discovering vulnerabilities with computing resources of volunteer hosts before the self-evolving botnets discover them. Through simulation experiments based on a continuous-time Markov chain, we evaluate the performance of the countermeasure model.**

Keywords–Botnet; machine learning; epidemic model; continuous-time Markov chain; countermeasure.

I. INTRODUCTION

Recently, machine learning techniques, such as deep learning [1][2], have been widely used and achieved significant results in various research areas. In addition, some researchers have been proposed vulnerability discovery methods that discover bugs and vulnerabilities with static code analysis and machine learning techniques [7][8]. Of course, the main purpose of these methods is to protect software. However, these methods can be used for discovering unknown security holes and exploited for illegal attacks by malicious attackers.

To perform illegal attacks, malicious attackers often infect hosts with malware. A botnet is a set of hosts infected by the botnet malware [6]. The zombie computers are controlled by a malicious attacker and perform illegal attacks. In the past, there have been some botnets that consist of more than a million zombie computers. The authors in [4][5] have introduced a new concept named self-evolving botnets, based on these facts. The self-evolving botnets discover vulnerabilities by performing distributed machine learning with computing resources of zombie computers and evolves autonomously exploiting the discovered vulnerabilities. Accordingly, they infect other hosts and make themselves bigger. The authors in [4][5] have provided an epidemic model of the self-evolving botnets, which formulates the infection dynamics of the self-evolving botnets as a continuous-time Markov chain. The authors have shown that the infectivity of self-evolving botnets is very high, compared with conventional botnets, through numerical experiments. In response, in [3], the authors have proposed basic ideas of countermeasures against self-evolving botnets and shown their effectiveness.

In this paper, we propose a countermeasure model against self-evolving botnets, which extends the basic ideas discussed in [3]. This model aims to counter the self-evolving botnets by discovering and repairing unknown vulnerabilities by utilizing computing resources of volunteer hosts before the self-evolving botnets discover them. Therefore, we call this model volunteer model hereafter. We represent the infection dynamics of self-evolving botnets with a continuous-time Markov chain under the situation where the volunteer model works. Through simulation experiments, we examine the behavior of the volunteer model.

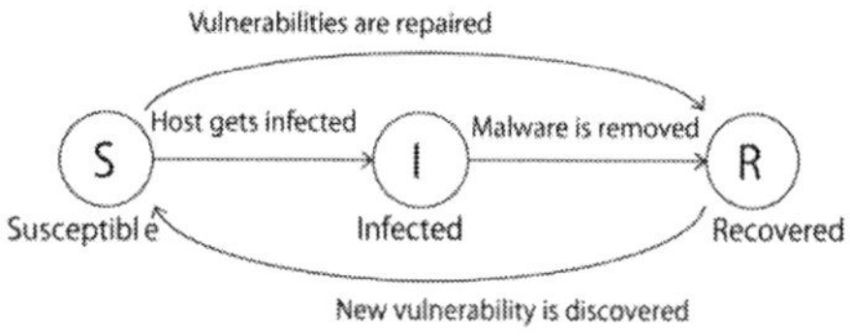

Figure 1. SIRS model.

The rest of this paper is organized as follows. Section II discusses the epidemic model for self-evolving botnets. In Section III, we explain the volunteer model. In Section IV, we discuss the behavior of the volunteer model with the results of simulation experiments. We state the conclusion of this paper in Section V.

II. BASIC EPIDEMIC MODEL FOR SELF-EVOLVING BOTNETS

In [4][5], in order to reveal threats of self-evolving botnets, the authors assumed situations where there is a self-evolving botnet in a network and proposed an epidemic model representing the infection dynamics of the self-evolving botnet. In this epidemic model, the state of each host in the network is represented by a Susceptible-Infected-Recovered-Susceptible (SIRS) model shown in Figure 1. In the SIRS model, "S" indicates that the host has vulnerabilities, "I" indicates that the host is infected, and "R" indicates that the host has no known vulnerabilities. Each host belongs to one of the states. We assume that hosts belonging to the recovered state R can get infected by unknown vulnerabilities which are discovered by the self-evolving botnet.

Hosts belonging to the susceptible state S transition to the infected state I when they get infected by attacks of the self-evolving botnet. Then the hosts are embedded in the self-evolving botnet. Hosts belonging to the susceptible state S and the infected state I transition to the recovered state R when known vulnerabilities and the botnet malware, respectively, removed from the hosts by, e.g., OS updates and anti-virus software. Note that we assume that all known vulnerabilities are simultaneously removed in these cases. When the self-evolving botnet discovers a new vulnerability by means of distributed machine learning using known vulnerabilities, all hosts belonging to the recovered state R transition to the susceptible state S because the botnet can infect the hosts by using the discovered vulnerability. The summary of the events in the SIRS model is as follows.

1) When a new vulnerability is discovered by the self-evolving botnet, all hosts belonging to the recovered state R transition to the susceptible state S.
2) When a host belonging to the susceptible state S removes its known vulnerabilities, it transitions to the recovered state R.
3) When a host belonging to the infected state I infects a host belonging to the susceptible state S and embeds it in the self-evolving botnet, the host getting infected transitions to the infected state I.
4) When a host belonging to the infected state I removes the botnet malware from itself, it transitions to the recovered state R.

In [5], the authors have formulated the infection process of a self-evolving botnet as a continuous-time Markov chain and evaluated its characteristic. In the Markov chain, the occurrence of each event 1)-4) described above, which is based on the SIRS model, follows a Poisson process.

III. VOLUNTEER MODEL

A. Modeling

Self-evolving botnets discover unknown vulnerabilities by utilizing the computing resources of zombie computers and attack susceptible hosts based on the discovered vulnerabilities. It is very difficult for each host to individually protect itself from such attacks. To overcome this difficulty, the volunteer model counters the self-evolving botnets by repairing vulnerabilities that are found with use of the computing resources of volunteer hosts before the self-evolving botnets discover them. In this paper, we represent the infection dynamics of the volunteer model under the following assumptions.

1) There is one volunteer group, to which all volunteer hosts belong, in a given network.
2) Each host in the susceptible state S or the recovered state R can become a volunteer host (i.e., join the volunteer group). The probability that a host becomes a volunteer host is proportional to the number of volunteer hosts. This assumption indicates that the effect of vulnerability discovery and protection increases with the number of volunteer hosts, so that the participation of new hosts to the volunteer group is encouraged.
3) Volunteer hosts share the information on vulnerability discovery each other and can repair the vulnerability. This is an incentive reward for participating the volunteer group. Therefore, the information is not shared with non-volunteer hosts.
4) Volunteer hosts can leave the volunteer group freely.

Figure 2 represents the state transition diagram of each host in the volunteer model, which follows these assumptions and is based on the SIRS model shown in Figure 1. In the volunteer model, the susceptible state S and the recovered state R are divided into two states "S_1", "S_2", "R_1", and "R_2", respectively. S_1 (resp. R_1) indicates that the host belongs to the susceptible state (resp. the recovered state) but does not belong to the volunteer group. On the other hand, S_2 (resp. R_2) indicates the host belongs to both the susceptible state (resp. the recovered state) and the volunteer group. In the volunteer model, the state of each host transitions according to the following event.

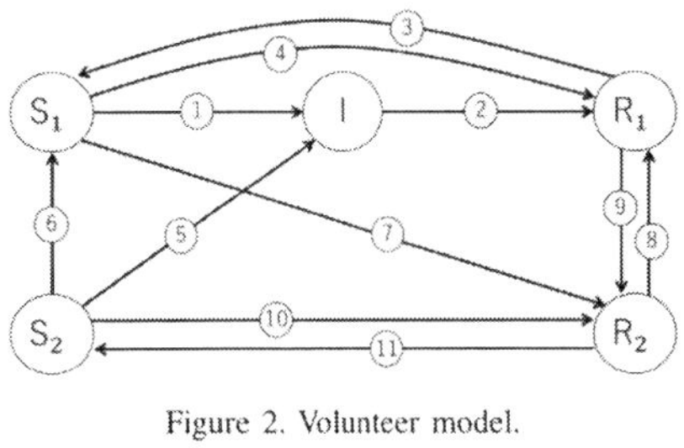

Figure 2. Volunteer model.

a) The host gets infected by an attack of an infected host (①, ⑤).
b) The host removes the botnet malware from itself (②).
c) The host removes known vulnerabilities from itself (④, ⑩).
d) The host leaves the volunteer group (⑥, ⑧).
e) The host join the volunteer group (⑦, ⑨).
f) The self-evolving botnet discovers a new vulnerability (③, ⑪).

In the event e), susceptible hosts transition to the recovered state R_2 immediately after they join the volunteer group because we assume that hosts belonging to the volunteer group share the information on vulnerabilities discovered by the volunteer group. We also assume that the volunteer group can discover unknown vulnerabilities with use of distributed machine learning, so that the probability that the transition ⑪ occurs is smaller than the probability that the transition ③ occurs in event f).

B. Continuous Markov chain

In this paper, we consider a continuous time Markov chain that represents the infection dynamics of the volunteer model, where each event occurs according to a Poisson process. Let $U_1(t)$, $U_2(t)$, $V(t)$, $W_1(t)$, and $W_2(t)$ denote the numbers of hosts belonging to the states S_1, S_2, I, R_1, and R_2, respectively at time t. The system state is represented by $(U_1(t), U_2(t), V(t), W_1(t), W_2(t))$. When the system state is $(U_1(t), U_2(t), V(t), W_1(t), W_2(t)) = (u_1, u_2, v, w_1, w_2) = \boldsymbol{\tau}$, the occurrence rate of each event is defined as follows.

a) When a host belonging to the state S_1 (resp. S_2) gets infected, the system state $\boldsymbol{\tau}$ transitions to $(u_1 - 1, u_2, v+1, w_1, w_2)$ (resp. $(u_1, u_2 - 1, v+1, w_1, w_2)$) (①, ⑤). The occurrence rates $\lambda_{\boldsymbol{\tau}}^{[1]}$ and $\lambda_{\boldsymbol{\tau}}^{[2]}$ of the respective events are given by

$$\lambda_{\boldsymbol{\tau}}^{[1]} = \alpha u_1 v, \tag{1}$$

$$\lambda_{\boldsymbol{\tau}}^{[2]} = \alpha u_2 v, \tag{2}$$

where α denotes the infection rate per host.

b) When a host belonging to the state I removes the botnet malware from itself, the system state $\boldsymbol{\tau}$ transitions to $(u_1, u_2, v-1, w_1+1, w_2)$ (②). The occurrence rate of this event is given by

$$\mu_{\boldsymbol{\tau}} = \delta_i v, \tag{3}$$

where δ_i denote the removal rate per host.

c) When a host belonging to the state S_1 (resp. S_2) repairs its own vulnerabilities, the system state $\boldsymbol{\tau}$ transitions to $(u_1 - 1, u_2, v, w_1 + 1, w_2)$ (resp. $(u_1, u_2 -$

$1, v, w_1, w_2 + 1))$ (④, ⑩). The occurrence rates $\psi_{\boldsymbol{\tau}}^{[1]}$ and $\psi_{\boldsymbol{\tau}}^{[2]}$ of the respective events are given by

$$\psi_{\boldsymbol{\tau}}^{[1]} = \delta_s u_1, \tag{4}$$

$$\psi_{\boldsymbol{\tau}}^{[2]} = \delta_s u_2, \tag{5}$$

where δ_s denote the repair rate per host.

d) When a host belonging to the state S_2 (resp. R_2) leaves the volunteer group, the system state $\boldsymbol{\tau}$ transitions to $(u_1 + 1, u_2 - 1, v, w_1, w_2)$ (resp. $(u_1, u_2, v, w_1 + 1, w_2 - 1)$) (⑥, ⑧). The occurrence rates $\zeta_{\boldsymbol{\tau}}^{[s]}$ and $\zeta_{\boldsymbol{\tau}}^{[r]}$ of the respective events are given by

$$\zeta_{\boldsymbol{\tau}}^{[s]} = \phi u_2, \tag{6}$$

$$\zeta_{\boldsymbol{\tau}}^{[r]} = \phi w_2, \tag{7}$$

where ϕ denotes the leave rate per host.

e) When a host belonging to the state S_1 (resp. R_1) joins the volunteer group, the system state $\boldsymbol{\tau}$ transitions to $(u_1 - 1, u_2, v, w_1, w_2 + 1)$ (resp. $(u_1, u_2, v, w_1 - 1, w_2 + 1)$) (⑦, ⑨). The occurrence rates $\epsilon_{\boldsymbol{\tau}}^{[s]}$ and $\epsilon_{\boldsymbol{\tau}}^{[s]}$ of the respective events are given by

$$\epsilon_{\boldsymbol{\tau}}^{[s]} = \theta(u_2 + w_2 + 1)u_1, \tag{8}$$

$$\epsilon_{\boldsymbol{\tau}}^{[r]} = \theta(u_2 + w_2 + 1)w_1, \tag{9}$$

where θ denotes the join rate per host. We assume that the probability that hosts join the volunteer group increases with the current size of the volunteer group.

f) When the self-evolving botnet discovers a new vulnerability, one of the following two event occurs. If the discovered vulnerability has been already repaired by the volunteer group, hosts belonging to the volunteer group do not transitions to the susceptible state. In this case, the system state $\boldsymbol{\tau}$ transitions to $(u_1 + w_1, u_2, v, 0, w_2)$ (③). The occurrence rate $\gamma_{\boldsymbol{\tau}}^{[1]}$ of this event is given by

$$\gamma_{\boldsymbol{\tau}}^{[1]} = \eta v \frac{\sigma(u_2 + w_2)}{\sigma(u_2 + w_2) + \eta v}, \tag{10}$$

where η and σ denote the vulnerability discovery rate per infected host and per volunteer host, respectively. If the discovered vulnerability has not been repaired by the volunteer group yet, hosts belonging to the volunteer group also transitions to the susceptible state. Therefore, the system state $\boldsymbol{\tau}$ transitions to $(u_1 + w_1, u_2 + w_2, v, 0, 0)$ (③, ⑪). The occurrence rate $\gamma_{\boldsymbol{\tau}}^{[2]}$ of this event is given by

$$\gamma_{\boldsymbol{\tau}}^{[2]} = \eta v \frac{\eta v}{\sigma(u_2 + w_2) + \eta v}. \tag{11}$$

We assume that the discovery capability of vulnerabilities of the self-evolving botnet (i.e., $\gamma_{\boldsymbol{\tau}}^{[1]} + \gamma_{\boldsymbol{\tau}}^{[2]} = \eta v$) is weakened according to the discovery capability of the volunteer group.

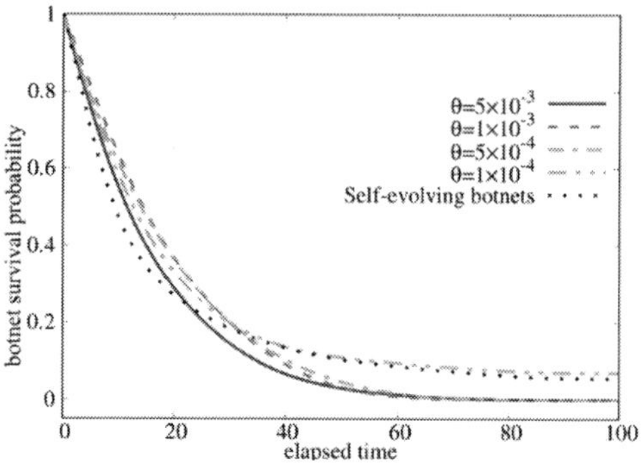

Figure 3. Botnet survival probability ($\eta = \sigma = 0.01$).

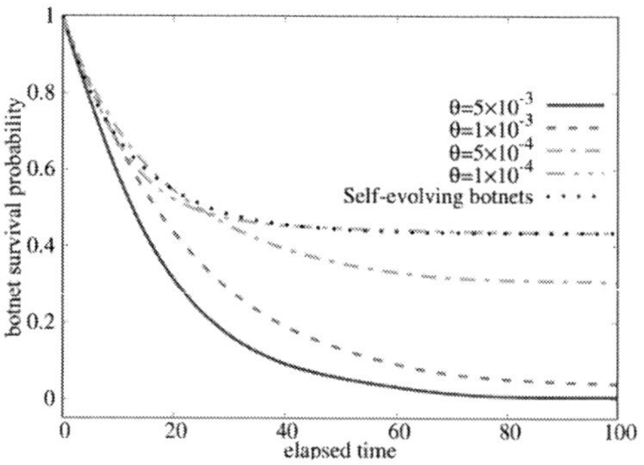

Figure 4. Botnet survival probability ($\eta = \sigma = 0.05$).

IV. EVALUATION

A. Model

In this paper, we examine the infection dynamics of the volunteer model through simulation experiments. The total number of hosts in a network is equal to 1,000. The initial state of the system is assumed to be $(U_1(t), U_2(t), V(t), W_1(t), W_2(t)) = (999, 0, 1, 0, 0)$. Specifically, there is one infected host and the other hosts have vulnerabilities, which do not belong to the volunteer group. The system parameters in (1)-(11) are set to be $\alpha = 0.001$, $\delta_i = 0.1$, $\delta_s = 1$, and $\phi = 0.1$. For each experiment, we collect 200 independent samples.

B. Results

We examine the infectivity of the self-evolving botnets under infection control environments. Figures 3 and 4 show the botnet survival probability as a function of the elapsed time t, where $\eta = \sigma = 0.01$ and 0.05, respectively. The botnet survival probability means the ratio of the number of samples where one or more infected hosts still exist at time t to the total number of samples. For the sake of comparison, we plot the results for the self-evolving botnet without the volunteer model in these figures. As shown in these figures, the botnet survival probability is very large when the volunteer model is not applied to the self-evolving botnet. We also observe that when the join rate θ to the volunteer group is low (i.e., $\theta = 1 \times 10^{-4}$), the botnet survival probability is almost the same as the self-evolving botnet without the volunteer model. On the other hand, the botnet survival probability decreases with the increase in the value of θ.

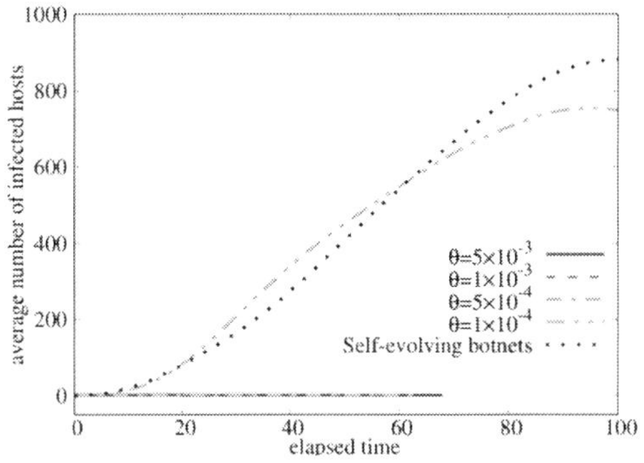

Figure 5. Average number of infected hosts ($\eta = \sigma = 0.01$).

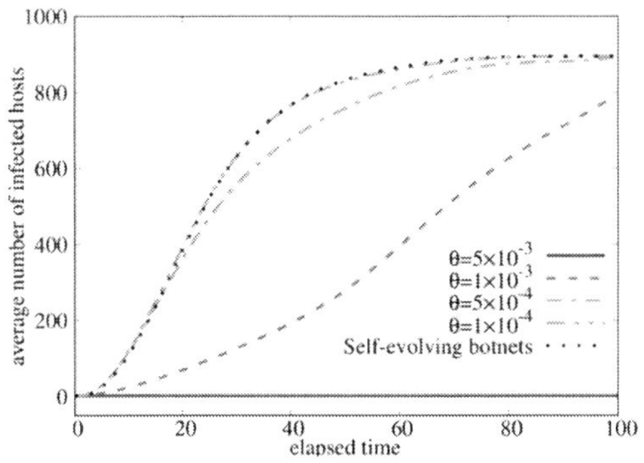

Figure 6. Average number of infected hosts ($\eta = \sigma = 0.05$).

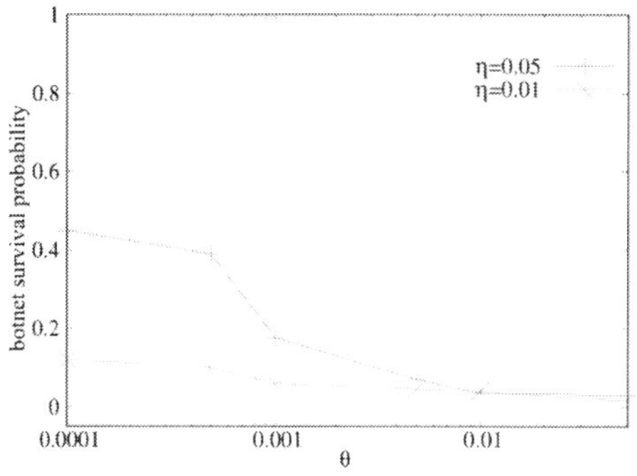

Figure 7. Botnet survival probability ($\eta = \sigma$).

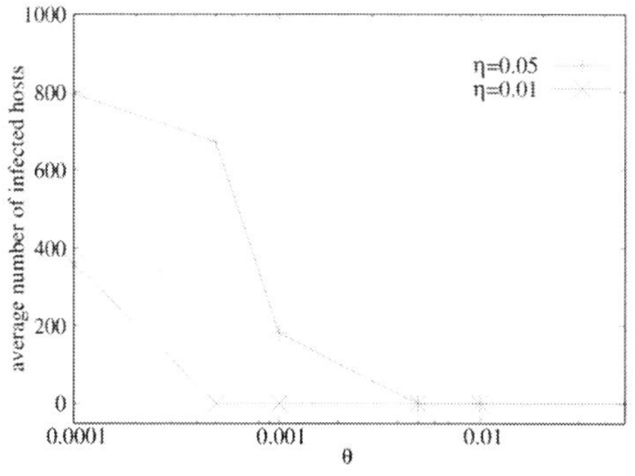

Figure 8. Average number of infected hosts ($\eta = \sigma$).

Figures 5 and 6 show the average number of infected hosts of samples in which infected hosts still exist at time t as a function of the elapsed time t, where $\eta = \sigma = 0.01$ and 0.05, respectively. From these figures, we observe that the average number of infected hosts rapidly increases when the volunteer model is not used or θ is low. Meanwhile, the volunteer model with large θ efficiently reduces the average number of infected host.

Figures 7 and 8 show the botnet survival probability and the average number of infected hosts, respectively, as a function of the value of θ, where $t = 40$ and $\eta = \sigma$. As we can see from these figures, the botnet survival probability and the average number of infected hosts decrease with the increase in the value of θ. These results mean that the volunteer model is effective for suppressing the spread of the self-evolving botnet.

V. CONCLUSION

This paper introduced a volunteer model to countermeasure self-evolving botnets. Through simulation experiments, we showed that the volunteer model efficiently reduces botnet survival probability and the average number of infected hosts. As future work, we will consider how hosts are encouraged to join the volunteer model. In this paper, we assume that the probability that a host becomes a volunteer host is proportional to the number of volunteer hosts. This is because the effect of vulnerability discovery and protection increases with the number of volunteer hosts. Volunteer hosts share the information on vulnerability discovery each other and can repair the vulnerability, which is an incentive reward for participating the volunteer group. However, the volunteer hosts should provide a certain amount of their computing resources, which degrade their performance. Therefore, we should consider this trade-off, using concepts such as the game theory.

Acknowledgement This is a product of research which was financially supported by the Kansai University Fund for Supporting Young Scholars, 2018, "Design of anti-malware systems against future malware evolution".

REFERENCES

[1] J. Dean et al., "Large scale distributed deep networks," in *Proc. Neural Information Processing Systems*, Lake Tahoe, NV, Dec. 2012, pp. 1–11.

[2] G. E. Hinton, S. Osindero, and Y. Teh, "A fast learning algorithm for deep belief nets," *Neural Computation*, vol. 18, no. 7, pp. 1527–1554, 2006.

[3] K. Hongyo, T. Kimura, T. Kudo, Y. Inoue, and K. Hirata, "Modeling of countermeasure against self-evolving botnets," in Proc. *IEEE International Conference on Consumer Electronics - Taiwan (IEEE ICCE-TW 2017)*, Taipei, Taiwan, Jun. 2017, pp. 1–2.

[4] T. Kudo, T. Kimura, Y. Inoue, H. Aman, and K. Hirata, "Behavior analysis of self-evolving botnets," in *Proc. the 2016 International Conference on Computer, Information, and Telecommunication Systems (CITS 2016)*, Kunming, China, Jul. 2016, pp. 1–6.

[5] T. Kudo, T. Kimura, Y. Inoue, H. Aman, and K. Hirata, "Stochastic modeling of self-evolving botnets with vulnerability discovery," *Computer Communications*, vol. 124, pp. 101–110, 2018.

[6] M. A. Rajab, J. Zarfoss, F. Monrose, and A. Terzis, "A multifaceted approach to understanding the botnet phenomenon," in *Proc. ACM SIGCOMM Conference on Internet measurement*, Rio de janeiro, Brazil, Oct. 2006, pp. 1–12.

[7] R. Scandariato, J. Walden, A. Hovsepyan, and W. Joosen, "Predicting vulnerable software components via text mining," *IEEE Transactions on Software Engineering*, vol. 40, no. 10, pp. 993–1006, 2014.

[8] F. Yamaguchi, F. Lindner, and K. Rieck, "Vulnerability extrapolation: assisted discovery of vulnerabilities using machine learning," in *Proc. USENIX conference on Offensive Technologies*, San Francisco, CA, Aug. 2011, pp. 1–10.

Detection of School Foundation Day Tweets
That Can Be Used to Distinguish Senders' Schools

Yasuhiko Watanabe, Hiroaki Onishi, Ryo Nishimura, and Yoshihiro Okada
Ryukoku University
Seta, Otsu, Shiga, Japan
Email: watanabe@rins.ryukoku.ac.jp, t150458@mail.ryukoku.ac.jp, r_nishimura@afc.ryukoku.ac.jp, okada@rins.ryukoku.ac.jp

***Abstract*—These days, many people use a Social Networking Service (SNS). When we use SNSs, we carefully protect the privacy of personal information: name, age, gender, address, telephone number, birthday, etc. However, we sometimes submit online messages that can threaten our privacy and security when combined with other information. In this study, we investigated tweets that can disclose senders' affiliations, especially, high schools to other people, including unwanted audiences, when combined with other public information. We collected 1,000 tweets including word "school foundation day" and found 46% of the collected tweets were ones disclosing foundation days of senders' schools. Furthermore, we found tweets including word "school foundation day" can be used to distinguish senders' schools when combined with event calendars in school web sites. Finally, we obtained 74% accuracy when we applied Support Vector Machine (SVM) to classify tweets including word "school foundation day" into ones disclosing the foundation days of senders' schools.**

***Keywords*–school foundation day; personal information; Twitter; SNS; privacy risk.**

I. INTRODUCTION

These days, many people use a Social Networking Service (SNS) to communicate with each other and try to enlarge their circle of friends. SNS users are generally concerned about potential privacy risks. To be specific, they are afraid that unwanted audiences will obtain information about them or their families, such as where they live, work, and play. As a result, SNS users are generally careful in disclosing their personal information. They disclose their personal information only when they think the benefits of doing it is greater than the potential privacy risks. For example, students are generally careful in disclosing which schools they go to. They are concerned that once unwanted audiences know which schools they go to, the unwanted audiences can obtain several kinds of their personal information: how old they are, where they live and study, who their friends and families are, and when they are at home or away. However, they often submit online messages that threaten their privacy and security when combined with other information. In this paper, we focus on school event messages submitted to Twitter. Student often submit tweets concerning school events, such as sports festival, culture festival, entrance ceremony, graduation ceremony, and foundation day. School event tweets often give students opportunities to start new communications on Twitter. However, they also give anyone, including unwanted audiences, opportunities to distinguish which schools they go to. Take a tweet concerning a school foundation day for example. Figure 1 shows a school foundation day tweet submitted by a high school student, *momone*. We retouched her photos in Figure 1 for protecting students' privacy. (exp 1) is the text of her tweet.

Figure 1. A school foundation day tweet submitted by a high school student, *momone*, on 6th October 2018.

(exp 1) *Souritsu kinenbi ha 6 nin. Nodo ga itaku naru kurai shabette waratta –*
(Six of us on foundation day. We talked so much and our throats were raspy –)

This tweet does not show which school *momone* went to. It only shows when she enjoyed the foundation day of her school. *Momone* might think that this tweet was not enough to distinguish which school she went to. In other words, there were too many schools and it was difficult to find schools whose foundation days were the day or just before she submitted this tweet. However, this tweet can threaten her privacy and security more than she expected. In this paper, we show that this tweet gave a chance to other people, including unwanted audiences, to distinguish which school she went to. In order to discuss the privacy risks caused by school event tweets, we show how school event tweets are used to distinguish which schools students go to. Furthermore, we discuss whether unwanted audiences can collect school event tweets by using machine learning techniques.

The rest of this paper is organized as follows: In Section II, we survey the related works. In Section III, we report school events and how school event tweets, especially school foundation day tweets, are used to distinguish which schools students go to. In Section IV, we discuss whether unwanted audiences can collect school foundation day tweets by using machine learning techniques. Finally, in Section V, we present our conclusions.

II. RELATED WORK

Personally identifiable information is defined as information which can be used to distinguish or trace an individual's identity such as social security number, biometric records, etc. alone, or when combined with other information that is linkable to a specific individual, such as date and place of birth, mother's maiden name, etc. [1] [2]. Internet users are generally concerned about unwanted audiences obtaining personal information. Fox et al. reported that 86% of Internet users are concerned that unwanted audiences will obtain information about them or their families [3]. Also, Acquisti and Gross reported that students expressed high levels of concern for general privacy issues on Facebook, such as a stranger finding out where they live and the location and schedule of their classes, and a stranger learning their sexual orientation, name of their current partner, and their political affiliations [4]. However, Internet users, especially young users, tend to disclose personal information on their profiles, for example, real full name, gender, hometown and full date of birth, which can potentially be used to identify details of their real life, such as their social security numbers. As a result, many researchers discussed the reasons why young users willingly disclose personal information on their SNS profiles. Dwyer concluded in her research that privacy is often not expected or undefined in SNSs [5]. Barnes argues that Internet users, especially teenagers, are not aware of the nature of the Internet and SNSs [6]. Hirai reported that many users had troubles in SNSs because they did not mind that strangers observed their communication with their friends [7]. Viseu et al. reported that many online users believe the benefits of disclosing personal information in order to use an Internet site is greater than the potential privacy risks [8]. On the other hand, Acquisti and Gross explain this phenomenon as a disconnection between the users' desire to protect their privacy and their actual behavior [4]. Also, Livingstone points out that teenagers' conception of privacy does not match the privacy settings of most SNSs [9]. Joinson et al. reported that trust and perceived privacy had a strong affect on individuals' willingness to disclose personal information to a website [10]. Also, Tufekci found that concern about unwanted audiences had an impact on whether or not students revealed their real names and religious affiliation on MySpace and Facebook [11]. The authors also think that most of students are seriously concerned about their privacy and security. However, they often underestimate the risk of their online messages and submit them. For example, many students submit online messages concerning school events. Most students do not mind that these messages can threaten their privacy and security. To be specific, these messages may give a chance to other people, including unwanted audiences, to distinguish which schools students go to. However, no studies have been made on the risk of online messages concerning school events.

III. RISK OF SCHOOL EVENT TWEETS

SNS users want to start new communication and enjoy it. As a result, they want good topics for starting new communication in SNS. For example, school events are good topics for starting new communication in SNS. Actually, many students submit tweets concerning school events. However, school event tweets may threaten students' privacy and security because most of them are submitted during or just after school events. Specifically, unwanted audiences can

- imagine when students in the target school submit school event tweets and
- use the dates of school event tweets as clues to distinguish which schools students go to.

Furthermore, it is easy to obtain school event calendars because many schools show their school event calendars in their web sites. In order to clarify the risks caused by school event tweets, in this paper, we discuss

- school events that are held every year and good topics for tweets, and
- how to distinguish which schools senders go to by using school event tweets and event calendars.

A. Annual school events frequently reported in tweets

Several kinds of events are held in schools. In this section, we discuss

- school festivals,
- school ceremonies, and
- school memorial days.

This is because these events are held every year in most schools in Japan and frequently reported in tweets by students. Furthermore, many schools show the dates of these school events in their web sites.

1) School festivals: We first discuss two major school festivals in Japan: sports festivals and culture festivals. In Japan, school sports festivals are mainly held in spring (May and June) or autumn (September and October). Many students submit tweets concerning sports festivals in their schools. Figure 2 shows a tweet concerning a sports festival submitted by a high school student, *ayane*, on 29th September 2018. On the other hand, in Japan, culture festivals are mainly held from September to December. Culture festivals are chances for students to show what they have learned in the year and create a performance for their parents, teachers, and in some cases, the public. As a result, many students submit tweets concerning culture festivals in their schools. Figure 3 shows a culture festival tweet. It was also submitted by *ayane* on 22nd September 2018.

Students often attach pictures to their tweets concerning sports festivals and culture festivals. As shown in Figure 2 and Figure 3, *ayane* attached many pictures to her sports festival tweet and culture festival tweet. Figure 4 shows pictures attached to *ayane*'s sports festival tweet. In the pictures, there were many students and we found a clue to distinguish which school these students and *ayane* went to: a girl student in the lower left picture wore an athletic uniform with the name of their school. The web site of their school showed that the sports festival and culture festival were held on 28th and 21st October 2018, respectively. As a result, *ayane* submitted her sports festival tweet and culture festival tweet on the next day of the sports festival and culture festival, respectively.

Sports festivals and culture festivals are held every year, however, the dates of them may change every year. For example, culture festival in *ayane*'s school was held on 21st October 2018 while it was held on 22nd October 2017.

Figure 2. A sports festival tweet submitted by a high school student, *ayane*, on 29th September 2018.

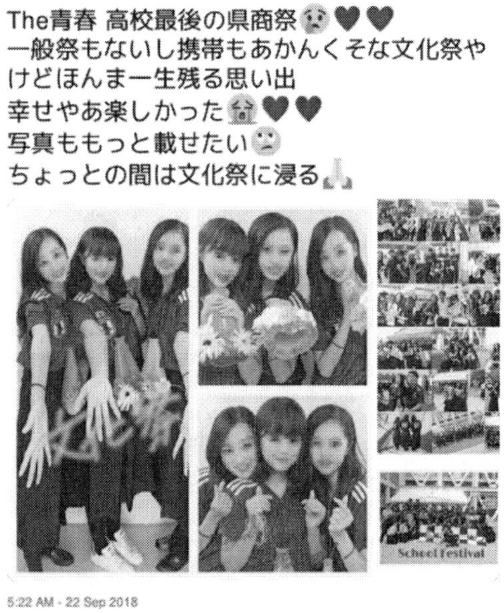

Figure 3. A culture festival tweet submitted by a high school student, *ayane*, on 22nd September 2018.

2) *School ceremonies:* We discuss two major school ceremonies in Japan: entrance ceremony and graduation ceremony. In Japan, entrance ceremonies are generally held in the first half of April. For example, in 2018, all public high schools in Kyoto held the entrance ceremonies on 9th or 10th April. On the other hand, graduation ceremonies are generally held in March. For example, in 2018, all public high schools in Kyoto held the graduation ceremonies on 1st March. The dates of entrance ceremonies and graduation ceremonies may change every year.

Figure 4. Pictures attached to *ayane*'s sports festival tweet (Figure 2).

Figure 5. A graduation ceremony tweet submitted by a high school student, *nanae*, on 7th March 2019.

Many students and their family members submit tweets with pictures concerning these ceremonies. Pictures attached to school ceremony tweets, just like those attached to school festival tweets, often give chances for readers to obtain several kinds of senders' personal information. Figure 5 shows a graduation ceremony tweet submitted by a high school student, *nanae*, on 7th March 2019. *Nanae* took pictures concerning her graduation ceremony and attached them to her tweet. In the pictures, we found a clue to distinguish which schools *nanae* went to: students were holding a signboard with the name of her school. It shows *nanae* went to the same school as *ayane*.

Entrance ceremonies and graduation ceremonies are held in short periods. Many schools hold these ceremonies on the same day. For example, in 2018, all public high schools in Kyoto held the graduation ceremonies on the same day. As a result, it is difficult to distinguish which schools senders go

Figure 6. A foundation day tweet submitted by a high school student, *ayane*, on 6th October 2018.

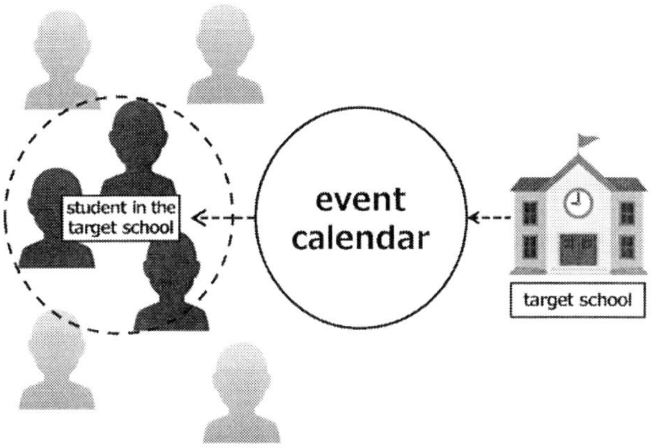

Figure 7. It is easy to detect school event tweets submitted by students in the target school on the day or just after the event was held.

to by using the submission date of tweets concerning entrance ceremonies and graduation ceremonies.

3) School memorial days: We discuss one major school memorial day in Japan, school foundation day. School foundation days are held all year around. Furthermore, school foundation days are fixed while the dates of school festivals and ceremonies may change every year. The important point is that many schools are closed on their foundation days. As a result, many students submit school foundation day tweets in order to show where they go, what they do, and who they are with in the special day. Figure 6 shows a foundation day tweet submitted by *ayane* on 6th October 2018. (exp 2) is a text message in her school foundation day tweet.

(exp 2) *Souritsu kinenbi ha suggoi shiawase na ichinichi yatta. chotto hayame no tanjyoubi oiwai shite kurete konna kawaii purezento moracchatta (;_;) daiji ni tsukawasete itadaki masu.*
(The foundation day was a very happy day. Thank you for an early birthday party and beautiful presents. I'll treasure them.)

B. How to use school event tweets for distinguishing which schools students go to

Many students submit their school event tweets. However, most of them may think that their school event tweets are not enough to distinguish which schools they go to. The reasons are as follows:

- There are many similar online messages. Their messages are not special. No one pays attention to them.
- There are many schools. It is difficult to find schools whose school events were held on the day or just before they submitted their school event tweets.

Take the tweet shown in Figure 3 for example. This culture festival tweet was submitted by *ayane* on 22nd September 2018. Most of students may think that it is hard to visit many school web sites and check whether the culture festival was held on 22nd September or just before. However, it is not difficult to detect school event tweets submitted by students in a particular school. To be specific, it is easy to obtain the event calendar from the web site of the target school and collect school event tweets that were submitted on the day or just after the target school held it. Figure 7 shows the overview of it.

In order to evaluate this method, take a high school in Kobe for example. We visited the web site of the target school and obtained the event calendar. According to the event calendar, in 2018, this school held

- the foundation day on 5th October,
- the sports festival on 28th September, and
- the culture festival on 21st September.

We think, the date of foundation day is more useful than those of sports festival and culture festival to collect tweets submitted by students of the target school. This is because the number of schools that have the same foundation day is less than those that have the same sport festival day or the same culture festival day. School foundation days are held all year round while sport festivals and culture festivals are not. As a result, we planned to collect foundation day tweets submitted on 5th October 2018, the foundation day of the target school, or just after it. In this paper, we used Twitter search and obtained 45 tweets that were submitted on 5th October or 6th October 2018 and included *kaiko kinenbi* (school foundation day) or *souritsu kinenbi* (foundation day). 15 tweets of them had pictures and two of them had pictures of young persons. We focused on these two tweets with pictures of young persons. One was shown in Figure 1 and submitted by *momone* on 6th October. The other was shown in Figure 6 and submitted by *ayane* on 6th October. Furthermore, *momone* submitted

- her sports festival tweet on 29th September (one day after the sports festival was held in the target school)
- her culture festival tweet on 21st September (the day when the culture festival was held in the target school)

Also, *ayane* submitted

- her sports festival tweet (Figure 2) on 29th September (one day after the sports festival was held in the target school)
- her culture festival tweet (Figure 3) on 22nd September (one day after the culture festival was held in the target school)

We think that it is not coincidence that the event dates of the target school were matched with the submission dates of these tweets. As a result, we concluded that *ayane* and *momone* went to the target school. Furthermore, we found a girl student wearing an athletic uniform with the name of the target school in the pictures attached to *ayane*'s sports festival tweet (Figure 2), submitted on 29th September.

We found that *ayane* sent birthday tweets to *momone* on her birthday. *Ayane* was *momone*'s friend. Furthermore, in 2018, not only *ayane* but three other users sent birthday tweets to *momone*. We could not detect these three users because they did not submit foundation day tweets. However, they submitted school festival tweets the dates of which were matched with those of the school festivals in the target school. As a result, we also concluded that they went to the same school as *momone* and *ayane*. Actually, one of them was *nanae*. The pictures attended to *nanae*'s graduation ceremony tweet (Figure 5) and *ayane*'s sports festival tweet (Figure 2) show that *nanae* and *ayane* went to the same school.

IV. Detection of Foundation Day Tweets

In order to collect school event tweets efficiently, it is important to detect them automatically. If school event tweets, especially foundation day tweets, are detected automatically, the detected tweets can be used for the following conflicting purposes.

- We can give warnings to users before they submit their school event tweets that threaten their privacy and security.
- Unwanted audiences can collect school event tweets and obtain several kinds of senders' personal information.

In this section, we discuss whether we can automatically detect foundation day tweets by using machine learning techniques.

In this study, we used the Support Vector Machine (SVM) for data training and classifying. Table I shows feature $s1 \sim s16$ used in machine learning on experimental data. $s1 \sim s7$ were obtained by using the results of morphological analysis on experimental data. In the experiments, we used a Japanese morphological analyzer, JUMAN, for word segmentation of Japanese tweets [12]. $s8 \sim s10$ and $s12 \sim s14$ were obtained by extracting character N-gram from experimental data. Odaka et al. reported that character 3-gram is good for Japanese processing [13]. $s4 \sim s7$ and $s12 \sim s15$ were obtained from first sentences of tweets. This is because, we thought, clue expressions of school events are often found at first sentences of tweets.

In this study, we used 1,000 Japanese tweets including "*kaiko kinenbi* (school foundation day)" for the experimental data. We collected these tweets by Twitter search from July to November 2018. These 1,000 tweets can be classified into two types:

TABLE I. Features used in SVM method for data training and classifying Japanese tweets including word "*kaiko kinenbi* (school foundation day)"

$s1$	word unigrams of the tweet
$s2$	word bigrams of the tweet
$s3$	the number of words in the tweet
$s4$	word unigrams of the first sentence of the tweet
$s5$	word bigrams of the first sentence of the tweet
$s6$	the number of words in the first sentence of the tweet
$s7$	the last word of the first sentence of the tweet
$s8$	character unigrams of the tweet
$s9$	character bigrams of the tweet
$s10$	character 3-grams of the tweet
$s11$	the length of the tweet
$s12$	character unigrams of the first sentence of the tweet
$s13$	character bigrams of the first sentence of the tweet
$s14$	character 3-grams of the first sentence of the tweet
$s15$	the length of the first sentence of the tweet
$s16$	whether the tweet is a reply

TABLE II. The details of the 1,000 Japanese tweets including "*kaiko kinenbi* (school foundation day)" (from July to November 2018).

	FD tweet	others	total
normal tweet	393	309	702
reply	66	232	298
retweet	0	0	0
total	459	541	1,000

- foundation day tweet
  foundation day tweets show when the foundation days of senders' schools are.
- others
  others do not show when the foundation days of senders' schools are although they include word "*kaiko kinenbi* (school foundation day)".

Furthermore, tweets can be classified into three types [14]:

- reply
  A reply is submitted to a particular person. It contains "@username" in the body of the tweet.
- retweet
  A retweet is a reply to a tweet that includes the original tweet.
- normal tweet
  A normal tweet is neither reply nor retweet. Normal tweets are generally submitted to general public.

Table II shows the numbers of normal tweets, replies, and retweets in the 1,000 tweets. Also, it shows the numbers of foundation day (FD) tweets and others in the 1,000 tweets. As shown in Figure II, there were no retweets in the 1,000 tweets. We conducted this experiment using TinySVM [15]. Table III shows the experimental result of the 1,000 Japanese tweets. The experimental result was obtained with 10-fold cross-validation. In order to discuss our method in more detail, we divided the experimental result of the 1,000 Japanese tweets

TABLE III. THE SVM CLASSIFICATION RESULT OF THE 1,000 JAPANESE TWEETS INCLUDING WORD "*kaiko kinenbi* (SCHOOL FOUNDATION DAY)".

human expert	SVM result		
result	FD tweet	others	recall
FD tweet	332	127	0.72
others	132	409	0.76
precision	0.72	0.76	

TABLE IV. THE SVM CLASSIFICATION RESULT OF THE 702 JAPANESE NORMAL TWEETS INCLUDING WORD "*kaiko kinenbi* (SCHOOL FOUNDATION DAY)".

human expert	SVM result		
result	FD tweet	others	recall
FD tweet	308	85	0.78
others	123	186	0.60
precision	0.71	0.69	

TABLE V. THE SVM CLASSIFICATION RESULT OF THE 298 JAPANESE REPLIES INCLUDING WORD "*kaiko kinenbi* (SCHOOL FOUNDATION DAY)".

human expert	SVM result		
result	FD tweet	others	recall
FD tweet	24	42	0.36
others	9	223	0.96
precision	0.73	0.84	

(Table III) into those of 702 normal tweets (Table IV) and 298 replies (Table V).

As shown in Table III, 741 Japanese tweets were classified correctly and 259 tweets incorrectly in this experiment. 332 tweets out of the 741 correctly classified tweets were ones where the foundation days of senders' schools were disclosed. As shown in Table III, both the recall and precision of tweets disclosing the foundation days of senders' schools were 72%. Furthermore, as shown in Table IV and Table V, the precision of normal tweets and replies disclosing the foundation days of senders' schools were 71% and 73%, respectively. Our method is useful for collecting foundation day tweets precisely. As a result, it is easy for unwanted audiences to collect tweets disclosing the foundation days of senders' schools by using our method. On the other hand, the recall of replies disclosing the foundation days of senders' schools was 36%. Our method could not detect many replies disclosing the foundation days of senders' schools. As a result, in order to give warnings to users before they submit their school event tweets that threaten their privacy and security, it is necessary to improve our method.

V. CONCLUSION

In this paper, we investigated school event tweets, especially foundation day tweets and showed that they should be treated carefully. This is because school event tweets can threaten students' privacy and security when combined with event calendars. We showed that foundation day tweets can be collected precisely by using machine learning techniques. On the other hand, anyone, including unwanted audiences, can obtain event calendars easily because they are often available on schools' web sites. In order to discuss how easy is it to obtain school event calendars, we are investigating the percentage of schools that let anyone obtain event calendars through their web sites. Finally, we should note that we retouched all the photos in this paper for protecting students' privacy.

REFERENCES

[1] C. Johnson III, Safeguarding against and responding to the breach of personally identifiable information, Office of Management and Budget Memorandum, 2007. [Online]. Available: http://www.whitehouse.gov/omb/memoranda/fy2007/m07-16.pdf [accessed: 2016-10-04]

[2] B. Krishnamurthy and C. E. Wills, "On the leakage of personally identifiable information via online social networks," Computer Communication Review, vol. 40, no. 1, 2010, pp. 112–117. [Online]. Available: https://doi.org/10.1145/1672308.1672328 [accessed: 2019-05-10]

[3] S. Fox et al., Trust and Privacy Online: Why Americans Want to Rewrite the Rules, The Pew Internet & American Life Project, 2000. [Online]. Available: http://www.pewinternet.org/2000/08/20/trust-and-privacy-online/ [accessed: 2019-05-10]

[4] A. Acquisti and R. Gross, Imagined Communities: Awareness, Information Sharing, and Privacy on the Facebook. Berlin, Heidelberg: Springer Berlin Heidelberg, 2006, pp. 36–58.

[5] C. Dwyer, "Digital relationships in the "myspace" generation: Results from a qualitative study," in Proceedings of the 40th Annual Hawaii International Conference on System Sciences, ser. HICSS '07. Washington, DC, USA: IEEE Computer Society, 2007, p. 19.

[6] S. B. Barnes, "A privacy paradox: Social networking in the united states," First Monday, vol. 11, no. 9, 2006. [Online]. Available: http://firstmonday.org/article/view/1394/1312 [accessed: 2019-05-10]

[7] T. Hirai, "Why does "Enjyo" happen on the Web? : An Examination based on Japanese Web Culture," Journal of Information and Communication Research, vol. 29, no. 4, mar 2012, pp. 61–71. [Online]. Available: http://doi.org/10.11430/jsicr.29.4_61 [accessed: 2019-05-10]

[8] A. Viseu, A. Clement, and J. Aspinall, "Situating privacy online: Complex perception and everyday practices," Information, Communication & Society, 2004, pp. 92–114.

[9] S. Livingstone, "Taking risky opportunities in youthful content creation: teenagers' use of social networking sites for intimacy, privacy and self-expression," New Media & Society, vol. 10, no. 3, 2008, pp. 393–411.

[10] A. N. Joinson, U.-D. Reips, T. Buchanan, and C. B. P. Schofield, "Privacy, trust, and self-disclosure online," Human-Computer Interaction, vol. 25, no. 1, 2010, pp. 1–24. [Online]. Available: https://www.tandfonline.com/doi/abs/10.1080/07370020903586662 [accessed: 2019-05-10]

[11] Z. Tufekci, "Can You See Me Now? Audience and Disclosure Regulation in Online Social Network Sites," Bulletin of Science, Technology & Society, vol. 28, no. 1, 2008, pp. 20–36.

[12] S. Kurohashi and D. Kawahara, JUMAN Manual version 5.1 (in Japanese). Kyoto University, 2005.

[13] T. Odaka et al., "A proposal on student report scoring system using n-gram text analysis method," The transactions of the Institute of Electronics, Information and Communication Engineers. D-I, vol. 86, no. 9, sep 2003, pp. 702–705.

[14] Y. Watanabe, K. Nakajima, H. Morimoto, R. Nishimura, and Y. Okada, "An investigation of a factor that affects the usage of unsounded code strings at the end of japanese and english tweets," in Proceedings of the Seventh International Conference on Evolving Internet (INTERNET 2015), Oct 2015, pp. 50–55. [Online]. Available: https://www.thinkmind.org/index.php?view=article&articleid=internet_2015_2_40_40038 [accessed: 2019-05-10]

[15] T. Kudoh. TinySVM: Support Vector Machines. [Online]. Available: http://chasen.org/taku/software/TinySVM/index.html [accessed: 2019-05-10]

Performance Analysis of Surveillance Camera System with Image Recognition Server

Goo Yeon Lee
leegyeon@kangwon.ac.kr
Dept. of Computer and Communication Eng.
Kangwon National University
Chuncheon-si, Gangwon-do, Korea

Hwa Jong Kim
hjkim@kangwon.ac.kr
Dept. of Computer and Communication Eng.
Kangwon National University
Chuncheon-si, Gangwon-do, Korea

Abstract—**In this paper, we study a performance analysis of a surveillance camera system with image recognition server based on frame discard rate and server utilization. The states of surveillance cameras are divided into recognition and silence states to analyze the parameters, such as the optimal number of image frames and cameras based on processing capacity of the recognition server. The result of the analysis will be useful for effective operation of the evolving surveillance camera systems.**

Keywords-surveillance camera; image recognition; network

I. INTRODUCTION

The image recognition server located in the central surveillance system can perform well when receiving as many image frames as possible from the surveillance cameras. However, the surveillance system operator may not allow frames to be transmitted continuously because it must pay a lot to the network depending on the number of transmitted image frames. Therefore, in this paper, we consider a system where the image recognition server analyzes the received image frames from surveillance cameras and determine whether there is an object of interest, and accordingly sets the state of each surveillance camera to a *recognition state* for transmitting a large number of frames and a *silence state* for transmitting a small number of frames. In such a surveillance camera network system, the system operator also needs to optimize the number of cameras arranged in accordance with the processing capacity of the image recognition server.

Many researches have been conducted on the number of transmission frames, network bandwidth and security method in surveillance camera systems. In [1], an optimal scheduling has been studied for storing the camera image data based on the network bandwidth and limited processing resources in the CCTV(Closed-Circuit TeleVision) system. In [2], the authors proposed a method to provide streaming service over HTTP (HyperText Transfer Protocol) by interworking with user and server. In this method, the user can predict the next segment resolution by providing current channel resource information.

In this paper, we perform a numerical analysis and discuss results in Section 2 and make a conclusion in Section 3.

II. ANALYTICAL MODEL AND NUMERICAL RESULTS

In the analysis, we assume that N surveillance cameras are connected to the image recognition server through the surveillance network. The image recognition server analyzes the arrived image frame and sets the camera to a recognition state with frame rate R_{rec} when the object of interest is recognized, otherwise sets it to a silence state with frame rate R_{sil} ($R_{rec} > R_{sil}$). Figure 1 shows the transition between the two states in surveillance cameras where the recognition and silence states of each camera alternate, and we assume that this transition process is independent of other cameras. This assumption is not appropriate when the surveillance cameras are concentrated at a short distance. However, in this study, we assume that the surveillance cameras are scattered in a large area. Also, for the sake of analysis, it is assumed that the state characteristics of all cameras are the same.

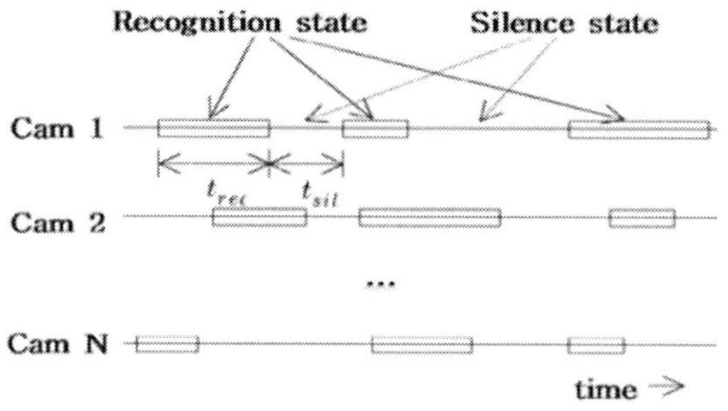

Figure 1. Transitions between recognition and silence states of surveillance cameras.

In Figure 1, we represent the recognition state interval length as a r.v. (random variable) t_{rec} and the silence state interval length as a r.v. t_{sil}. We assume that the number of frames processed per second in the image recognition server (processing capacity) is C. Generally, the surveillance system is effective in real-time monitoring, therefore we assume that the image recognition server has a small waiting queue to guarantee real-time performance and we also assume that for the sake of analysis, any frames received beyond the server capacity C in seconds are discarded.

Based on the above assumptions, the probability of a surveillance camera being in the recognition state and in the silence state are given as $P_{rec} = \frac{E(t_{rec})}{E(t_{rec})+E(t_{sil})}$ and $P_{sil} = 1 - P_{rec}$, where $E(\cdot)$ is the expected value. Also, the probability that k cameras are in the recognition state can be calculated as $P_k = \binom{N}{k}(P_{rec})^k(1-P_{rec})^{N-k}$, $(0 \le k \le N)$. In terms of reasonable operation, the minimum total number of transmitted frames per second should be equal to or less than the processing capacity C. Also, processing capacity C should be equal to or less than the maximum total number of transmitted frames per second. That is $N \cdot R_{sil} \le C \le N \cdot R_{rec}$.

The average total number of frames transmitted per second is $N{\cdot}P_{rec}{\cdot}R_{rec}$ + $N{\cdot}(1-P_{rec}){\cdot}R_{sil}$. If the server processing capacity C is designed to be equal to $N{\cdot}R_{rec}$, there will be no frames that are not processed by the server and discarded. However, in this case, the waste of processing capacity of the server is on average $C - N{\cdot}P_{rec}{\cdot}R_{rec} - N{\cdot}(1-P_{rec}){\cdot}R_{sil}$ frames per second. Therefore, it is necessary to increase the utilization of the server by allowing some frames to be discarded. Thus, we analyze the relationship between the processing capacity of the server, the number of discarded frames, and the number of cameras. Given the server capacity C, the corresponding number of cameras m can be calculated using $C=m{\cdot}R_{rec}+(N-m){\cdot}R_{sil}$ where m is an integer that is equal to $m=\left\lfloor\frac{C-N{\cdot}R_{sil}}{R_{rec}-R_{sil}}\right\rfloor$. Now the expected average number of frames that are discarded without processing at the server is:

$$F_{discarded} = \sum_{k=m+1}^{N} P_k{\cdot}[k{\cdot}R_{rec} + (N-k){\cdot}R_{sil} - C] \quad (1)$$

In this study, two performance measures are considered. The first is the ratio of the number of frames that are discarded at the server to the server's processing capacity that we call Discarded Ratio (DR). The discarded frames consume network resources without being processed at the server. So the larger the number, the greater the inefficiency. The second is the utilization of the server, ρ, which is expressed as a ratio of the number of frames actually processed by the server to the capacity of the server. High utilization means the high operation efficiency of the server.

DR is calculated as $\frac{F_{discarded}}{C}$, and we have

$$DR = \frac{1}{C}{\cdot}\sum_{k=m+1}^{N} P_k{\cdot}[k{\cdot}R_{rec} + (N-k){\cdot}R_{sil} - C] \quad (2)$$
$$= \sum_{k=m+1}^{N}\binom{N}{k}(P_{rec})^k(1-P_{rec})^{N-k}\left[\frac{k{\cdot}R_{rec}+(N-k){\cdot}R_{sil}}{C}-1\right].$$

Then ρ can be calculated as

$$\rho = \frac{1}{C}{\cdot}[\sum_{k=0}^{m} P_k{\cdot}[k{\cdot}R_{rec} + (N-k){\cdot}R_{sil}] + \sum_{k=m+1}^{N} P_k{\cdot}C]$$
$$= 1 - \sum_{k=0}^{m}\binom{N}{k}(P_{rec})^k(1-P_{rec})^{N-k}\left[1-\frac{k{\cdot}R_{rec}+(N-k){\cdot}R_{sil}}{C}\right]. \quad (3)$$

Figures 2 and 3 are numerical results of the analysis when C=100, R_{rec} =5, R_{sil} = 1 and P_{rec} = 0.1, 0.2, 0.3, 0.4, 0.5.

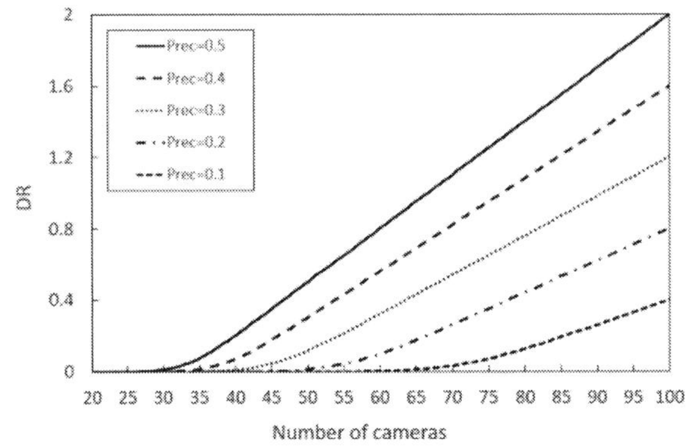

Figure 2. Relation between N and DR when C=100, R_{rec} =5, R_{sil} = 1, P_{rec} = 0.1, 0.2, 0.3, 0.4, 0.5.

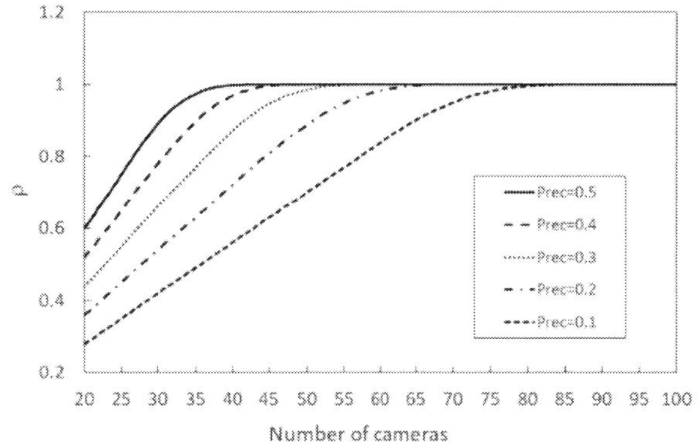

Figure 3. Relation between N and ρ when C=100, R_{rec} =5, R_{sil} = 1, P_{rec} = 0.1, 0.2, 0.3, 0.4, 0.5.

Figure 2 shows the relationship between DR and N, and Figure 3 shows the relationship between ρ and N. As shown in Figures 2 and 3, when designing DR = 0 which means no frames to be discarded at the server, the number of surveillance cameras is limited to N = 20. However, in this case, the utilization, ρ, is 28%, 36%, 44% 52%, 60% for P_{rec} = 0.1, 0.2, 0.3, 0.4, 0.5 respectively, which means the server efficiency is not high as one expects. To increase the server efficiency, we need to allow some value of DR. For example, when DR=0.01 (1%), and P_{rec}= 0.1, 0.2, 0.3, 0.4, 0.5, the number of cameras can be increased to N= 64, 49, 40, 34, 29, respectively. In this case, the server utilization is 88.8%, 87.3%, 87.1%, 87.4%, 86.4% respectively. Hence, as we allow the number of unprocessed and thus discarded frames at the server to be 1% of the server processing capacity, the utilization of the server rapidly increases to 86% through 89%.

III. CONCLUSION

In this study, we analyzed two performance factors that are required for an efficient surveillance camera system with image recognition server, i.e., server utilization and frame discard rate. We believe the results obtained in this study will be useful for the efficient design and operation of surveillance camera system, which has been widely used recently.

ACKNOWLEDGMENT

This work was supported by Institute for Information & communications Technology Promotion (IITP) grant funded by the Korea government (MSIT) (No: 2018-0-00261, GDPR Compliant Personal Identifiable Information Management Technology for IoT Environment)

REFERENCES

[1] K. J. Lin, T. K. Hou, and R. J. Chiu, "Jitter-Constrained Camera Scheduling in CCTV Surveillance Networks", 2016 IEEE International Conference on Signal and Image Processing(ICSIP), pp. 650-654, Aug. 2016.

[2] E. Khorov, A. Krasilov, M. Liubogoshchev, and S. Tang, "SEBRA: SAND-Enabled Bitrate and Resource Allocation algorithm for network assisted video streaming", in Proc. of IEEE WiMob, Rome, Italy, pp. 1-8, Nov. 2017.

Managing Path Switching in Multipath Video Streaming

Shinichi Nagayama, Dirceu Cavendish, Daiki Nobayashi, Takeshi Ikenaga
Department of Computer Science and Electronics
Kyushu Institute of Technology
Fukuoka, Japan
e-mail: {o108076s@mail}.kyutech.jp {cavendish@ndrc, nova@ecs, ike@ecs}.kyutech.ac.jp

***Abstract*—Video streaming has become the major source of Internet traffic nowadays. Considering that content delivery network providers utilize Video over Hypertext Transfer Protocol/Transmission Control Protocol (HTTP/TCP) as the preferred protocol stack for video streaming, understanding TCP performance in transporting video streams has become paramount. Recently, multipath transport protocols have allowed video streaming over multiple paths to become a reality. In this paper, we analyze the impact of path switching on multipath video streaming and network performance, and propose new schedulers which minimize the number of path switching. We utilize network performance measures, as well as video quality metrics, to characterize the performance and interaction between network and application layers of video streams for various network scenarios.**

***Keywords*—Video streaming; high speed networks; TCP congestion control; TCP socket state; Multipath TCP; Packet retransmissions; Packet loss.**

I. INTRODUCTION

Transmission Control Protocol (TCP) is the dominant transport protocol of the Internet, providing reliable data transmission for the large majority of applications. For data applications, the perceived quality of service is the total transport time of a given file. For real time (streaming) applications, the perceived quality of experience involves not only the total transport time, but also the amount of data discarded at the client due to excessive transport delays, as well as rendering stalls due to the lack of timely data. Transport delays and data starvation depend on how TCP handles flow control and packet retransmissions. Therefore, video streaming user experience depends heavily on TCP performance.

Recently, multipath transport has allowed video streams over multiple IP interfaces and network paths. Multipath streaming not only augments aggregated bandwidth, but also increases reliability at the transport level session even when a specific radio link coverage gets compromised. An important issue in multipath transport is the path (sub-flow) selection; a path scheduler is needed to split traffic to be injected on a packet by packet basis onto available paths. For video streaming applications, head of line blocking may cause incomplete or late frames to be discarded at the receiver, as well as stream stalling. In this work, we analyze the effect of path switching on the quality of video stream delivery. In addition, we propose path switch aware schedulers, which strive to minimize the number of path switches during a video stream delivery session while improving video performance. We show that, by selectively controlling path switching, video streaming performance improvements can be obtained for widely deployed TCP variants and network scenarios.

The material is organized as follows. Related work discussion is provided on Section II. Section III describes video streaming over TCP system. Section IV introduces the TCP variants addressed in this paper. Section V analyzes path switching effects on video performance, and introduces our new path scheduling proposals, generically called sticky schedulers. Section VI addresses multiple path video delivery performance evaluation using default path scheduler vis a vis several sticky schedulers, for each TCP variant and multiple packet schedulers. Our empirical results show that most TCP variants deliver better video performance when sticky scheduling is utilized. Section VII addresses directions we are pursuing as follow up to this work.

II. RELATED WORK

Although multipath transport studies are plenty in the literature, there has been limited prior work on video performance over multiple paths [4] [14] [19]. Regarding multipath schedulers, there has been recent research activity, propelled by the availability of Multipath Transmission Control Protocol (MPTCP) transport stack. Most of them focus on specific sub-flow characterization to support smart path selection. For instance, Yan et al. [21] propose a path selection mechanism based on estimated sub-flow capacity. Their evaluation is centered on throughput performance, as well as reducing packet retransmissions. Hwang et al. [9] propose a blocking scheme of a slow path when delay difference between paths is large, in order to improve data transport completion time on short lived flows. Ferlin et al. [6] introduce a path selection scheme based on a predictor of the head-of-line blocking of a given path. They carry out emulation experiments with their scheduler against the minimum Round Trip Time (RTT) default scheduler, in transporting bulk data, Web transactions and Constant Bit Rate (CBR) traffic, with figure of merits of goodput, completion time and packet delays, respectively. More recently, Kimura et al. [11] have shown throughput performance improvements on schedulers driven by path sending rate and window space, focusing on bulk data transfer applications. Also, Dong et al. [5] have proposed a path loss estimation approach to select paths subject to high and bulk loss rates. Although they have presented some video streaming experiments, they do not measure streaming performance from an application perspective. Xue et al. [20] has proposed a path scheduler based on prediction of the amount of data a path is able to transmit and evaluated it on simulated

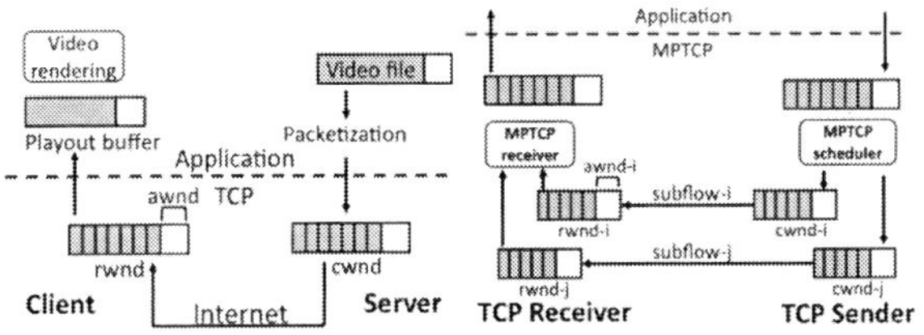

(a) TCP (b) MPTCP

Figure 1: Video Streaming over TCP/MPTCP

network scenarios with respect to throughput performance. A different approach, at which different sub-flows are used for segregating prioritized packets of Augmented Reality/Virtual Reality streams has been proposed by Silva et al. [18]. Finally, Frommgen et al. [8] have shown that stale round trip time (rtt) information interferes with path selection of small streams such as HTTP traffic. The authors then propose an rtt probing and one way delay based path selection to improve latency and throughput performance of thin streams.

In contrast, our current work seeks multipath path scheduling principles that can be applied to different path schedulers to specifically improve the quality of video streams. Previously [12], we have proposed new Multipath TCP path schedulers based on dynamic path characteristics, such as congestion window space and estimated path throughput, and evaluated multipath video streaming using these proposed schedulers. Recently [13], we have also proposed to enhance path schedulers with TCP state information, such as whether a path is in fast retransmit and fast recovery state, to improve video quality in lossy network scenarios. In this work, we propose one more principle to path selection, the minimization of path switching. We evaluate new path schedulers, called sticky schedulers, on video stream applications using widely deployed TCP variants on open source network experiments over WiFi an wired access links.

III. Video Streaming over TCP

Video streaming over HTTP/TCP involves an HTTP server, where video files are made available for streaming upon HTTP requests, and a video client, which places HTTP requests to the server over the Internet, for video streaming. Figure 1 (a) illustrates video streaming components.

An HTTP server stores encoded video files, available upon HTTP requests. Once a request is placed, a TCP sender is instantiated to transmit packetized data to the client machine. At TCP transport layer, a congestion window is used for flow controlling the amount of data injected into the network. The size of the congestion window, $cwnd$, is adjusted dynamically, according to the level of congestion in the network, as well as the space available for data storage, $awnd$, at the TCP client receiver buffer. Congestion window space is freed only when data packets are acknowledged by the receiver, so that lost packets are retransmitted by the TCP layer. At the client side, in addition to acknowledging arriving packets, TCP receiver sends back its current available space $awnd$, so that at the sender side, $cwnd \leq awnd$ at all times. At the client application layer, a video player extracts data from a playout buffer, filled with packets delivered by TCP receiver from its buffer. The playout buffer is used to smooth out variable data arrival rate.

A. Interaction between Video streaming and TCP

At the server side, the HTTP server retrieves data into the TCP sender buffer according to $cwnd$ size. Hence, the injection rate of video data into the TCP buffer is different than the video variable encoding rate. In addition, TCP throughput performance is affected by the round trip time of the TCP session. This is a direct consequence of the congestion window mechanism of TCP, where only up to a $cwnd$ worth of bytes can be delivered without acknowledgements. Hence, for a fixed $cwnd$ size, from the sending of the first packet until the first acknowledgement arrives, a TCP session throughput is capped at $cwnd/RTT$. For each TCP congestion avoidance scheme, the size of the congestion window is computed by a specific algorithm at time of packet acknowledgement reception by the TCP source. However, for all schemes, the size of the congestion window is capped by the available TCP receiver space $awnd$ sent back from the TCP client.

At the client side, the video data is retrieved by the video player into a playout buffer and delivered to the video renderer. Playout buffer may underflow, if TCP receiver window empties out. On the other hand, playout buffer overflow does not occur, since the player will not pull more data into the playout buffer than it can handle.

In summary, video data packets are injected into the network only if space is available at the TCP congestion window. Arriving packets at the client are stored at the TCP receiver buffer and extracted by the video playout client at the video nominal playout rate.

IV. Transmission Control Protocol Variants

TCP protocols fall into two categories, delay and loss based. Advanced loss based TCP protocols use packet loss as primary congestion indication signal, performing window regulation as $cwnd_k = f(cwnd_{k-1})$, being ack reception paced. Most f functions follow an Additive Increase Multiplicative Decrease (AIMD) strategy, with various increase and decrease parameters. TCP NewReno [1] and Cubic [16] are examples of AIMD strategies. Delay based TCP protocols, on the other hand, use queue delay information as the congestion indication signal, increasing/decreasing the window if the delay is small/large, respectively. Compound [17] and Capacity and Congestion Probing (CCP) [3] are examples of delay based protocols.

Most TCP variants follow TCP Reno phase framework: slow start, congestion avoidance, fast retransmit and fast recovery. For TCP variants widely used today, congestion avoidance phase is sharply different. We will be introducing specific TCP variants' congestion avoidance phase shortly.

A. Cubic TCP Congestion Avoidance

TCP Cubic is a loss based TCP that has achieved widespread usage as the default TCP of the Linux operating system. During congestion avoidance, its congestion window adjustment scheme is:

$$
\begin{aligned}
AckRec: \quad cwnd_{k+1} &= C(t-K)^3 + Wmax \\
K &= (Wmax\frac{\beta}{C})^{1/3} \\
PktLoss: \quad cwnd_{k+1} &= \beta cwnd_k \\
Wmax &= cwnd_k
\end{aligned} \tag{1}
$$

where C is a scaling factor, Wmax is the cwnd value at time of packet loss detection and t is the elapsed time since the last packet loss detection (cwnd reduction). Parameters K drives the cubic increase away from Wmax, whereas β tunes how quickly cwnd reduction happens on packet loss. This process ensures that its $cwnd$ quickly recovers after a loss event.

B. Compound TCP Congestion Avoidance

Compound TCP is the TCP of choice for most deployed Wintel machines. It implements a hybrid loss/delay based congestion avoidance scheme, by adding a delay congestion window dwnd to the congestion window of NewReno [17]. Compound TCP cwnd adjustment is as per (2):

$$
\begin{aligned}
AckRec: \quad cwnd_{k+1} &= cwnd_k + \frac{1}{cwnd_k + dwnd_k} \\
PktLoss: \quad cwnd_{k+1} &= \frac{cwnd_k}{2}
\end{aligned} \tag{2}
$$

where the delay component is computed as:

$$
\begin{aligned}
AckRec: dwnd_{k+1} &= \begin{cases} dwnd_k + \alpha dwnd_k^K - 1, & \text{if } diff < \gamma \\ dwnd_k - \eta diff, & \text{if } diff \geq \gamma \end{cases} \\
PktLoss: dwnd_{k+1} &= dwnd_k(1-\beta) - \frac{cwnd_k}{2}
\end{aligned} \tag{3}
$$

where $diff$ is an estimated number of backlogged packets, γ is a threshold parameter which drives congestion detection sensitivity and α, β, η and K are parameters chosen as a tradeoff between responsiveness, smoothness and scalability.

Compound TCP dynamics is dominated by its loss based component, presenting a slow responsiveness to network available bandwidth variations, which may cause playout buffer underflows.

C. Multipath TCP

MPTCP is a transport layer protocol, currently being evaluated by IETF, which makes possible data transport over multiple TCP sessions [7]. The key idea is to make multipath transport transparent to upper layers, hence presenting a single TCP socket to applications. Under the hood, MPTCP works with TCP variants, which are unaware of the multipath nature of the overall transport session. To accomplish that, MPTCP supports a packet scheduler that extracts packets from the MPTCP socket exposed to applications and injects them into TCP sockets belonging to a "sub-flow" defined by a single path TCP session. MPTCP transport architecture is represented in Figure 1 (b).

MPTCP packet scheduler works in two different configuration modes: uncoupled and coupled. In uncoupled mode, each sub-flow congestion window $cwnd$ is adjusted independently. In coupled mode, MPTCP couples the congestion control of the sub-flows, by adjusting the congestion window $cwnd_k$ of a sub-flow k according with parameters of all sub-flows. Although there are several coupled mechanisms, we focus on Linked Increase Algorithm (LIA) [15] and Opportunistic Linked Increase Algorithm (OLIA) [10]. In both cases, a MPTCP scheduler selects a sub-flow for packet injection according to some criteria among all sub-flows with large enough $cwnd$ to allow packet injection.

D. Linked Increase Congestion Control

LIA [15] couples the congestion control algorithms of different sub-flows by linking their congestion window increasing functions, while adopting the standard halving of $cwnd$ window upon packet loss detection. More specifically, LIA cwnd adjustment scheme is as per (4):

$$
\begin{aligned}
AckRec: cwnd^i_{k+1} &= cwnd^i_k + min(\frac{\alpha B_{ack} Mss^i}{\sum_0^n cwnd^p}, \frac{B_{ack} Mss^i}{cwnd^i}) \\
PktLoss: cwnd^i_{k+1} &= \frac{cwnd^i_k}{2}
\end{aligned} \tag{4}
$$

where α is a parameter regulating the aggressiveness of the protocol, B_{ack} is the number of acknowledged bytes, Mss^i is the maximum segment size of sub-flow i and n is the number of sub-flows. Equation (4) adopts $cwnd$ in bytes, rather than in packets (Maximum Segment Size - MSS), in contrast with TCP variants equations to be described shortly, because here we have the possibility of diverse MSSs on different sub-flows. However, the general idea is to increase $cwnd$ in increments that depend on $cwnd$ size of all sub-flows, for fairness, but no more than a single TCP Reno flow. The min operator in the increase adjustment guarantees that the increase is at most the same as if MPTCP was running on a single TCP Reno sub-flow. Therefore, in practical terms, each LIA sub-flow increases $cwnd$ at a slower pace than TCP Reno, still cutting $cwnd$ in half at each packet loss.

E. Opportunistic Linked Increase Congestion Control

OLIA [10] also couples the congestion control algorithms of different sub-flows, but with the increase based on the quality of paths. OLIA cwnd adjustment scheme is as per (5):

$$
\begin{aligned}
AckRec: cwnd^i_{k+1} &= cwnd^i_k + \frac{\frac{cwnd^i}{(RTT^i)^2}}{(\sum_0^n \frac{cwnd^p}{RTT^p})^2} + \frac{\alpha^i}{cwnd^i}; \\
PktLoss: cwnd^i_{k+1} &= \frac{cwnd^i_k}{2}
\end{aligned} \tag{5}
$$

where α is a positive parameter for all paths. The general idea is to tune $cwnd$ to an optimal congestion balancing point (in the Pareto optimal sense). In practical terms, each OLIA sub-flow increases $cwnd$ at a pace related to the ratio of its RTT and RTT of other subflows, still cutting $cwnd$ in half at each packet loss.

V. Path Switching Aware MPTCP Packet Schedulers

MPTCP scheduler selects which sub-flow to inject packets into the network on a packet by packet basis. The default strategy is to select the path with shortest average packet delay. However, this greedy shortest delay strategy may increase the number of path switches on a streaming session. Lets first analyze the impact of path switching on application streaming performance.

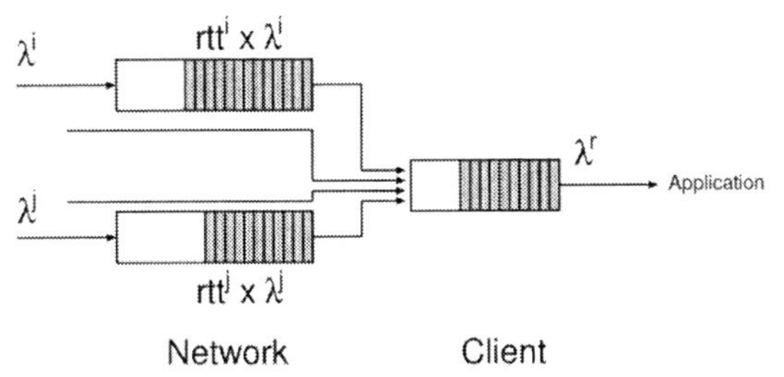

Figure 2: Path i to j Switching Model

Let λ^i, λ^j be the packet injection rates of a video stream session into path i and path j, respectively, as in Figure 2. Let also rtt^i, rtt^j be their respective round trip times. In addition, let λ^r be the playout buffer draining rate. Then:

- **Buffer underflow:** At the moment of path i to j switch, there are roughly $\lambda^i rtt^i$ packets in transit. As these packets get serviced at λ^r rate, for buffer underflow to occur, all these packets need to be serviced before the first packet injected at path j arrives. Assuming it takes rtt^j amount of time for this first packet to arrive, the condition for buffer underflow upon switching from path i to path j is: $rtt^i\lambda^i < rtt^j\lambda^r$. That is, buffer underflow probability is proportional to the ratio rtt^j/rtt^i. Hence, buffer underflow is more likely on path switches from smaller path rtt to larger path rtt.
- **Picture discard:** Assume F packets are needed to re-assemble a frame. Let F^i and $F - F^i$ be the number of packets transmitted on path i and path j, respectively. Then, in a transition from path i to path j, it takes F^i/λ^i to deliver these packets to playout buffer. By this time, the rest of the frame must have arrived at playout buffer, or some packets will be missing and the frame will not be able to be reassembled. It takes $(F - F^i)/\lambda^j$ to inject these packets, and another rtt^j delay for them to arrive at the playout buffer. So, the condition for frame discard is: $F^i/\lambda^i < (F - F^i)/\lambda^j + rtt^j$, or $F^i < (F - F^i)\lambda^i/\lambda^j + rtt^j\lambda^i$. That is, picture discard probability is proportional to the ratio λ^i/λ^j.

We study three path schedulers, seeking to minimize the number of path switches, as follows. On the onset of a video streaming session, the path with smallest rtt is chosen, as with the default path scheduler. However, once a new path is selected (due to congestion of previous path), three strategies for path switch minimization are studied: i) the scheduler stays on a new path for as long as it can, until the new path experiences congestion. We call this path scheduler greedy sticky scheduler - GR-STY; ii) the scheduler checks whether $\lambda^i/\lambda^j < 1$ before committing to stick to a new path. We call this version throughput sticky scheduler - TP-STY; iii) In addition to previous condition, the scheduler checks whether $rtt^i < rtt^j$. We call this version throughput RTT sticky scheduler - TR-STY. We evaluate these path schedulers against the minimum rtt default scheduler - DFT. Notice that our ultimate goal is to minimize buffer underflow and picture discards at the video receiver.

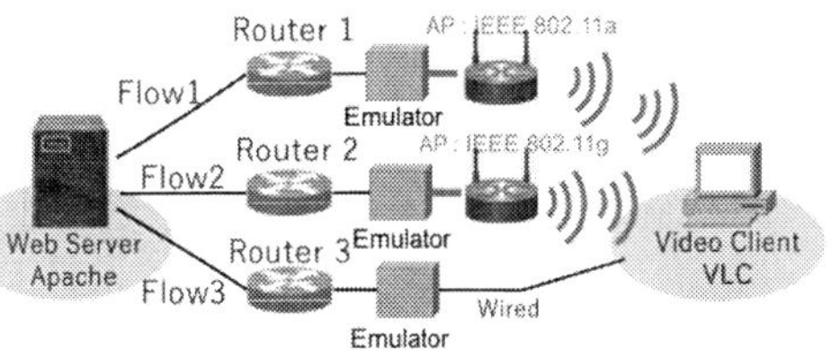

Figure 3: Video Streaming Emulation Network

TABLE I: EXPERIMENTAL NETWORK SETTINGS

Element	Value
Video size	409 MBytes
Video rate	5.24 Mbps
Playout time	10 mins 24 secs
Video Codec	H.264 MPEG-4 AVC
MPTCP variants	Cubic, Compound, LIA, OLIA
MPTCP schedulers	DFT, GR-STY, TP-STY, TR-STY

TABLE II: EXPERIMENTAL NETWORK SCENARIO

Scenario	Emulator configuration (RTT, Bandwidth, Random loss rate)
3 path Equal Loss Rate (Base Line Scenario)	Flow1) RTT 50 ms, BW 2 Mb/s, Loss 0 % Flow2) RTT 100 ms, BW 2 Mb/s, Loss 0 % Flow3) RTT 100 ms, BW 2 Mb/s, Loss 0 %
3 path Differential Loss Rate (3p-50)	Flow1) RTT 50 ms, BW 2 Mb/s, Loss 2.0 % Flow2) RTT 100 ms, BW 2 Mb/s, Loss 0 % Flow3) RTT 100 ms, BW 2 Mb/s, Loss 0 %
3 path Differential Loss Rate (3p-150)	Flow1) RTT 150 ms, BW 2 Mb/s, Loss 2.0 % Flow2) RTT 200 ms, BW 2 Mb/s, Loss 0 % Flow3) RTT 200 ms, BW 2 Mb/s, Loss 0 %

VI. Video Streaming Performance of Sticky Multipath Schedulers

In Figure 3, we describe the network testbed used for emulating a network path with wireless and wired access links. An HTTP Apache video server is connected to three access switches, which are connected to link emulators, used to adjust path delay and inject controlled random packet loss. A VLC client machine is connected to two Access Points, a 802.11a and 802.11g, on different bands (5GHz and 2.4GHz, respectively), as well as a wired link. All wired links are 1Gbps. No cross traffic is considered, as this would make it difficult to isolate the impact of TCP congestion avoidance schemes on video streaming performance. This simple topology and isolated traffic allows us to better understand the impact of differential delays and packet loss on streaming performance.

We list network settings and scenarios generated by network emulator in Tables I and II, respectively. Video settings are typical of a video stream. Its size is short enough to enable multiple streaming trials within a reasonable amount of time. For each scenario, path bandwidth capacity is tuned so as to force the use of all three paths to stream a video playout rate of 5.24Mbps. We also inject 2.0 % of packet loss on the shortest path of each scenario except the baseline scenario, so as to contrast default packet scheduler (shortest RTT) with other schedulers. TCP variants used are: Compound, Cubic, LIA and OLIA.

Performance measures adopted are:

- **Picture discards:** number of frames discarded by the video decoder. This measure defines the number of frames skipped by the video rendered at the client side.

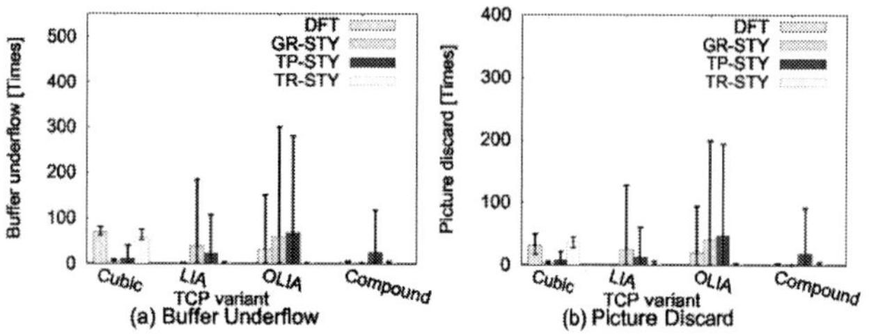

Figure 4: Scheduler Streaming Perf.; Base Line Scenario

- **Buffer underflow:** number of buffer underflow events at video client buffer. This measure defines the number of "catch up" events, where the video freezes and then resumes at a faster rate until all late frames have been played out.
- **Sub-flow throughput:** the value of TCP Throughput on each sub-flow. This measure captures how MPTCP operates its scheduling packet injection and whether it is able to maintain a high enough throughput for the video playout rate.
- **Number of path switches:** number of path switches executed during a video streaming session. A path switch is counted every time two consecutive packets are injected into the network via two different subflows.

We organize our video streaming experimental results in three network scenarios: i) A baseline scenario, with no injected packet loss and differential delay; ii) Three path MPTCP under medium round trip delay; iii) Three path MPTCP under long round trip delay. Results are reported as average and min/max deviation bars.

A. Baseline Scenario

In Figures 4, a and b report on video streaming and TCP performance of baseline scenario, where 50, 100, and 100 msec delays are small, with only random packet loss from the wireless links. For Cubic variant, there is clearly a buffer underflow and picture discard performance improvement when GR-STY and TP-STY schedulers are used. TR-STY delivers similar performance to default scheduler, which can be explained by too low stickiness of TR-STY. On the other hand, LIA, OLIA and Compound TCP variants deliver best performance under default and TR-STY schedulers. We note that these three TCP variants are less aggressive in adjusting *cwnd* than Cubic, as per respective equations of Section IV. Hence, it takes longer for these variants to grab newly available bandwidth of a new path.

In Figure 5, we report on the number of path switches executed for each scheduler, under various TCP variants. Firstly notice that GR-STY, TP-STY, and TR-STY schedulers have different levels of stickiness, GR-STY being the least restrictive. Hence, GR-STY delivers the lowest number of path switches, and TR-STY delivers the highest, closely following the number of path switches of the default scheduler. Notice also that the scheduler that delivers the lowest number of path switches is not necessarily the one that delivers best video performance in Figure 4. This shows the performance tradeoff

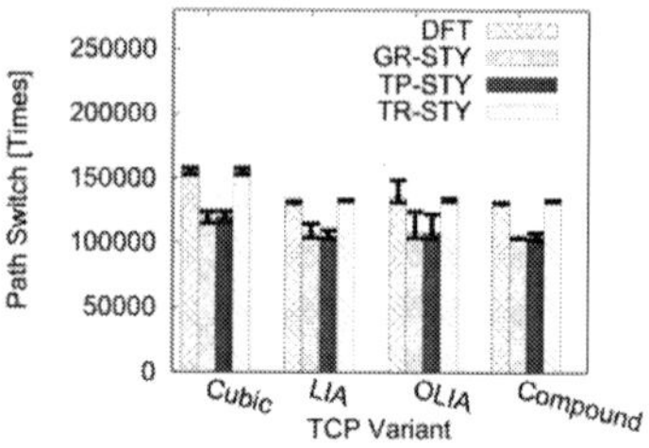

Figure 5: Path Switch.; Base Line Scenario

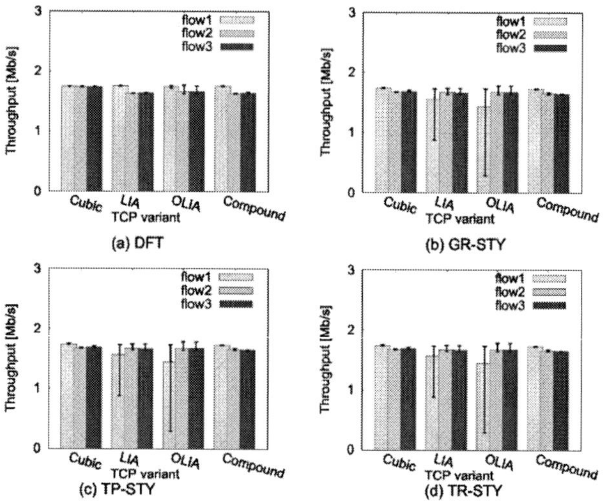

Figure 6: Throughput.; Base Line Scenario

between sticking to a given path, versus changing back to another path of perhaps better quality.

In Figures 6 a, b, c, and d we report on throughput results of the various TCP variants operating under the several schedulers. For this analysis, it is important to call to attention that flow 3 is the best quality flow, as it is a wired path with no wireless random packet loss; flow 1 and flow 2 present random packet losses due to wireless link interference. So, from a throughput efficiency point of view, flow 3 should be preferred in detriment of the other ones. Notice that the default scheduler in Figure 6 a favors flow 1, due to its smaller rtt, whereas the other sticky schedulers divert more traffic away from flow 1 into flow 3, especially for slow to react LIA and OLIA TCP variants (in Figures 6 b, c, and d). This causes less overall retransmission (graphs omitted), resulting in a better transport efficiency.

B. Small delay with packet loss scenario

In Figures 7, a and b reports on video streaming performance under network scenario 3p-50, with short path delays of 50, 100, and 100 msecs, where 2.0 % random packet loss is injected into the shortest delay path. First notice how a relatively small packet loss rate causes significant buffer underflow and picture discard degradation as compared to the baseline scenario. About TCP variants, Cubic and Compound TCP improve their buffer underflow and picture discard performances under TR-STY schedulers, whereas LIA and OLIA variants present similar performance across all schedulers.

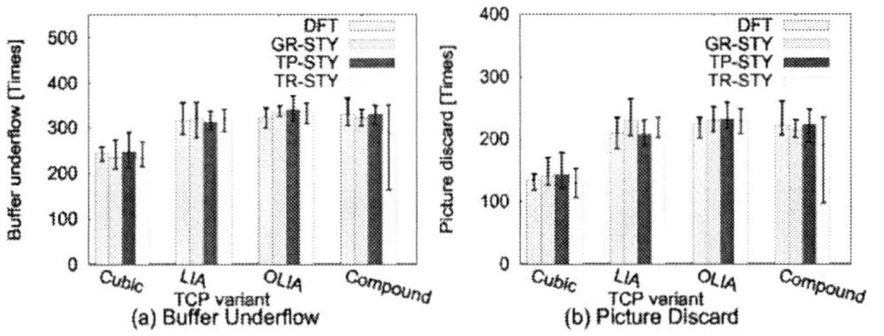

Figure 7: Scheduler Streaming Perf.; Scenario 3p-50

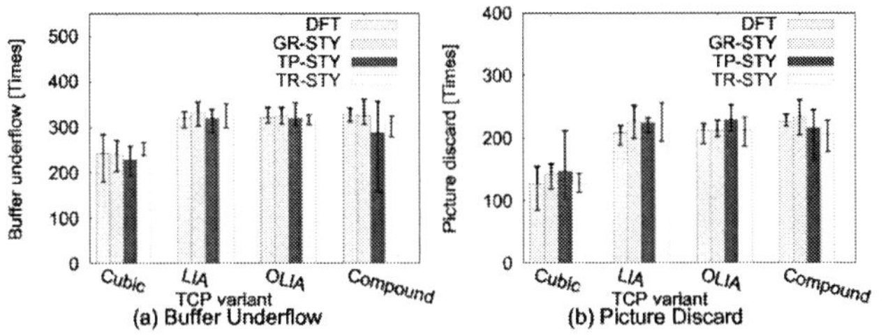

Figure 8: Scheduler Streaming Perf.; Scenario 3p-150

C. Large delay with packet loss scenario

In Figures 8, a and b reports on video streaming and TCP performance under scenario 3p-150, a three path scenario with large delays of 150, 200, and 200 msecs, respectively, with a 2.0 % random loss on shortest path. We can see that, when compared with previous scenarios, Cubic and Compound TCP variants have smaller buffer underflow and picture discard improvements between using different versions of Sticky scheduler and the default scheduler. LIA and OLIA present similar performance accross all schedulers. We conjecture that the larger the path delays are, the less performance improvement gains.

Overall, the above results show that video streaming performance improvement can be obtained by reducing path switching among available paths while avoiding path switches with high probability of causing buffer underflow and picture discards at the video receiver side. In addition, there seems to be a point of diminishing returns when paths have very long round trip times. Although these results were obtained for specific testbed topology and network scenarios, we believe similar improvements can be attained on more generic network scenarios.

VII. Conclusion and Future work

In this paper, we have proposed packet schedulers that reduce path switching among available paths to improve the quality of streaming video over MPTCP. We have evaluated MPTCP performance with default and packet schedulers which avoid path switching when the probability of buffer underflow and picture discard is high. Our results have shown that a clever path switch reduction may improve video streaming for Cubic and Compound Linux and Windows TCP variants, respectively, while not impacting performance of coupled LIA and OLIA variants. We believe that avoiding path switching may be applicable across a wide variety of network scenarios. We are currently investigating the integration of path switching management with other path scheduling mechanisms to improve video streaming performance.

Acknowledgments

Work supported by JSPS KAKENHI Grant # 16K00131.

References

[1] M. Allman, V. Paxson, and W. Stevens, "TCP Congestion Control," IETF RFC 2581, April 1999.

[2] Arzani et al., "Deconstructing MPTCP Performance," In Proceedings of IEEE 22nd ICNP, pp. 269-274, 2014.

[3] D. Cavendish, K. Kumazoe, M. Tsuru, Y. Oie, and M. Gerla, "Capacity and Congestion Probing: TCP Congestion Avoidance via Path Capacity and Storage Estimation," IEEE Second International Conference on Evolving Internet, pp. 42-48, September 2010.

[4] X. Corbillon, R. Aparicio-Pardo, N. Kuhn, G. Texier, and G. Simon, "Cross-Layer Scheduler for Video Streaming over MPTCP," ACM 7th International Conference on Multimedia Systems, May 10-13, 2016, Article 7.

[5] E. Dong et. al., "LAMPS: A Loss Aware Scheduler for Multipath TCP over Highly Lossy Networks," *Proceedings of the 42th IEEE Conference on Local Computer Networks*, pp. 1-9, October 2017.

[6] S. Ferlin et. al., "BLEST: Blocking Estimation-based MPTCP Scheduler for Heterogeneous Networks," In Proceedings of IFIP Networking Conference, pp. 431-439, 2016.

[7] A. Ford et. al., "Architectural Guidelines for Multipath TCP Development," IETF RFC 6182, 2011.

[8] A. Frommgen, J. Heuschkel and B. Koldehofe, "Multipath TCP Scheduling for Thin Streams: Active Probing and One-way Delay-awareness," IEEE Int. Conference on Communications (ICC), pp.1-7, May 2018.

[9] J. Hwang and J. Yoo, "Packet Scheduling for Multipath TCP," IEEE 7th Int. Conference on Ubiquitous and Future Networks, pp.177-179, July 2015.

[10] R. Khalili, N. Gast, and J-Y Le Boudec, "MPTCP Is Not Pareto-Optimal: Performance Issues and a Possible Solution," IEEE/ACM Trans. on Networking, Vol. 21, No. 5, pp. 1651-1665, Aug. 2013.

[11] Kimura et al., "Alternative Scheduling Decisions for Multipath TCP," IEEE Communications Letters, Vol. 21, No. 11, pp. 2412-2415, Nov. 2017.

[12] Matsufuji et al., "Multipath TCP Packet Schedulers for Streaming Video," IEEE Pacific Rim Conference on Communications, Computers and Signal Processing (PACRIM) , August 2017, pp. 1-6.

[13] Nagayama et al., "TCP State Driven MPTCP Packet Scheduling for Streaming Video," IARIA 10th International Conference on Evolving Internet, pp. 9-14, June 2018.

[14] J-W. Park, R. P. Karrer, and J. Kim,, "TCP-Rome: A Transport-Layer Parallel Streaming Protocol for Real-Time Online Multimedia Environments," In Journal of Communications and Networks, Vol.13, No. 3, pp. 277-285, June 2011.

[15] C. Raiciu, M. Handly, and D. Wischik, "Coupled Congestion Control for Multipath Transport Protocols," IETF RFC 6356, 2011.

[16] I. Rhee, L. Xu, and S. Ha, "CUBIC for Fast Long-Distance Networks," Internet Draft, draft-rhee-tcpm-ctcp-02, August 2008.

[17] M. Sridharan, K. Tan, D. Bansal, and D. Thaler, "Compound TCP: A New Congestion Control for High-Speed and Long Distance Networks," Internet Draft, draft-sridharan-tcpm-ctcp-02, November 2008.

[18] F. Silva, D. Bogusevschi, and G-M. Muntean, "A MPTCP-based RTT-aware Packet Delivery Prioritization Algorithm in AR/VR Scenarios," In Proceedings of IEEE Intern. Wireless Communications & Mobile Computing Conference - IWCMCC 18, pp. 95-100, June 2018.

[19] J. Wu, C. Yuen, B. Cheng, M. Wang, and J. Chen, "Streaming High-Quality Mobile Video with Multipath TCP in Heterogeneous Wireless Networks," IEEE Transactions on Mobile Computing, Vol.15, Issue 9, pp. 2345-2361, 2016.

[20] Xue et al., "DPSAF: Forward Prediction Based Dynamic Packet Scheduling and Adjusting With Feedback for Multipath TCP in Lossy Heterogeneous Networks," IEEE/ACM Trans. on Vehicular Technology, Vol. 67, No. 2, pp. 1521-1534, Feb. 2018.

[21] F. Yan, P. Amer, and N. Ekiz, "A Scheduler for Multipath TCP," In Proceedings of IEEE 22nd ICCCN, pp. 1-7, 2013.

The Meaning of 'Accountability', 'Responsibility,' and 'Liability' in the GDPR: Proposal for an Ontology

Nicola Fabiano

Studio Legale Fabiano
Roma, Italy
Email: info@fabiano.law

***Abstract*—The contribution starts from the European Regulation 2016/679 to analyse the terms 'accountability', 'responsibility' and 'liability' and their meaning. Accountability is the key to verify that there is an ethical implication in the GDPR through the evaluation of the related human actions. Every action can qualify the behaviour as 'accountability' and hence confer an ethical connotation. We consider the differences among the meaning of the mentioned terms as a starting point to define an ontology of the GDPR.**

Keywords–Data Protection; Ethics; Accountability; Responsibility; Liability.

I. INTRODUCTION

The present contribution aims to investigate on some terms laid down by the European Regulation 2016/679 (General Data Protection Regulation - GDPR) [1], highlighting how their meaning is not the same in all the official languages of the European Union. We think that the deepening on the sense of the terms 'accountability', 'responsibility' and 'liability' is a relevant focus both to clarify what each term should explain in the data protection context and a good starting point for working on an ontology of the GDPR. We demonstrate that the meaning of the terms above is not the same in all the official languages (especially in Italian), where the true sense belongs to the English languages. Once demonstrating the correct meaning, it is possible to address the ontology that is a complex process anyway. Here, we do not explain the ontology, but we would introduce this topic for the following works.

II. THE EUROPEAN REGULATION N. 2016/679

The European Regulation 2016/679 (General Data Protection Regulation - GDPR) *"on the protection of natural persons with regard to the processing of personal data and on the free movement of such data, and repealing Directive 95/46/EC (General Data Protection Regulation)"* has been published on 4 May 2016 in the Official Journal of the European Union and entered into force on 25 May 2016, but it applies from 25 May 2018. According to the Article 94, this Regulation repeals the Directive 95/46/EC [18] with effects from 25 May 2018. The GDPR mentions the Charter of Fundamental Rights of the European Union [2] in the first Whereas (The protection of natural persons in relation to the processing of personal data is a fundamental right. Article 8(1) of the Charter of Fundamental Rights of the European Union (the 'Charter') and Article 16(1) of the Treaty on the Functioning of the European Union (TFEU) provide that everyone has the right to the protection of personal data concerning him or her).

One of the primary goals of the European regulator was to harmonise the legislation of each Member State: the GDPR is directly applicable in each European State, to avoid possible confusion among each domestic law. The aim of the European regulator, conscious of the high value of the personal information, was to protect the natural person with regard to the processing of personal data; the GDPR recognises several rights to the 'data subject' (Article 4.1 says: "an identified or identifiable natural person ('data subject'); an identifiable natural person is one who can be identified, directly or indirectly, in particular by reference to an identifier such as a name, an identification number, location data, an online identifier or to one or more factors specific to the physical, physiological, genetic, mental, economic, cultural or social identity of that natural person").

The main rights of the 'data subject' laid down by the GDPR are:

(a) *right to request from the controller access to and rectification or erasure of personal data;*
(b) *right to withdraw consent at any time;*
(c) *right to lodge a complaint with a supervisory authority;*
(d) *right of access;*
(e) *right to rectification;*
(f) *right to erasure (âĂŸright to be forgottenâĂŹ);*
(g) *right to restriction of processing;*
(h) *right to data portability;*

The listed rights show how relevant is the role of the 'data subject' and hence the high value of the personal data.

Regarding the processing of personal data the GDPR lays down specific obligations for the controller (Article 4(1) number (7) says: 'controller' means the natural or legal person, public authority, agency or other body which, alone or jointly with others, determines the purposes and means of the processing of personal data; where the purposes and means of such processing are determined by Union or Member State law, the controller or the specific criteria for its nomination may be provided for by Union or Member State law), and the processor (Article 4(1) number (8) says: 'processor' means a natural or legal person, public authority, agency or other body which processes personal data on behalf of the controller), mainly observing the principles according to the articles 5 and 6 and implementing "appropriate technical and organisational measures to ensure a level of security appropriate to the risk" (Article 32).

The GDPR is a milestone because it brings a new approach to the protection of natural persons with regard to the processing of personal data, introducing numerous changes, such as, inter alia, the accountability principle, the Data Protection Impact Assessment (DPIA), the Data Protection by Design and by Default principle, the data breach notification, the Data Protection Officer (DPO), the very high administrative fines in respect of infringements of the Regulation, and so on.

It is clear that technology and law are not at the same level because the first one (technology) is always ahead than the second one (law). The actions on the part of the legislator always followed the technological solutions, and so the rules have to be able to consider the technology evolution.

Apart from the law, there is also the "soft-law" that consists of opinions issued by Data Protection Supervisory Authorities and the European Data Protection Board (former Article 29 Working Party). The opinions are not binding but provides clarification contributing to interpret the data protection law.

III. The terms 'Accountability', 'Responsibility' and 'Liability' in the official languages of the European Union

According to the Treaty on the functioning of the European Union [3] and the Treaty on European Union, the official European languages are those mentioned in the Treaties and hence all those of the States member of the Union. Unfortunately, due to the language localisation, in some versions of the GDPR, we cannot see the same terms mentioned above.

In the English version of the GDPR we find three terms:

1) 'Accountability' (Article 5);
2) 'Responsibility';
3) 'Liability'.

In the Italian version of the GDPR, for example, we see only the term 'responsibility'. In fact, the before mentioned words are typical only of the common law systems, and each one of them has different meanings from the other. In civil law systems, the only used word is 'responsibility', and hence it is quite difficult to translate in other languages, different from English, the words 'accountability', 'responsibility' and 'liability' each one with its specific meaning. Hence, the meaning of the terms above might depend on the context, the legislation, the jurisdiction and also from the geographic area.

On the one hand, applying the GDPR in Europe, and especially in civil law systems, it is hard due to the identification of the correct word to adapt in a specific case of responsibility. On the other hand, the GDPR applies in Europe but also all over the world according to the territorial scope laid down by Article 3, under the conditions set out in paragraph 2. Therefore, to understand the meaning of the three terms 'accountability', 'responsibility' and 'liability' it is necessary to consider, also in the national context, only the English version of the EU Regulation 2016/679.

This approach could be the first step for the best qualification of an ontology of the GDPR.

What does the term '**accountability**' mean? The GDPR uses the term 'accountability' referring to the controller and especially to the principle laid down by the Article 5, paragraph 2, where we read *The controller shall be responsible for, and be able to demonstrate compliance with, paragraph 1 (âĂŸaccountabilityâĂŹ)*. The topic is complex. The first reference we used to understand the correct meaning of the term 'accountability' in Europe is the Interactive Terminology for Europe (IATE) that is the EU's terminology database [4]. The IATE contains several definitions for specific domains or area, and we chose the meanings closer to the data protection field. Checking the word 'accountability' into the IATE database, we found some results, among which the European Data Protection Supervisor (EDPS) vocabulary, with the following definitions that seem more relevant, even if they are taken from different fields:

Data protection: *principle intended to ensure that controllers are more generally in control and in the position to ensure and demonstrate compliance with data protection principles in practice. Accountability requires that controllers put in place internal mechanisms and control systems that ensure compliance and provide evidence âĂŞ such as audit reports âĂŞ to demonstrate compliance to external stakeholders, including supervisory authorities.*

Public sector: *the obligations of persons or entities, including public enterprises and corporations, entrusted with public resources to be answerable for the fiscal, managerial and program responsibilities that have been conferred on them, and to report to those that have conferred these responsibilities on them* [7]. The above definitions show that, depending on the area, the meaning of the term 'accountability' might be different. Nevertheless, apart from the sector or area, the definitions have something in common. In fact, among the most important dictionaries, we found the same definitions or the same concept of 'accountability' always derived by the root 'accountable' (The term 'accountability' is defined: a) the quality or state of being accountable, especially: an obligation or willingness to accept responsibility or to account for one's actions: Merriam-Webster Dictionary online [6], or b) the the fact or condition of being accountable: English Oxford Living Dictionary [7], or c) the fact of being responsible for what you do and able to give a satisfactory reason for it, or the degree to which this happens: Cambridge Dictionary online [8]. Analysing the term accountable we see that the word 'accountability' is strictly related to an action by a person (these are the definitions of the term accountable: a) subject to giving an account (subject to giving an account) [9], or b) required or expected to justify actions or decisions; responsible (ministers are accountable to Parliament) [10], or c) someone who is accountable is completely responsible for what they do and must be able to give a satisfactory reason for it (In settings where responsibility for policy making is most clear, incumbent politicians are held accountable for macroeconomic performances) [11], or d) responsible to someone or for some action; answerable (The council that represents them is funded by the public to serve the public - and must be accountable to the public) [12]. In common law systems, the term "accountability" is closely related to the "responsibility", and the distinction is a thin line of demarcation. The characteristic of "responsibility" is autonomy, that is, a person - in his function - can act without external pressures or interference and therefore be free to make motivated decisions associated with his / her role while being bound to duties or obligations. A person "responsible" can make choices according to his intentions and is not under the control of others, and he or she is free to decide also about moral or social choices. The connection between role or function and the effects of the subject's actions or omissions characterise precisely the "responsibility").

We believe that it is possible to attribute to the term "responsibility" an ethical connotation on the basis of the the decisions that a "responsible actor" can freely assume. Someone [13] describes the "responsible actor" as «[...] one whose job involves a predetermined set of obligations that must be met in order for the job to be accomplished. [...] In many cases, simply discharging this primary obligation (the function associated with the role) may be sufficient unto itself; however, responsibility can also include moral obligations that are in addition and usually related to the functional obligations of the role. Thus, responsibility assumes that the actor becomes also a moral agent possessed of a certain level of moral maturity and an ability to reason».

An "accountable" subject, hence, is obliged to respect external conditions for which he does not have a power of self-determination and lacks the autonomy of the "responsible" subject but he or she is accountable for the consequences of his work anyway. Thus, an "accountable" subject is obliged to maintain a behaviour bound by sources external to himself, which are beyond his control and the power of self-determination. An "accountable" subject is also "responsible". The data controller, therefore, is "accountable" and hence conditioned by factors external to himself (the regulation to be respected), although he is capable of self-determination and has autonomy of action. Similarly, the controller is also "responsible" as he is free to evaluate the actions to be taken to comply with the GDPR rules.

Coming back on accountability, according to Thomas Bivins [13] "*The simplest formula is that a person can be held accountable if (1) the person is functionally and/or morally responsible for an action, (2) some harm occurred due to that action, and (3) the responsible person had no legitimate excuse for the action. Ideally, the assumption would then be to hold a person who is responsible for an action also accountable for the results of that action*". Bivins [13] continues with the following statement: "*In other words, accountability is a response to the human acts that one has performed. If it is a good act, the person deserves praise and if it is a bad act a person deserves blame. The idea of responsibility and accountability are closely linked, however are they slightly different by definition or moral implication*". According to T. Bivins [13] "*accountability might be defined as "blaming or crediting someone for an action" âĂŤ normally an action associated with a recognized responsibility*". **The term 'accountability', hence, is related to the effects of an action for which a person is not able to excuse**. The characteristic of accountability is the autonomy, and namely, a person can act without pressures or interferences hence being free to make decisions associated with his or her role. Furthermore, 'accountability' is linked to a behaviour typified by a moral or social connotation. Considering the moral and social connotation of accountability, we think that it is possible to evaluate implications in the ethical field.

Paragraph 2 of the article 5, in the English version, uses different terms as compared to the Italian translation, where we read: "The controller shall be responsible for, and be able to demonstrate compliance with, paragraph 1 ("accountability ")". We read, instead, in the English version of the GDPR two ontologically and legally different terms: on the one hand, the controller shall be: "**responsible** for ... (paragraph 1)" and on the other hand "able to demonstrate compliance with ... (paragraph 1)", qualifying this behaviour as "**accountability**".

In light of what has been said, the data controller, is "responsible" (for the power of self-determination to demonstrate compliance with the regulation) and free to act and take decisions of moral importance, that is to say, respect or not the norms. The controller is also "accountable" and bound by the principle expressed in paragraph 2 of article 5 and responds, under article 83 for the violation of this principle.

"Accountability" has been translated into Italian with "responsibility", and the term "responsible" in the first part of paragraph 2 of article 5, is translated as "competent". The Italian jurist could remain disoriented and confused, having to qualify juridically "competence" and "responsibility".

In the Italian juridical system, indeed, there is only a concept: "responsibility". The important aspect is related to the identification of the juridical nature of the behaviour, related to the role of a subject (the data controller), against the law (mainly action or omission - The controller shall be responsible for, and be able to demonstrate compliance with, paragraph 1 ('accountability')). The data controller could act (poorly, and therefore not respect the principles set out in paragraph 1) or not act (omit to comply).

The burden of being "able to demonstrate compliance with" (respect for principles) finds other references in the GDPR and specifically in article 24, Paragraph 3 where we read "*Adherence to approved codes of conduct as referred to in Article 40 or approved certification mechanisms as referred to in Article 42 may be used as an element by which to demonstrate compliance with the obligations of the controller*". The legislator, in the English version, used the term "responsibility" precisely to indicate the status of the 'responsible actor' who is free to decide whether to use the certification mechanisms to be able to demonstrate compliance with the obligations laid down by the GDPR. According to the common law systems approach, here we are not faced with a hypothesis of "accountability" for the reasons explained above on the qualification of the two different roles "responsible actor" and "accountable actor".

Moreover, there are differences between the English version and the Italian one of Article 82 of the GDPR titled "Right to compensation and liability". The European legislator used in the English version the term "liability" to highlight a situation where, in case of damages, there are different consequences instead of the administrative fees. Liability, instead, is a legal obligation. In the Italian juridical system, instead, we qualify the "liability" always as responsibility.

According to the article 83 paragraph 5, infringements of the principles laid down by Article 5 "shall be subject to to administrative fines up to 20 000 000 EUR or in the case of an undertaking, up to 4% of the total worldwide annual turnover of the preceding financial year, whichever is higher". Therefore, the sanction explains how the GDPR, considers 'accountability' as a high-value principle, layding down 'responsibility' and 'liability' for its infringement. Responsibility, thus, is related to a person and it refers to the outcomes of actions and it is strictly related to accountability.

In light of this, it is clear the choice of the term 'accountability' adopted by the European legislator in the GDPR because, despite being typical of the common law systems, has the aim to highlight and stress exactly the actions (or omissions) of the controller in respecting of the EU Regulation 2016/679.

IV. Ethics and Data Protection

The European Data Protection Supervisor (EDPS), during the 40th International Conference [14] said [15]:
"*What then is the relationship of ethics and the law?*
From my perspective, ethics come before, during and after the law.
It informs how laws are drafted, interpreted and revised.
It fills the gaps where the law appears to be silent.
Ethics is the basis for challenging laws".

The mentioned statement was perfectly aligned with the theme of the conference (Debating Ethics: dignity and respect in data driven life). Ethics is the new challenge in the field of the protection of personal data, where the primary goal is to guarantee the data subject's rights paying attention, particularly to human dignity.

The attention of the Data Protection and Privacy Commissioners, the stakeholders and the civil society, is moving from purely technical aspects towards more high-level ones, focusing, hence, on concepts strictly related to human values: human dignity. The risk is that a natural person becomes pure data, debasing and losing so the exemplary aspects belonging to a human. Ethics is the correct path to preserve the ontological nature of human.

In light of this, the question is: What is ethics? There are no easy answers because we have several definitions. We want to refer to a way of thinking that can help us to distinguish, generally speaking, what is wrong from what is right, finding the right key to conferring a natural person the exact value belonging to him or her. Accountability is an element related to ethics on the basis of the behaviour of a person and his or her choice to take action or not.

We must investigate ethical specific aspects to allow us having an efficient approach discovering the correct pathway towards a balance between Data Protection and Ethics. Robert Goodin [16] talks about the 'Vulnerability Principle' which he thus defined: "Moral agents acquire special responsibilities to protect the interests of others to the extent that those others are specially vulnerable or in some way dependent on their choices and actions". The Goodin's definition of 'vulnerability principle' mentions terms (moral agents, responsibilities, vulnerable, choices and actions) that are very close to the accountability definition as explained in the previous paragraph. Hence, in ethical behaviour, people should pay attention to avoiding to make choices and action that could be a vulnerability cause for others. In the data protection field, it is mandatory to avoid any detriment to the data subject.

The GDPR does not lay down any specific rules on Ethics. Nevertheless, we think that it is possible to start applying the GDPR principles thinking ethical: it is a matter of approach even without any norm.

V. Ethics and Practical Applications in the Data Protection Domain

The main question is "How is it possible in practice to respect Ethics in the Data Protection?" Also, in this case, the answer is not simple, but we can indeed refer to the 'Data protection by design and by default' principle laid down in article 25 of the GDPR. In fact, according to the article 25, paragraph 1, of the GDPR "the controller shall, both at the time of the determination of the means for processing and at the time of the processing itself, implement appropriate technical and organisational measures".

Accountability is the main reference in this case because any infringement of the mentioned principle entails administrative fee "up to 10 000 000 EUR, or in the case of an undertaking, up to 2% of the total worldwide annual turnover of the preceding financial year, whichever is higher". The controller have to respect the GDPR accountably. In a case, for example, where developers work on a project to carry out an algorithm, they respect the 'data protection by design' principle paying attention during the design phase to norms and rules on the protection of personal data.

Nowadays, we assist in an increase in the technical resources that use Artificial Intelligence (AI). Ethics is much important especially where - through the AI - software works getting data, often not either provided directly by the data subject, processing so massive amount of personal information. Ethics entails the respect of the principles 'Data protection by design and by default' and hence, also here, the controller has to be accountable.

Each natural person, giving his or her personal data, trust the 'controller' who must adopt the appropriate technical and organisational measures and respect the data protection laws. The misuse of personal data, due to the inappropriate use of personal information belonging to a natural person, is a data breach. Any misuse is a breach of trust, and it entails an ethical violation and, above all, the infringement of the data protection laws. The AI Now Report 2018 [17] from AI Now Institute, New York University shows ten points on the Artificial Intelligence and in point 5 and point 10 we find reference to Ethics (AI Now Report 2018, New York, 2018 - Point 5. "Technology companies should provide protections for conscientious objectors, employee organizing, and ethical whistleblowers. 10. University AI programs should expand beyond computer science and engineering disciplines").

VI. Conclusion

In conclusion, we demonstrated how the meaning of the terms 'accountability', 'responsibility' and 'liability' are related to a common law system and their translation in other languages does not find useful to explain the appropriate sense. Thus, our research describes how and why in the GDPR, we read three different terms related to responsibility, and this is the reason to refer to the English version to better understand the sense. We also highlighted the ethical characters that connotate 'accountability' in choices taken by a natural person. Dealing with data protection and privacy should always suggest to people considering the ethical approach in every single case, analysing human behaviour - actions (or omission) - as a part of the 'accountability'. Furthermore, this research, at the same time, shows how we can consider the terms mentioned above as a part of the ontology of the GDPR. We are carrying out a full analysis of the terms laid down by the EU Regulation 2016/679 hoping to publish soon specific research on the GDPR ontology.

REFERENCES

[1] Regulation (EU) 2016/679 of the European Parliament and of the Council of 27 April 2016 on the protection of natural persons with regard to the processing of personal data and on the free movement of such data, and repealing Directive 95/46/EC (General Data Protection Regulation). https://eur-lex.europa.eu/legal-content/EN/TXT/PDF/?uri=CELEX:32016R0679&from=EN [retrieved: June, 2019]

[2] Charter of Fundamental Rights of the European Union, 2016. https://www.ecb.europa.eu/ecb/legal/pdf/oj_c_2016_202_full_en_txt.pdf [retrieved: June, 2019]

[3] The Treaty on the functioning of the European Union (2016/C 202/01), 2016. https://www.ecb.europa.eu/ecb/legal/pdf/oj_c_2016_202_full_en_txt.pdf [retrieved: June, 2019]

[4] European Union Terminology. IATE (Interactive Terminology for Europe) is the EU's terminology database. https://iate.europa.eu/home [retrieved: June, 2019]

[5] From: the Oxford Handbook of Public Management, Edited by E. Ferlie, L. E. Lynn Jr., and C. Pollitt, Oxford Handbooks Online

[6] Merriam-Webster Dictionary online https://www.merriam-webster.com/dictionary/accountability [retrieved: June, 2019];

[7] English Oxford Living Dictionary https://en.oxforddictionaries.com/definition/accountability [retrieved: June, 2019];

[8] Cambridge Dictionary online https://dictionary.cambridge.org/dictionary/english/accountability [retrieved: June, 2019].

[9] Merriam-Webster Dictionary online https://www.merriam-webster.com/dictionary/accountable [retrieved: June, 2019]

[10] English Oxford Living Dictionary https://en.oxforddictionaries.com/definition/accountable [retrieved: June, 2019]

[11] Cambridge Dictionary online https://dictionary.cambridge.org/dictionary/english/accountable [retrieved: June, 2019]

[12] Collins English Dictionary online *https://www.collinsdictionary.com/dictionary/english/accountable* [retrieved: June, 2019]

[13] T. H. Bivins, Responsibility and Accountability, in Ethics in Public Relations: Responsible Advocacy, chapter 2, Edited by: K. Fitzpatrick - C. Bronstein, SAGE Publications Inc., 2006 http://homepages.se.edu/cvonbergen/files/2012/12/Resonsibility-and-Accountability1.pdf [retrieved: June, 2019]

[14] 40th International Conference of Data Protection and Privacy Commissioners - Brussels, 2018 www.privacyconference2018.org [retrieved: June, 2019]

[15] G. Buttarelli - European Data Protection Supervisor, Choose Humanity: Putting Dignity back into Digital, 2018. https://www.privacyconference2018.org/system/files/2018-10/Choose%20Humanity%20speech_0.pdf [retrieved: June, 2019]

[16] R. Goodin, Protecting the Vulnerable: A Reanalysis of Our Social Responsibilities, Chicago, University of Chicago Press, 1985

[17] AI Now Report 2018, New York, 2018 https://ainowinstitute.org/AI_Now_2018_Report.pdf [retrieved: June, 2019]

[18] Directive 95/46/EC of the European Parliament and of the Council of 24 October 1995 on the protection of individuals with regard to the processing of personal data and on the free movement of such data. https://eur-lex.europa.eu/legal-content/EN/TXT/PDF/?uri=CELEX:31995L0046&from=EN [retrieved: June, 2019]

[19] European Data Protection Supervisor - EDPS, Artificial Intelligence, Robotics, Privacy and Data Protection, 2016. https://edps.europa.eu/sites/edp/files/publication/16-10-19_marrakesh_ai_paper_en.pdf [retrieved: June, 2019]

[20] 40th International Conference of Data Protection and Privacy Commissioners, Declaration on Ethics and Data Protection in Artificial Intelligence, 2018. https://icdppc.org/wp-content/uploads/2018/10/20180922_ICDPPC-40th_AI-Declaration_ADOPTED.pdf [retrieved: June, 2019]

[21] European Parliament, European Parliament resolution of 16 February 2017 with recommendations to the Commission on Civil Law Rules on Robotics (2015/2103(INL)), 2017. http://www.europarl.europa.eu/sides/getDoc.do?pubRef=-//EP//NONSGML+TA+P8-TA-2017-0051+0+DOC+PDF+V0//EN [retrieved: June, 2019]

[22] European Commission, Communication from the Commission to the European Parliament, the European Council, the Council, the European Economic and Social Committee and the Committee of the Regions - Artificial Intelligence for Europe - COM(2018) 237 final, 2018. https://ec.europa.eu/digital-single-market/en/news/communication-artificial-intelligence-europe [retrieved: June, 2019]

[23] European Group on Ethics in Science and New Technologies, Statement onArtificial Intelligence, Robotics and âĂŸAutonomousâĂŹ Systems, 2018. https://ec.europa.eu/research/ege/pdf/ege_ai_statement_2018.pdf#view=fit&pagemode=none [retrieved: June, 2019]

[24] European Data Protection Supervisor (EDPS), Opinion 4/2015 - Towards a new digital ethics. Data, dignity and technology, 2015. https://edps.europa.eu/sites/edp/files/publication/15-09-11_data_ethics_en.pdf [retrieved: June, 2019]

[25] 32nd International Conference of Data Protection and Privacy Commissioners, Resolution on Privacy by Design. 32nd International Conference of Data Protection and Privacy Commissioners, Jerusalem, 2010. https://edps.europa.eu/sites/edp/files/publication/10-10-27_jerusalem_resolutionon_privacybydesign_en.pdf [retrieved: June, 2019]

Ethics in AI and Automated Decisions

Filippo Bianchini
Studio Legale Bianchini
Perugia, Italy
e-mail: info@bianchini.legal

Abstract—**The use of Artificial Intelligence is increasingly pervasive in our lives and this poses technological, legal and ethical problems; the definition of the term itself is not unique and evokes different contexts. The protection of human dignity and the safeguarding of fundamental rights and freedoms pass through a correct information on the use both of personal data and of algorithms for processing them, which must be knowable and their results contestable. The ethical approach to these issues is particularly relevant where it does not exclude the law but manages to overcome it by ensuring that it can keep pace with a tumultuous technological development. A proposed solution is that of an assessment that considers the ethical and social impact as well as a complete possibility of access by the data subject.**

Keywords-artificial intelligence; ethics; personal data; GDPR; data protection; automated decision; profiling.

I. INTRODUCTION

John McCarthy first coined the term "Artificial Intelligence" (AI) in 1955 when he invited a group of researchers from a variety of disciplines including language simulation, neuron nets, complexity theory and more to a summer workshop called the "Dartmouth Summer Research Project on Artificial Intelligence" to discuss what would ultimately become the field of AI [1].

Artificial intelligence systems are becoming increasingly common in everyday life, strongly influencing the habits and behaviour of both individuals and communities. Nowadays, we increasingly speak of "datafication" (the trend to turn a phenomenon into a quantitative form, i.e., into data) [2], a phenomenon that enables us to analyse and store enormous amounts of data, thus setting the stage for the *Big Data* economy. This notion has been traditionally outlined by D. Laney using the so-called 3V-model, i.e., volume, velocity and variety [3]. A fourth "V" can be identified in veracity, or truthfulness. In turn, these combined features generate a fifth one: value, profit.

Datafication makes it possible to correlate the collected data for profiling purposes: on the one hand, this enables the profiling controller to tap their informative potential, with benefits in terms of streamlining and savings; on the other hand, it seriously threatens the rights and freedoms of the individual, with potential repercussions not only on their behaviour but also on their knowledge, choices and feelings. In addition, new "inferred" data are generated from the first batch, and they too require protection.

Major concerns arise involving complex algorithms, which can process considerable amounts of data and are therefore increasingly used to dig into the personality of the individual and lay bare its innermost recesses, thus enabling their users to make potentially impactful decisions on the data subject. Suffice it to think about the negative legal and personal implications that the processing of incorrect or outdated data can have for a given individual [4]: this may well trigger a *garbage in, garbage out* mechanism, whereby the processing of poor data inevitably leads to misleading results.

Today, modern dictionary definitions focus on AI being a sub-field of computer science and how machines can imitate human intelligence (being human-like rather than becoming human). The English Oxford Living Dictionary gives this definition: "The theory and development of computer systems able to perform tasks normally requiring human intelligence, such as visual perception, speech recognition, decision-making, and translation between languages" [5]. Merriam-Webster defines artificial intelligence this way: "1. A branch of computer science dealing with the simulation of intelligent behaviour in computers. 2. The capability of a machine to imitate intelligent human behaviour" [6]. The Encyclopedia Britannica states, "artificial intelligence (AI), the ability of a digital computer or computer-controlled robot to perform tasks commonly associated with intelligent beings" [7] Intelligent beings are those that can adapt to changing circumstances.

The Council of Europe offers the following definition of AI: "A set of sciences, theories and techniques whose purpose is to reproduce by a machine the cognitive abilities of a human being. Current developments aim, for instance, to be able to entrust a machine with complex tasks previously delegated to a human" [8]; while the European Commission gives this one: "Artificial intelligence (AI) refers to systems that display intelligent behaviour by analysing their environment and taking actions – with some degree of autonomy – to achieve specific goals. AI-based systems can be purely software-based, acting in the virtual world (e.g., voice assistants, image analysis software, search engines, speech and face recognition systems) or AI can be embedded in hardware devices (e.g., advanced robots, autonomous cars, drones or Internet of Things applications)" [9].

Arend Hintze, an assistant professor of integrative biology and computer science and engineering at Michigan State University, categorizes AI into four types, from the kind of AI systems that exist today to sentient systems, which do not yet exist [10]. His categories are as follows:

Type 1: Reactive machines. An example is Deep Blue, the IBM chess program that beat Garry Kasparov in the 1990s. Deep Blue can identify pieces on the chess board and make predictions, but it has no memory and cannot use past experiences to inform future ones: it analyses possible moves - its own and its opponent - and chooses the most strategic move.

Type 2: Limited memory. These AI systems can use past experiences to inform future decisions. Some of the decision-making functions in self-driving cars are designed this way. Observations inform actions happening in the not-so-distant future, such as a car changing lanes. These observations are not stored permanently.

Type 3: Theory of mind. This psychology term refers to the understanding that others have their own beliefs, desires and intentions that impact the decisions they make. This kind of AI does not yet exist.

Type 4: Self-awareness. In this category, AI systems have a sense of self, have consciousness. Machines with self-awareness understand their current state and can use the information to infer what others are feeling. This type of AI does not yet exist.

The rest of this paper is organized as follows. Section II describes the contribution of the Convention 108+ and the Regulation (EU) 2016/679. Section III describes the contribution of the High-Level Expert Group on AI. Section IV describes the contribution of the Organization for Economic Co-operation and Development. Section V explores some practical uses of AI. The conclusion closes the article.

II. The Contribution of the Convention 108 and the Regulation (EU) 2016/679

Earlier this January, the Consultative Committee of the Convention for the Protection of Individuals with regard to the Processing of Personal Data (Convention 108 [11]) has published its "Guidelines on Artificial Intelligence and Data Protection" [12]. In this document the Committee confirms that "The protection of human dignity and safeguarding of human rights and fundamental freedoms, in particular the right to the protection of personal data, are essential when developing and adopting AI applications that may have consequences on individuals and society". The Committee also acknowledges that the development of AI should be based on the principles of the Convention 108, signed in Strasbourg on 28 January 1981 and recently modernised as Convention 108+

While the core principles contained in Convention 108 have stood the test of time and its technologically-neutral, principle-based approach constitutes an undeniable strength, the Council of Europe considered necessary to modernize its landmark instrument.

The modernization of Convention 108 pursued two main objectives: to deal with challenges resulting from the use of new information and communication technologies and to strengthen the Convention's effective implementation [13].

A. *Information and Access to Personal Data*

The principles enumerated in the Convention are the basis of the current legislation on the protection of personal data and, in particular, of the "Regulation (EU) 2016/679 of the European Parliament and of the Council of 27 April 2016 on the protection of natural persons with regard to the processing of personal data and on the free movement of such data, and repealing Directive 95/46/EC" (General Data Protection Regulation, GDPR [14]), as it can be seen by a quick comparison of Article 5 in both texts (see Table I below).

TABLE I. COMPARISION BETWEEN CONVENTION 108 AND GDPR

Convention 108+	GDPR
3. Personal data undergoing processing shall be processed lawfully. 4. Personal data undergoing processing shall be: a. processed fairly and in a transparent manner;	1. Personal data shall be: (a) processed lawfully, fairly and in a transparent manner in relation to the data subject ('lawfulness, fairness and transparency');
b. collected for explicit, specified and legitimate purposes and not processed in a way incompatible with those purposes; further processing for archiving purposes in the public interest, scientific or historical research purposes or statistical purposes is, subject to appropriate safeguards, compatible with those purposes;	(b) collected for specified, explicit and legitimate purposes and not further processed in a manner that is incompatible with those purposes; further processing for archiving purposes in the public interest, scientific or historical research purposes or statistical purposes shall, in accordance with Article 89(1), not be considered to be incompatible with the initial purposes ('purpose limitation');
c. adequate, relevant and not excessive in relation to the purposes for which they are processed;	(c) adequate, relevant and limited to what is necessary in relation to the purposes for which they are processed ('data minimisation');
d. accurate and, where necessary, kept up to date;	(d) accurate and, where necessary, kept up to date; every reasonable step must be taken to ensure that personal data that are inaccurate, having regard to the purposes for which they are processed, are erased or rectified without delay ('accuracy');
e. preserved in a form which permits identification of data subjects for no longer than is necessary for the purposes for which those data are processed.	(e) kept in a form which permits identification of data subjects for no longer than is necessary for the purposes for which the personal data are processed; personal data may be stored for longer periods insofar as the personal data will be processed solely for archiving purposes in the public interest, scientific or historical research purposes or statistical purposes in accordance with Article 89(1) subject to implementation of the appropriate technical and organisational measures required by this Regulation in order to safeguard the rights and freedoms of the data subject ('storage limitation');
	(f) processed in a manner that ensures appropriate security of the

	personal data, including protection against unauthorised or unlawful processing and against accidental loss, destruction or damage, using appropriate technical or organisational measures ('integrity and confidentiality').

Articles 13(2) and 14(2) of the GDPR say that "the controller shall provide the data subject with the following information necessary to ensure fair and transparent processing in respect of the data subject: (g) the existence of automated decision-making, including profiling, referred to in Article 22(1) and (4) and, at least in those cases, meaningful information about the logic involved, as well as the significance and the envisaged consequences of such processing for the data subject". However, it is not entirely clear why the safeguards were limited to fully automated decision-making processes.

Further protection is granted by the right of access under Article 15(1) GDPR, which provides for the possibility of obtaining information about "(h) the existence of automated decision-making, including profiling, referred to in Article 22(1) and (4) and, at least in those cases, meaningful information about the logic involved, as well as the significance and the envisaged consequences of such processing for the data subject".

B. Automated Individual Decision-Making, including Profiling

Moreover, Article 9(1) of the Convention 108+ has that "Every individual shall have a right: a. not to be subject to a decision significantly affecting him or her based solely on an automated processing of data without having his or her views taken into consideration" while Article 22(1) of the GDPR says that "The data subject shall have the right not to be subject to a decision based solely on automated processing, including profiling, which produces legal effects concerning him or her or similarly significantly affects him or her".

In my opinion, the expression "right not to be subject" must be considered addressed to the data controller, being automatically applicable (by default) except in the case of exceptions foreseen in paragraph 2. This way, AI applications should always allow meaningful control by data subjects over the data processing and related effects on individuals and on society.

III. The Contribution of the High-Level Expert Group on AI (AI HLEG)

The High-Level Expert Group on Artificial Intelligence (AI HLEG) is an independent expert group that was set up by the European Commission in June 2018. The group has been set up in order to support the implementation of the European strategy on Artificial Intelligence, including the elaboration of recommendations on future-related policy development and on ethical, legal and societal issues related to AI [15]. Moreover, the AI HLEG will serve as the steering group for the European AI Alliance's work, interact with other initiatives, help stimulate a multi-stakeholder dialogue, gather participants' views and reflect them in its analysis and reports.

The group has given its definition of AI: "Artificial intelligence (AI) systems are software (and possibly also hardware) systems designed by humans that, given a complex goal, act in the physical or digital dimension by perceiving their environment through data acquisition, interpreting the collected structured or unstructured data, reasoning on the knowledge, or processing the information, derived from this data and deciding the best action(s) to take to achieve the given goal. AI systems can either use symbolic rules or learn a numeric model, and they can also adapt their behaviour by analysing how the environment is affected by their previous actions.

As a scientific discipline, AI includes several approaches and techniques, such as machine learning (of which deep learning and reinforcement learning are specific examples), machine reasoning (which includes planning, scheduling, knowledge representation and reasoning, search, and optimization), and robotics (which includes control, perception, sensors and actuators, as well as the integration of all other techniques into cyber-physical systems)" [16].

In its "Ethics guidelines for trustworthy AI" [17], the AI HLEG has found that "trustworthy AI has three components, which should be met throughout the system's entire life cycle:

1. it should be lawful, complying with all applicable laws and regulations;
2. it should be ethical, ensuring adherence to ethical principles and values; and
3. it should be robust, both from a technical and social perspective, since, even with good intentions, AI systems can cause unintentional harm".

Speaking about ethics, it is necessary to observe that "laws are not always up to speed with technological developments, can at times be out of step with ethical norms or may simply not be well suited to addressing certain issues. For AI systems to be trustworthy, they should hence also be ethical, ensuring alignment with ethical norms".

And what these norms are? The AI HLEG has specified four principles, in form of ethical imperatives:

i. Respect for human autonomy
ii. Prevention of harm
iii. Fairness
iv. Explicability

In my opinion, all these explications should be considered *by design and by default* (that is "both at the time of the determination of the means for processing and at the time of the processing itself", see Article 25 GDPR), so as to establish a real protection for the individual.

IV. The Contribution of the Organization for Economic Co-operation and Development (OECD)

On 22 May 2019 the Organization for Economic Co-operation and Development (OECD) and partner countries formally adopted the first set of intergovernmental policy guidelines on Artificial Intelligence, agreeing to uphold international standards that aim to ensure AI systems are designed to be robust, safe, fair and trustworthy [18].

The OECD's 36 member countries, along with Argentina, Brazil, Colombia, Costa Rica, Peru and Romania, signed up to the OECD Principles on Artificial Intelligence at the Organization's annual Ministerial Council Meeting that took place in Paris and was focused on "Harnessing the Digital Transition for Sustainable Development". Elaborated with guidance from an expert group formed by more than 50 members from governments, academia, business, civil society, international bodies, the tech community and trade unions, the Principles comprise five values-based principles for the responsible deployment of trustworthy AI and five recommendations for public policy and international co-operation. They aim to guide governments, organizations and individuals in designing and running AI systems in a way that puts people's best interests first and ensuring that designers and operators are held accountable for their proper functioning.

In summary, the Principles state that:

1. AI should benefit people and the planet by driving inclusive growth, sustainable development and well-being;
2. AI systems should be designed in a way that respects the rule of law, human rights, democratic values and diversity, and they should include appropriate safeguards – for example, enabling human intervention where necessary – to ensure a fair and just society;
3. there should be transparency and responsible disclosure around AI systems to ensure that people understand when they are engaging with them and can challenge outcomes;
4. AI systems must function in a robust, secure and safe way throughout their lifetimes, and potential risks should be continually assessed and managed;
5. organisations and individuals developing, deploying or operating AI systems should be held accountable for their proper functioning in line with the above principles.

The OECD recommends that governments:

a) facilitate public and private investment in research & development to spur innovation in trustworthy AI;
b) foster accessible AI ecosystems with digital infrastructure and technologies, and mechanisms to share data and knowledge;
c) create a policy environment that will open the way to deployment of trustworthy AI systems;
d) equip people with the skills for AI and support workers to ensure a fair transition,
e) co-operate across borders and sectors to share information, develop standards and work towards responsible stewardship of AI.

V. Practical Uses

As any human instrument, AI can be used in good as well as in bad ways.

A. *Good Applications of AI*

Artificial intelligence is beginning to be applied in the medical setting and has potential to improve workflows and errors, impacting patients and clinicians alike.

The European Commission, for instance, has a strong history of project involving AI aimed at improving people's quality of life.

Among others:

- DE-ENIGMA: using play to help autistic children recognize and express emotions.
  A humanoid robot known as Zeno helps to teach school-aged autistic children, who have additional intellectual disabilities or limited spoken communication, to express emotions. It will be able to process children's movements, vocalizations and facial expressions in order to adaptively present activities linked to emotions, and engage in feedback, support and play.
- Alfred: a virtual assistant helping older people stay active.
  The project created a virtual "butler" to which people can talk, ask questions or give commands, and developed systems to encourage older people to socialize by suggesting and managing events, to monitor their state of health, and to help them stay physically and mentally active via personalized games. It produced 25 apps, both for immediate use and to inspire developers interested in designing new services that target the needs of senior citizens.
- Bots2Rec (Robots to Re-Construction): using robots to clear asbestos and keep workers safe.
  The project is developing robots that can clear asbestos – which, when inhaled by humans in the form of fibers or dust, can cause serious lung diseases – from contaminated buildings. The robots act autonomously in a building's rooms, but an operator can also control them to perform specific tasks, with the help of a virtual representation of the site.
- MURAB (MRI and Ultrasound Robotic Assisted Biopsy): using AI to detect cancer.
  The project is developing technology that will make it possible to take more precise and effective biopsies (tissue samples) and diagnose cancer and other illnesses faster. It is creating a robot that will scan a patient's body using a combination of Magnetic Resonance Imaging (MRI) and ultrasound technology and select the right location for a biopsy. This will be quicker and more comfortable for patients and will have the potential to identify early-stage signs of cancer that conventional ultrasounds may not pick up as well as reduce the likelihood of false negative results.

Recent studies show that facial analysis technologies measured up to the capabilities of expert clinicians in syndrome identification. However, these technologies identified only a few disease phenotypes, limiting their role in clinical settings, where hundreds of diagnoses must be considered. A group of researchers presented a facial image analysis framework that quantifies similarities to hundreds of syndromes using computer vision and deep-learning algorithms [19]. On the final experiment reflecting a real clinical setting problem, this structure achieved 91% top-10 accuracy in identifying the correct syndrome on 502 different images. The model was trained on a dataset of over 17,000 images representing more than 200 syndromes, curated through a community-driven phenotyping platform.

B. (Possible) Bad Applications of AI

There is also a dark side in facial recognition. On May 2019, San Francisco has become the first city in the United States to ban the use of facial recognition technology by the police and local government agencies. The "Stop Secret Surveillance" ordinance [20], set to take effect one month later, also requires city agencies to gain the board's approval before buying new surveillance technology and an audit of any existing surveillance tech in use by the city. The ban does not cover use of the technology by individuals or businesses.

Critics of facial recognition say the technology is not reliable enough to be in the hands of law enforcement. The American Civil Liberties Union (ACLU) is one of many civil-rights groups supporting the ordinance. Matt Cagle, a technology and civil liberties attorney at the ACLU of Northern California, said that this technology "provides government with unprecedented power to track people going about their daily lives. That's incompatible with a healthy democracy" [21].

Concerns about the technology aren't unfounded. In a study published by the MIT Media Lab earlier this year [22], researchers found facial analysis software made mistakes when identifying the gender of female or dark-skinned individuals.

All this echoes the "Correctional Offender Management Profiling for Alternative Sanctions" (COMPAS) risk assessment [23], a presentencing investigation report (PSI) – the documents that typically provide background information on offenders to sentencing courts – mainly known for the "State v. Loomis" case [24] [25].

The COMPAS was analyzed by ProPublica, a Non-Governmental Organization, which found that black defendants were far more likely than white defendants to be incorrectly judged to be at a higher risk of recidivism, while white defendants were more likely than black defendants to be incorrectly flagged as low risk [26].

VI. Conclusion

Following an exploration of the different meanings of AI, the present work has described the various contributions offered by the Convention 108+, the Regulation (EU) 2016/679, the High-Level Expert Group on AI and the Organization for Economic Co-operation and Development. Subsequently it has presented some practical applications of AI, both good and (possibly) bad.

Postulating the absolute value of the human beings and the protection of their personal data as a consequent fundamental right, it is necessary to observe that the Data Protection Impact Assessment (DPIA) introduced by Article 35 GDPR can evolve into a Privacy, Ethical and Social Impact Assessment (PESIA), which takes into account not only the aforementioned data protection but also its ethical and social impact, i.e., the collective nature of the risk [27].

Furthermore, it seems appropriate to establish a full 'right to explanation', whereby the data subject is not only made aware of the rationale behind the algorithm's automated decision-making but is also given a full explanation of the outcome – and thus the specific decision taken.

Thus, the compliance with ethical norms, as well with positive ones, will have the effect of expanding the protection of natural persons with regard to the processing of personal data, notably in relation to automated individual decision-making processes, with the advantage of not necessarily having to wait for a legislative provision which may arrive too late to regulate the tumultuous technological development.

Acknowledgment

The Author sincerely thanks Mr Nicola Fabiano for his constant inspiration in the field of Data Protection.

References

[1] J. McCarthy, M. L. Minsky, N. Rochester and C.E. Shannon, "A Proposal for the Dartmouth Summer Research Project on Artificial Intelligence". Available from: http://www-formal.stanford.edu/jmc/history/dartmouth/dartmouth.html [retrieved: 2019-05-31]

[2] V. Mayer-Schönberger and K. Cukier, "Big Data: a revolution that transforms how we work, live, and think", Houghton Mifflin Harcourt, 2012

[3] D. Laney, "3D Data Management: Controlling Data Volume, Velocity, and Variety". Available from: https://blogs.gartner.com/doug-laney/files/2012/01/ad949-3D-Data-Management-Controlling-Data-Volume-Velocity-and-Variety.pdf [retrieved: 2019-05-31]

[4] C. O'Neil, "Weapons of Math Destruction", Crown 2016. She is also author of the blog mathbabe.org

[5] Online, available from: https://en.oxforddictionaries.com/definition/artificial_intelligence [retrieved: 2019-05-31]

[6] Online, available from: https://www.merriam-webster.com/dictionary/artificial%20intelligence [retrieved: 2019-05-31]

[7] B.J. Copeland , "Artificial intelligence", Available from: https://www.britannica.com/technology/artificial-intelligence [retrieved: 2019-05-31]

[8] Online, available from: https://www.coe.int/en/web/human-rights-rule-of-law/artificial-intelligence/glossary [retrieved: 2019-05-31]

[9] Communication from the Commission to the European Parliament, the European Council, the Council, the European Economic and Social Committee and the Committee of the Regions on Artificial Intelligence for Europe, Brussels, 25.4.2018 COM(2018) 237 final, online, Available from: https://ec.europa.eu/transparency/regdoc/rep/1/2018/EN/COM-2018-237-F1-EN-MAIN-PART-1.PDF [retrieved: 2019-05-31]

[10] A. Hintze, "Understanding the four types of AI, from reactive robots to self-aware beings", online, available from: https://theconversation.com/understanding-the-four-types-of-ai-from-reactive-robots-to-self-aware-beings-67616 [retrieved: 2019-05-31]

[11] Details of Treaty No.108, Convention for the Protection of Individuals with regard to Automatic Processing of Personal Data, online, available from: https://www.coe.int/en/web/conventions/full-list/-/conventions/treaty/108 [retrieved: 2019-05-31]

[12] Consultative Committee of the Convention for the Protection of Individuals with regard to Automatic Processing of Personal Data (Convention 108), "Guidelines on Artificial Intelligence and Data Protection", online, available from: https://rm.coe.int/guidelines-on-artificial-intelligence-and-data-protection/168091f9d8 [retrieved: 2019-05-31]

[13] Council of Europe, "Explanatory Report to the Protocol amending the Convention for the Protection of Individuals with regard to Automatic Processing of PersonalData", online, available from: https://rm.coe.int/cets-223-explanatory-report-to-the-protocol-amending-the-convention-fo/16808ac91a [retrieved: 2019-05-31]

[14] Regulation (EU) 2016/679 of the European Parliament and of the Council of 27 April 2016 on the protection of natural persons with regard to the processing of personal data and on the free movement of such data, and repealing Directive 95/46/EC (General Data Protection Regulation), online, available from: https://eur-lex.europa.eu/legal-content/EN/TXT/HTML/?uri=CELEX:32016R0679&from=IT#d1e1797-1-1 [retrieved: 2019-05-31]

[15] High-Level Expert Group on Artificial Intelligence, online, available from: https://ec.europa.eu/digital-single-market/en/high-level-expert-group-artificial-intelligence [retrieved: 2019-05-31]

[16] AI HLEG, "A Definition of AI: Main Capabilities and Disciplines", online, available from: https://ec.europa.eu/newsroom/dae/document.cfm?doc_id=56341 [retrieved: 2019-05-31]

[17] AI HLEG, "Ethics Guidelines for Trustworthy AI", online, available from: https://ec.europa.eu/newsroom/dae/document.cfm?doc_id=58477 [retrieved: 2019-05-31]

[18] OECD, "Recommendation of the Council on Artificial Intelligence", OECD/LEGAL/0449, online, available from: https://legalinstruments.oecd.org/api/print?ids=648&lang=en [retrieved: 2019-05-31]

[19] Y. Gurovich, Y. Hanani, O. Bar, N. Fleischer, D. Gelbman, L. Basel-Salmon, P. Krawitz, S.B Kamphausen, M. Zenker, L.M. Bird and K.W. Gripp, "Identifying facial phenotypes of genetic disorders using deep learning", Nature Medicine 25, 60–64 (2019), available from: https://arxiv.org/abs/1801.07637 and also https://www.nature.com/articles/s41591-018-0279-0#article-info and also available at https://www.eff.org/files/2019/05/07/leg_ver3.pdf [both retrieved: 2019-05-31]

[20] Online, available from: https://sfgov.legistar.com/View.ashx?M=F&ID=7206781&GUID=38D37061-4D87-4A94-9AB3-CB113656159A and also available from: https://www.eff.org/files/2019/05/07/leg_ver3.pdf [both retrieved: 2019-05-31]

[21] K. Conger, R. Fausset and S.F. Kovaleski, "San Francisco Bans Facial Recognition Technology", online, available from: https://www.nytimes.com/2019/05/14/us/facial-recognition-ban-san-francisco.html [retrieved: 2019-05-31]

[22] I.D. Raji and J. Buolamwini, "Actionable Auditing:Investigating the Impact of Publicly Naming Biased Performance Results of Commercial AI Products", online, available from: http://www.aies-conference.com/wp-content/uploads/2019/01/AIES-19_paper_223.pdf [retrieved: 2019-05-31]

[23] T. Brennan, D. William and E. Beate, "Evaluating the Predictive Validity of the Compas Risk and Needs Assessment System." Criminal Justice and Behavior 36, no. 1 (January 2009), available from: http://www.northpointeinc.com/files/publications/Criminal-Justice-Behavior-COMPAS.pdf [retrieved: 2019-05-31]

[24] Supreme Court of Wisconsin, State of Wisconsin, Plaintiff–Respondent, v. Eric L. Loomis, Defendant–Appellant, 881 N.W.2d 749 (Wis. 2016), online, available from: https://caselaw.findlaw.com/wi-supreme-court/1742124.html [retrieved: 2019-05-31]

[25] "Wisconsin Supreme Court Requires Warning Before Use of Algorithmic Risk Assessments in Sentencing", Harvard Law Review, March 2017, Vol. 130, No. 5, available from: http://harvardlawreview.org/wp-content/uploads/2017/03/1530-1537_online.pdf [[retrieved: 2019-05-31]

[26] J. Larson, S. Mattu, L. Kirchner and J. Angwin, "How We Analyzed the COMPAS Recidivism Algorithm", online, available from: https://www.propublica.org/article/how-we-analyzed-the-compas-recidivism-algorithm [retrieved: 2019-05-31]. For the whole story, see: J. Angwin, J. Larson, S. Mattu and L. Kirchner, "Machine Bias – There's software used across the country to predict future criminals. And it's biased against blacks", online, available from: https://www.propublica.org/article/machine-bias-risk-assessments-in-criminal-sentencing [retrieved: 2019-05-31]

[27] Virt-EU project, "What's the PESIA framework?", online, available from: https://medium.com/@VIRT_EU/whats-the-pesia-framework-912bf0a12a4e [retrieved: 2019-05-31]

Privacy Risk in the IoT Environment: the Need for a Multiple Approach According to the GDPR Principles

Giovanni De Marco

Freelance Engineer - Data Protection Consultant
UNIDPO associate
Napoli, Italy
Email: gdemarco@demarcoconsulting.it

Abstract—**The Internet of Things environment poses many problems of technological, socio-technical and legal nature. Many efforts have been made to solve the several technical challenges and issues arising from the peculiar characteristics of IoT devices, but none of them seems to be decisive at present. Moreover, the user's behaviour is almost always excluded from the premises of these approaches, causing them to be systematically weak towards non-proactive attitudes of end users. In particular, the relationship between risk awareness and the attitude towards privacy preserving behaviours seems to be undervalued. Outside of that, the centralized system on which common Internet devices work is not suitable in the IoT environment, asking for decentralized methods. Referring to the principles of the General Data Protection Regulation UE/679/2016 may be the key to a global approach to both the technical and non-technical challenges that the IoT environment presents. The objective of the paper is to delimit the problem's contours, as they emerge from the analysed technical, legal and sociological contributions, and therefore to propose an optimization of the management strategies for the protection of personal data in the Internet of Things ecosystem.**

Keywords–IoT; GDPR; Privacy by Design; Data Protection by Design and by Default; Privacy Risk Awareness

I. Introduction

Under the acronym IoT -standing for *Internet of Things*- are grouped several technologies from a vast variety of contexts and an ultimate definition of the ecosystem going under this term is not easy. An effective logical synthesis is given in [1]: *"an IoT system can be depicted as a collection of smart devices that interact on a collaborative basis to fulfil a common goal."*. These devices are smart in the sense that they have (at least) one sensor and are capable of interacting with other devices, IoT or not IoT, connected to them via a network. IoT technologies have already started flooding our daily life, but their endemic diffusion is yet to come; should there be as much as 20 billions or 47 billions [2] connected devices in 2020, it will make no difference: the set of problems to be faced will be the same. This new kind of technology has distinct peculiarities translating into completely new sets of problems, related to their huge multiplicity, their pervasiveness and ubiquity and their primary function, i.e., gathering (personal) data from the physical environment. Consequently, the potential harm that the spreading of IoT devices can cause in terms of privacy and data protection is really high. Many efforts have been made to solve the several technical challenges and issues arising from the peculiar characteristics of IoT devices, but none of them seems to be decisive at present (see, for instance, [1]). Moreover, approaching these issues only from a technical point of view may be not effective, both because these problems are not only technical problems, and because the intrinsic dynamism of these technologies requires a structured strategy covering socio-technical and legal aspects alongside the technical ones. In particular, the relationship between risk awareness and the attitude towards privacy preserving behaviours should be taken into account. The paper is structured as follows: in section II the technical issues proper of the IoT environment are enumerated and legal requirements for data protection are analysed. In section III the focus is on the interaction between these new technologies and user's behaviour. In section IV a synthesis of the various aspects of the problem is presented and a proposal of management strategy compliant to the principles of the European Union *General Data Protection Regulation EU/679/2016* (GDPR) is suggested, as the key to a global approach to both the technical and non-technical challenges that the IoT environment poses. Finally, in section V, the critical points of the suggested strategy are underlined and the path to the future needed work is indicated.

II. Technical and Legal aspects

The peculiarities of IoT devices result in specific arguments to be addressed in order to keep this technological blossoming under control, in terms of practical usability, security and privacy protection; even if an exhaustive catalogue cannot be determined, due to the intrinsic dynamical and very varied nature of devices falling under the IoT category, the following can reasonably be the list of principal topics (see [3]-[5] for detailed analysis):

A. *Physical and resource restraints*

Particular types of IoT technologies, such as wearable devices or equipment designed to carry out tasks in contexts of high mobility and lack of sources of supply, are characterized by very limited physical resources [3][4]; reduced form factors implying small or no user interface and limited processing and/or supply power are very common features to many IoT products [6][7]. These limitations have immediate repercussions on the security aspects, since many consolidated strategies and techniques prove to be inapplicable due to lack of resources.

B. *Heterogeneity and scale*

IoT products are extremely various, in terms of field of application, conditions of use, physical and technical properties

[3], and their number will be unprecedented [6]. These peculiarities mean big challenges to be faced, such as an adequate network infrastructure able to manage an enormous number of connections and a robust frame to permit the correct interaction between very different IoT devices and between these devices and the infrastructure itself [4][5][8].

C. Authentication and confidentiality

The IoT ecosystem will be an overpopulated world blurring physical and virtual reality. In such a context the usual techniques of authentication lose any effectiveness and, in relation to the heterogeneity aspect, multiple solutions have been and will be implemented; thus, authentication and consequently confidentiality become a much bigger problem to manage compared to the usual Internet context [3][4][9].

D. Updating and accountability

Even though these two points can appear as fringe issues, their impact can be devastating, considering the huge number of devices and, hence, of manufacturers [10]. In the daily usage of the "common" connected devices, like desktop and laptop computers, tablets and smartphones, we take for granted the surveying of basic and application software and the consequent releases of patches and updates [11]. This is going to be even more true in the IoT environment, exactly because of the big heterogeneity of manufacturers and of products. In this scenario, accountability conflicts are an obvious side effect [3][12].

In various percentages, all these aspects contribute to give rise to threats for the personal data processed in the IoT environment; hence, one of the main goals to be achieved in the IoT ecosystem is to provide adequate *trust* strategies and practical solutions. As everything else in the IoT world, this question is very complex, too. For sake of simplicity, we will detect two macro-areas of relationships occurring in the IoT world: the trust of the end user towards the IoT system itself and the trust between different devices collaborating and exchanging data in the network. Both areas have been thoroughly examined in several researches, and many solutions have been proposed (see surveys [1][3]-[5][13]); the central point is that many of these works start from existing technologies and try their best to adapt them to the context of IoT.

The negative side effect of this approach is dual: first, many solutions developed for the "traditional" Internet security scenario, such as encryption protocols [3][4] or IP (Internet Protocol) standard addressing [8] are literally not suitable in the IoT context; second, and even more important, adapting some existing technique or paradigm in an effort to manage unprecedented challenges, as those posed by the IoT environment are, is in conflict with the principles of *Data Protection by Design and by Default*, prescribed in the *General Data Protection Regulation EU/679/2016* (GDPR, [14]) – Article 25.

As explained in [15], these principles are slightly different from the *Privacy by Design* (PbD) principle [16], since the approach adopted in the GDPR focuses on the data protection rather than on privacy. Nevertheless, without any prejudice towards this important distinction, the two concepts are strictly related; so to say, the prescriptions in Article 25 of the GDPR are in a child-parent relationship with the PbD, and, in this context, it's much more useful to focus on the common idea that connects them. In other words, any technical or organisational measure to be undertaken must have as a cornerstone the privacy protection itself. To be even more clear, and referring to the last of the 7 foundational principles of PbD [16], the *mantra* is ***keep it user-centric***.

GDPR compliant solutions should consequently consider, for instance, data preprocessing, i.e., data minimisation, data anonymisation and data pseudonymisation, as told in Recital n. 26, 28 and in Articles 25 and 32 of the Regulation, to reduce the risks *at source*. In any case, the cited countermeasures are not the only possible ones, since the Regulation describes them simply as some amongst many remedies. An important suggestion about further countermeasures to be undertaken comes from the *European Data Protection Supervisor* (EDPS) opinion on online manipulation [17], in which one of the biggest current problems in the context of cybersecurity is identified in the centralisation of personal data in few private hands: *"[...] Big data analytics and artificial intelligence systems have made it possible to gather, combine, analyse and indefinitely store massive volumes of data. Over the past two decades, a dominant business model for most web-based services has emerged which relies on tracking people online and gathering data on their character, health, relationships and thoughts and opinions with a view to generating digital advertising revenue. These digital markets have become concentrated around a few companies that act as effective gatekeepers to the internet and command higher inflation-adjusted market capitalisation values than any companies in recorded history."*. The endemic diffusion of IoT products is an obvious aggravating circumstance to these worries; hence, in a *proactive* approach [16], the decentralisation of databases is a fundamental criterion for data protection, in addition to the aforementioned countermeasures. Moreover, strictly related to the issues emerging from this EDPS opinion, there is another very important and challenging novelty introduced with the GDPR, i.e., the *right to be forgotten*, as per article 17 of the Regulation. The practical implementation of this new right of the data subject, i.e., the right to ask for (and to obtain) a complete and definitive cancellation of her/his data held by a specific data controller, would be largely facilitated and better granted by the use of decentralised databases in addition with anonymisation techniques, since a large part of personal data would be, in this scheme, stored locally rather than in a remote server managed by the data controller.

Nevertheless, it is very important to underline that the *ex ante* approach required by the PbD and embedded in the GDPR, is of crucial importance also when the trust problem in IoT is addressed in innovative ways, and thus the proposed solution is the effect of a fresh start. Starting from scratch does not lead, by itself, to achieve the goal: for instance an authentication system relying on the blockchain is *per se* compliant with the decentralization idea, being the blockchain an intrinsically decentralized technology; furthermore the example of the blockchain sounds particularly striking to address the trust management, given the capability of blockchains to ensure trust between participants without relying on a supervising authority. Nevertheless, a blockchain solution could reveal itself to be non-compliant with the PbD principles. For instance, in [18] a very interesting trust system for IoT is developed exploiting the blockchain technology; the system hinges on "promises to be honored" between a *service provider* and a *service consumer*, and the "reputation" of each participant to the chain is brilliantly built up not only from the previous history already stored in the chain, but it is also linked to other trust indicators coming from external environment, so that a new participant to the chain is not obliged to start from "zero trust", but can inherit his (good) reputation from other contexts. All the transactions are encrypted *"[...] to provide confidentiality between the parties [...]"*, but the side effect of this *ex post* privacy countermeasure is that the encryption could also be exploited by malicious consumers to keep their bad reputation hidden; the problem is solved *"[...] publishing the obligations that were not fulfilled in an unencrypted form [...] and linking them to the previous encrypted ones."*. The result is that *"[...] all the non-fulfilled obligations are public."*, and this solution, since the non-fulfilled obligations have immediate negative impact on the reputation of the participant, is hardly acceptable, being the blockchain records immutable and not subject to any impartial trust agency, making it impossible to erase a potential *perp walk* effect caused by the disclosure of non-fulfilled obligations to all other participants.

Moreover, as explained again in [15], not all blockchain systems are compatible with the GDPR (only *private*, i.e. *permissioned*, blockchains and *combined* blockchains can be GDPR compatible) and this means that any measure developed without accounting these legal constraints will be almost useless in a global interconnected virtual market in which the GDPR becomes day by day the main normative reference. This one is far from being a secondary detail: there have been several works addressing the trust issue in IoT through the blockchain technology [19] but, unfortunately, those adopting *public*, i.e., *permissionless* blockchains are intrinsically non-compliant with the GDPR. The risk can be that some technically effective solutions may be implemented and spread, and possibly become established as reference solutions, while they cause in the approach itself a compliance problem.

III. SOCIO-TECHNICAL ASPECTS

As we have seen, the security and trust challenges presented by the growing IoT ecosystem are really arduous; but there are even more problems to be taken into account. Let us refer to another concept expressed in [15], i.e., the fundamental relation:

$$security \neq privacy.$$

This inequality summarizes the real possibility of scenarios in which, despite the computer security countermeasures, no effective privacy protection has been achieved. From this point of view, the aforementioned examples are perfectly suitable.

Another remarkable and extremely concrete example of this kind is the so called *privacy paradox*; this expression refers to a recurring finding of several researchers: very often individuals who claim to be really concerned about their privacy, actually behave in strong contradiction with their statements [3][6][20][21].

As it is clearly understandable, such a phenomenon cannot be easily limited by standard security countermeasures of any kind, being it a disrupting attitude, capable of undermining the system from the inside. An end user who would correctly fulfil all the established security and trust criteria though behaving according to the privacy paradox, could however put her/his personal data under threat, considering that she/he acts with full privileges and authorizations: a perfect example of security without privacy. Furthermore, as stated in [6], the limited resources typical of many IoT devices, in combination with the huge scale of data exchange that we expect with the further diffusion of these technologies, can only worsen this gap between intentions and actual behaviour [22].

These socio-technical aspects seem to be at least as important as the strictly technical ones; in any case, it must be pointed out once more that the consideration of the behaviour of individuals when facing these new technologies is far from being totally clear. In [20], the complexity of these problems is well documented, and the intrinsic difficulty to identify the cause of the phenomenon is underlined. Some studies even question the actual existence of the privacy paradox [23], however, further and more recent evidence, and more strongly related to the IoT blossoming, suggests the contrary [22].

In any case, notwithstanding the fact that the privacy paradox phenomenon must always be estimated while taking into account all the biasing parameters, such as age [22], digital literacy and skills [6], convenience and context [20][24][25], a robust privacy protection strategy cannot afford to ignore it.

Moreover, these behavioural issues interact and intertwine themselves with other aspects of individual's behaviour in articulated technological environments, such as the *herding effect* [26][27], where, in a nutshell, individual's decisions are strongly biased by decisions previously taken by other subjects in a closed social group or category. As underlined in [6], the interaction between these two attitudes of the end users represents a serious threat to any security frame, being these weaknesses *outside* the security system.

As already said, in order to understand the nature of these phenomena, several works have addressed the problem; amongst various interesting aspects emerging from these works, three of them seem particularly relevant in the IoT context: the correlation between individual's digital skills and risk awareness [6][28], the correlation between individual's risk awareness and how coherent are her/his attitude and behaviour in terms of privacy [28] and the "privacy for convenience" mechanism [20][25]. In short, in the sociological literature a direct proportionality relation is detected between digital skills and privacy risks awareness [6]; furthermore, in [29]-[31] the relation between risk awareness and choices in terms of privacy is outlined. Even if no definitive results come out of these researches, the aforementioned aspects are very interesting clues to try to understand which the parameters favouring proactive user's behaviours are.

In addition, in [28], a further interesting assumption is made, i.e., that the incoherence of some behaviours can be explained with the concept of *privacy cynicism*: *"[...] an attitude of uncertainty, powerlessness and mistrust towards the handling of personal data by online services, rendering privacy protection behavior subjectively futile."*. The results of the study seem to confirm the hypothesis, and this sheds even more worries in view of the definitive diffusion of the IoT technologies. This research is also directly linked to other works, like [32][33], in which the tendency to ignore terms and condition of online services is underlined, and it results to be the standard behaviour; moreover the common experience of the average user do aims to a substantial feeling of impotence, being the so called EULA (*End User License Agreement*) perceived as pretty mocking for their length and complexity [34]-[37]. On the Internet, it is even possible to listen for hours and hours to a guy reading some appliance's terms and conditions [38].

Last but not least, the trading of privacy for convenience must be considered in relation to the two previously remarked aspects. This mechanism, analysed in [39], is summarized by the authors stating: *"[...] small incentives, costs or misdirection can lead people to safeguard their data less [...]. Moreover, whenever privacy requires additional effort or comes at the cost of a less smooth user experience, participants are quick to abandon technology that would offer them greater protection. This suggests that privacy policy and regulation has to be careful about regulations that inadvertently lead consumers to be faced with additional effort or a less smooth experience in order to make a privacy-protective choice."*.

IV. Discussion

The scenario described in the previous sections is really complex and challenging, as well as worrying. The unprecedented number of devices that will more and more permeate our daily experience, their multiplicity and the consequent variety of ways of interaction pose very big issues to be solved, in order to have concrete benefits from the IoT ecosystem, rather than achieving an ungovernable myriad of devices collecting, transmitting, comparing and processing personal data without control.

In many cases, the problems are mostly technical [40], and it comes out that much better could have been done by simply applying basic security countermeasures, such as, for instance, data encryption. Nevertheless, the complex relations between new hyper-connected technologies and human behaviour pose even bigger problems. Many researches reveal disconcerting attitude towards the possible use and misuse of personal data widespread on the Internet, to the point where individual's behaviours become really difficult to understand and explain [41][42], but these events cannot be regarded as totally conscious and aware behaviours.

Once again, it is appropriate to refer to the GDPR principles and prescriptions in order to correctly address the whole set of problems. Besides the already mentioned principles of Data Protection by Design and by Default, we should consider another fundamental prescription of the GDPR, i.e., the necessity of a risk assessment for any potential harmful data processing in order to support the central concept of accountability of the data controller, on which the whole regulation hinges.

Indeed, the Data Protection Impact Assessment (DPIA) is a legal obligation under Article 35 of the regulation. This obligation, together with the Data Protection by Design and by Default principle, can be taken as a jumping-off point to imagine a solution, which may be seen as a natural application of the GDPR prescriptions.

- *Data management model in relation to privacy risks intrinsic to IoT technologies and compliance criteria to the privacy by design and privacy by default principles*

  Article 35, paragraph 1 of the GDPR prescribes: *"Where a type of processing in particular using new technologies, and taking into account the nature, scope, context and purposes of the processing, is likely to result in a high risk to the rights and freedoms of natural persons, the controller shall, prior to the processing, carry out an assessment of the impact of the envisaged processing operations on the protection of personal data. A single assessment may address a set of similar processing operations that present similar high risks."*. It looks pretty clear that this prescription does apply to IoT technologies; this means that any data controller dealing with IoT devices is obliged to undergo a DPIA process and to evaluate its results in order to comply with the EU/679/2016 Regulation. Moreover, in article 35, paragraph 7, is told that: *"The assessment shall contain at least:*

  (a) *a systematic description of the envisaged processing operations and the purposes of the processing, including, where applicable, the legitimate interest pursued by the controller;*

  (b) *an assessment of the necessity and proportionality of the processing operations in relation to the purposes;*

  (c) *an assessment of the risks to the rights and freedoms of data subjects referred to in paragraph 1; and*

  (d) *the measures envisaged to address the risks, including safeguards, security measures and mechanisms to ensure the protection of personal data and to demonstrate compliance with this Regulation taking into account the rights and legitimate interests of data subjects and other persons concerned."*.

In other words, an evaluation of the risk inherent in personal data processing intrinsic to the usage of an IoT device is necessarily included into any compliance process to the GDPR; the evaluation must detail and specify the techniques adopted in order to ensure personal data protection during the operation of the device. In this sense, amongst the DPIA results, the countermeasures put in place to respond to the basic principles of *privacy by design and by default* must also appear. All these DPIA outcomes can be stored in a database managed by a third party Authority (it could be, for instance, the EDPS, or a further Authority related to the EDPS). In this way, any (new) IoT device would be automatically classified and archived in this public database, and, alongside the device, the database would register the details of the risk level for each processing and of the countermeasures implemented to mitigate those risks; the crucial task of the managing Authority would be the harmonisation of each device's DPIA results, so to have an evaluation scale as homogeneous as possible. Something similar already happens with many privacy-friendly services, such as, for instance, the *DuckDuckGo* browsing service [43]; however, in order to ensure real impartiality, the involvement of a supervisory Authority appears necessary, as was the case, for example, with the *Privacy Flag* project [44]. The harmonization process is for sure a critical point of the whole management strategy; nevertheless, in accordance with Articles 40 et seq. of the GDPR, the diffusion of common *codes*

of conduct could be the shared background on which to build a widely supported reference frame for the comparison of different services and devices in terms of privacy risk. Indeed, respecting determined codes of conduct approved by the EDPS, would mean, by itself, ensuring the compliance to well known, shared and detailed data protection criteria.
For how much it concerns, instead, possible cases of unreliable or untruthful DPIAs, they come under the more general casuistry of infringements of the GDPR, and they must be treated as breaches of the accountability principle; in the same way, here is not considered the extreme case in which the use of a prior consultation is needed (article 36 of the GDPR).

- *Basic risk mitigation criteria*
Given that a detailed description of each specific situation would be unachievable, precisely because of the already examined extreme heterogeneity of the IoT ecosystem, it is, in any case, possible to identify two macro-categories: indoor devices and outdoor devices. For devices belonging to the first category, they will, in almost all cases, be connected to a trusted Local Area Network (LAN); thus, for these equipments, the basic criterion for risk reduction must include the implementation of strict anonymisation and/or pseudonymisation procedures which, together with the use of a local database for data storage, must lead to a standard for the transmission of data outside the LAN on the basis of which only data rendered appropriately anonymous must be able to reach the central management server of the device. In other words, inside of the trusted LAN the user's personal data are normally processed in order to safeguard the quality of the service provided through the device and its customization by means of the progressive learning of user's tastes and preferences, so that the appeal and the convenience of the specific IoT device are not compromised. On the other hand, only data made anonymous according to the techniques indicated above will be sent to the main external server of the considered equipment, thus safeguarding the possibility, for the manufacturer, to carry out statistical processing on the data processed by his own devices, but in anonymous form. For the second category, namely that of outdoor devices, the problems are greater, as they cannot rely on the support of a trusted LAN. However, there is nothing to prevent from reproducing the previous scheme by sending user's personal data to a private server, that is to say inside of the user's trusted LAN; at this point an application related to the device and operating locally in the trusted LAN, provides for the anonymization and/or pseudonymisation of the data and the subsequent sending of the data made anonymous to the central server of the device. Alternatively, a second personal device could play the role of the trusted LAN and of the local storage space, for instance taking advantage of a smartphone generated Personal Area Network (PAN) or through some other sort of short range connection between the IoT device and the user's smartphone. In addition, for such equipment, the default setting should provide for the deletion of all data whose sharing with the central server of the device is indispensable for the use of the service itself (e.g., geolocation data in the navigation devices) at the end of every single usage. This kind of data processing policy would be of great help also to fulfil the obligations in terms of *right to be forgotten*. These countermeasures obviously have nothing to do with the security issues of data transmission, which must be addressed and resolved beforehand, so that this granular privacy management system can be based on a solid foundation of computer security, avoiding incurring cases like that illustrated in [40]. For instance, symmetric cryptography could be the right choice due to cost and power restraints [7], and an OTP (One Time Password) second security level may be the solution to improve security by pairing the IoT device with the user's smartphone. However, this aspect has no trivial solution, given that, as already mentioned, IoT devices are almost never suitable for the application of standardized security methods due to their limited resources; therefore this aspect must certainly be deepened, although this deepening goes beyond the scope of this contribution.

- *Real time signalling of the risk level based on the settings in terms of protection of personal data of the device*
As already seen, to obtain adequate levels of protection of personal data it is absolutely essential to take into due account the behavioural aspects of the end user. From what we have seen in section III, it appears necessary to implement a mechanism that, with immediacy and without interfering with the functions of the device, is able to signal in real time to the user the level of risk to which the user is exposed. Furthermore, this indicator must take into account all the possible modifications to the device settings that impact on data protection, so that the signalling changes instantaneously and consistently according to the specific settings chosen, so to allow the user an effective, rapid and conscious balancing between practicality of use and risk for personal data. In consideration of the scheme illustrated in the previous two points, this can be achieved through a chromatic signalling system on board the device, or shown through an application specifically related to the device, by correlating to each different setting of the personal data management parameters (which is normally a possibility already included in almost all network devices or applications) a different colour signal. For example, imagining a scale on five levels, you would have:
(1) Bright green: high personal data protection level and privacy safeguarding.
(2) Yellow-green: medium-high personal data protection level. Good privacy safeguarding.
(3) Yellow: medium personal data protection level. Privacy safeguarding acceptable: some risks.
(4) Orange: medium-low personal data protection level. Privacy safeguarding weak: significant risk.
(5) Red: low personal data protection level. Bad privacy safeguarding: high risk.

The scale can obviously be deepened by adding more levels and the corresponding colour nuances beyond these five sample levels. This dynamic signalling system would allow the user to choose the balance point between practicality of use and data protection that best suits her/his needs. In other words, with reference to the previous point, the level of protection chosen may or may not include anonymisation as well as automatic deletion of navigation data, but these choices, accompanied by the corresponding signal indicating the level of risk, would certainly be more aware, even in the case of "unscrupulous" users who, knowingly, choose the most dangerous settings for the protection of their personal data.

In this way, associating in real time with each change in the settings a signal of the corresponding level of protection of personal data, it is possible to actively oppose the tendency of users to yield to the dynamics of *privacy for convenience*, which, as the literature on this topic shows, are often not very conscious dynamics because of the lack of perception of the risks to which the users are exposing themselves. Such a privacy risk management frame, explicitly thought to maximize the protection of user's data, could nevertheless be of great convenience for the manufacturers too, since any choice made in a context of maximum understandability of the privacy risk could hardly leave room for litigations seizing on the lack of awareness. In other words, an increase in user's privacy risk awareness can be the most effective strategy not only to let individuals make their choices in the most conscious way, but also to build up a proactive environment involving users and manufacturers, in order to reduce the sense of impotence in front of personal data violations and misuses that, in the long term, could ultimately bring to a "lose-lose" situation, into which, obviously, no one would be glad to get.

Nevertheless, the obvious premise to all these considerations is the compliance to the GDPR and the fair play of all manufacturers and players in the cyber-market.

V. Conclusion and Future Work

The IoT technologies are expected to become a pervasive aspect of the life of us all in the very near future. Its special characteristics, such as the unprecedented number of devices, their ubiquitous nature and the capability of making virtual and physical world blur together, outline an intrinsic duplicity in this incoming revolution: it promises to drastically transform our way of living, but it also poses threats to the privacy of us all end users as never before. The profound interaction, almost a symbiosis, between IoT devices and the surrounding world, including human beings, forces a multiple approach in order to frame the problem and then have chances of solving it; in this regard, the principles stated in the GDPR appear even more as the correct guidance to lead the way. Waiting for ambitious, visionary and fascinating projects of self-protecting personal data to come true [45], we need to develop right now an effective strategy to manage this paradigm shift.

This contribution proposes a general strategy of approach to these problems which puts the respect of norms on the protection of personal data, first of all the GDPR, above the identification of technical solutions. Moreover, the strict interaction between IoT technologies and human beings also means a strict interaction between user's behaviour and personal data protection, this reflecting itself in the need of integrating, into the technical solution, practical and effective signalling of the risks to which the user is exposed when using a specific IoT device or equipment. The proposed strategy tries to solve these problems by means of rearrangement and optimisation of already existing technologies and solutions. The legal obligation to undergo a DPIA is a very important starting point, since, at least in markets in which the data protection regulation is the GDPR or a *GDPR like* regulation, it can be the starting point on which to build the crucial component of the strategy proposed, i.e., the existence of a common standard for the evaluation of risk levels between different IoT devices. As already underlined, this task should include the involvement of a supervisory Authority to ensure the necessary level of impartiality for all parties involved; nevertheless, the current panorama already offers systems that compare various services in terms of privacy protection, and these examples can act as a reference point for a comparison platform as broad and shared as possible. Hence, amongst many possible and needed next steps to be made, two appear more urgent: the development of a prototype application which implements the signalling system taking into account any possible configuration of the data parameters of a significant selection of IoT device, and the testing of this prototype application in therms of usability and risk awareness increase on a sample of users.

Acknowledgment

The author would like to sincerely thank the reviewers for the great help given. Their ability in highlighting critical points and in indicating all necessary modifications has been decisive to improve this contribution.

References

[1] S. Sicari, A. Rizzardi, L. A. Grieco, and A. Coen-Porosini, "Security, privacy and trust in Internet of Things: The road ahead," Computer Networks, vol. 76, 2015, pp. 146–164.

[2] "IoT numbers vary drastically: devices and spending in 2020," 2017, URL: https://www.wespeakiot.com/iot-numbers-devices-spendings-2020/ [retrieved: may, 2019].

[3] C. Maple, "Security and privacy in the internet of things," Journal of Cyber Policy, vol. 2, no. 2, 2017, pp. 155–184.

[4] Z. Yan, P. Zhang, and A. V. Vasilakos, "A survey on trust management for Internet of Things," Journal of network and computer applications, vol. 42, 2015, pp. 120–134.

[5] A. Al-Fuqaha, M. Guizani, M. Mohammadi, M. Aledhari, and M. Ayyash, "Internet of things: A survey on enabling technologies, protocols, and applications," IEEE Communications Surveys & Tutorials, vol. 17, no. 4, 2015, pp. 2347–2376.

[6] M. Williams, J. R. C. Nurse, and S. Creese, "The Perfect Storm: The Privacy Paradox and the Internet-of-Things," in 2016 11th International Conference on Availability, Reliability and Security (ARES), 2016, pp. 644–652.

[7] K. A. RafidhaRehiman and S. Veni, "Security, Privacy and Trust for Smart Mobile devices in Internet of Things – A Literature Study," IJARCET, vol. 4, no. 5, 2015, pp. 1775–1779.

[8] H. Ma, "Internet of Things: Objectives and Scientific Challenges," Journal of Computer Science and Technology, vol. 26, no. 6, 2011, pp. 919–924.

[9] "Internet of Things Security and Privacy Challenges," 2018, URL: https://reolink.com/internet-of-things-security-privacy-challenges/ [retrieved: may, 2019].

[10] "The Internet of Things will be vulnerable for years, and no one is incentivized to fix it," 2014, URL: https://venturebeat.com/2014/08/23/the-internet-of-things-will-be-vulnerable-for-years-and-no-one-is-incentivized-to-fix-it/ [retrieved: may, 2019].

[11] "IoT Security Upgradability and Patching," 2016, URL: https://www.ntia.doc.gov/files/ntia/publications/ota_ntia.pdf [retrieved: may, 2019].

[12] "IoT and Blockchain Convergence: Benefits and Challenges - IEEE Internet of Things," 2017, URL: https://iot.ieee.org/newsletter/january-2017/iot-and-blockchain-convergence-benefits-and-challenges.html retrieved: may, 2019].

[13] A. S. Neeraj and A. Singh, "Internet of Things and Trust Management in IoT - Review," IRJET, vol. 03, no. 6, 2016, pp. 761–767.

[14] "Regulation (EU) 2016/679 of the European Parliament and of the Council of 27 April 2016 on the protection of natural persons with regard to the processing of personal data and on the free movement of such data, and repealing Directive 95/46/EC (General Data Protection Regulation) ," 2016, URL: https://eur-lex.europa.eu/legal-content/EN/TXT/PDF/?uri=CELEX:32016R0679&from=EN [retrieved: may, 2019].

[15] N. Fabiano, "Internet of things and blockchain: Legal issues and privacy. the challenge for a privacy standard," in 2017 IEEE International Conference on Internet of Things (iThings) and IEEE Green Computing and Communications (GreenCom) and IEEE Cyber, Physical and Social Computing (CPSCom) and IEEE Smart Data (SmartData). IEEE, Jun. 2017, pp. 727–734.

[16] A. Cavoukian, "Privacy by Design The 7 Foundational Principles," 2016, URL: https://www.ipc.on.ca/wp-content/uploads/resources/7foundationalprinciples.pdf [retrieved: may, 2019].

[17] "Opinion3/2018EDPS Opinion on online manipulation and personal data," 2018, URL: https://edps.europa.eu/sites/edp/files/publication/18-03-19_online_manipulation_en.pdf [retrieved: may, 2019].

[18] R. Di Pietro, X. Salleras, M. Signorini, and E. Waisbard, "A blockchain-based trust system for the internet of things," in Proceedings of the 23Nd ACM on Symposium on Access Control Models and Technologies. ACM, Jun. 2018, pp. 77–83. [Online]. Available: http://doi.acm.org/10.1145/3205977.3205993

[19] X. Zhu and Y. Badr, "Identity Management Systems fot the Internet of Things: A Survey Towards Blockchain Solutions," Sensors, vol. 18, no. 12, 2018. [Online]. Available: http://www.mdpi.com/1424-8220/18/12/4215

[20] S. Barth and M. D. T. de Jong, "The privacy paradox: Investigating discrepancies between expressed privacy concerns and actual online behavior - A systematic literature review," Telematics and Informatics, vol. 34, no. 7, 2017, pp. 1038–1058.

[21] "The EMC Privacy Index," 2014, URL: https://www.emc.com/collateral/brochure/privacy-index-global-in-depth-results.pdf [retrieved: may, 2019].

[22] M. Williams, J. R. C. Nurse, and S. Creese, " *"Privacy is the boring bit"*: User Perceptions and Behaviour in the Internet-of-Things," in Proceedings of the 15th Annual Conference on Privacy, Security and Trust (PST) Aug. 28–30, 2017, Calgary, AB, Canada. IEEE Computer Society, Aug. 2017, pp. 181–190, ISBN: 978-1-5386-2487-6.

[23] T. Dienlin and S. Trepte, "Is the privacy paradox a relic of the past? an in-depth analysis of privacy attitudes and privacy behaviors," European Journal of Social Psychology, vol. 45, no. 3, 2015, pp. 285–297.

[24] A. Gambino, J. Kim, S. S. Sundar, J. Ge, and M. B. Rosson, "User disbelief in privacy paradox: Heuristics that determine disclosure," in Proceeding of the 2016 CHI Conference Extended Abstracts. ACM, May 2016, pp. 2837–2843.

[25] S. Kokolakis, "Privacy attitudes and privacy behaviour: A review of current research on the privacy paradox phenomenon," Computers & Security, vol. 34, Jan. 2015, pp. 122–134.

[26] H. Sun, "A longitudinal study of herd behavior in the adoption and continued use of technology," MIS Quarterly: Management Information Systems, vol. 37, 12 2013, pp. 1013–1041.

[27] Y. E. Huh, J. Vosgerau, and C. K. Morewedge, "Social defaults: Observed choices become choice defaults," Journal of Consumer Research, vol. 41, Oct. 2014, pp. 746–760.

[28] C. P. Hoffmann, C. Lutz, and G. Ranzini, "Privacy cynicism: A new approach to the privacy paradox," Cyberpsychology: Journal of Psychosocial Research on Cyberspace, vol. 10, no. 4, 2016.

[29] L. M. Coventry, D. Jeske, and P. Briggs., "Perceptions and actions : Combining privacy and risk perceptions to better understand user behaviour," in Symposium on Usable Privacy and Security (SOUPS) 2014. USENIX Association, Jul. 2014, pp. 443–457.

[30] I. Oomen and R. Leenes, Privacy Risk Perceptions and Privacy Protection Strategies. Springer, 05 2008, vol. 261, pp. 121–138.

[31] L. Shepherd, J. Archibald, and I. Ferguson, "Perception of risky security behaviour by users: Survey of current approaches," in Human Aspects of Information Security, Privacy, and Trust: First International Conference, HAS 2013, Held as Part of HCI International 2013, Las Vegas, NV, USA, July 21-26, 2013. Proceedings, vol. 8030. 0302-9743, 07 2013, pp. 176–185.

[32] Y. Bakos, F. Marotta-Wurgler, and D. R. Trossen, "Does anyone read the fine print? consumer attention to standard-form contracts," The Journal of Legal Studies, vol. 43, no. 1, 2014, pp. 1–35.

[33] J. A. Obar and A. Oeldorf-Hirsch, "The biggest lie on the internet: ignoring the privacy policies and terms of service policies of social networking services," Information, Communication & Society, vol. 0, no. 0, 2018, pp. 1–20.

[34] "How Silicon Valley Puts the 'Con' in Consent," 2019, URL: https://www.nytimes.com/2019/02/02/opinion/internet-facebook-google-consent.html [retrieved: may, 2019].

[35] A. M. McDonald and L. F. Cranor, "The cost of reading privacy policies," A Journal of Law and Policy for the Information Society, vol. 4, no. 3, 2008, pp. 543–568.

[36] "You're not alone, no one reads terms of service agreements," 2017, URL: https://www.businessinsider.com/deloitte-study-91-percent-agree-terms-of-service-without-reading-2017-11 [retrieved: may, 2019].

[37] "Reading the Privacy Policies You Encounter in a Year Would Take 76 Work Days," 2012, URL: https://www.theatlantic.com/technology/archive/2012/03/reading-the-privacy-policies-you-encounter-in-a-year-would-take-76-work-days/253851/ [accessed: 2019-03-04].

[38] "Here's nine hours of a guy reading the entire terms and conditions for the Amazon Kindle," 2017, URL: https://news.avclub.com/here-s-nine-hours-of-a-guy-reading-the-entire-terms-and-1798259191 [retrieved: may, 2019].

[39] S. Athey, C. Catalini, and C. Tucker, "The digital privacy paradox: Small money, small costs, small talk," National Bureau of Economic Research, Working Paper w23488, Jun. 2017.

[40] "European Commission orders mass recall of creepy, leaky child-tracking smartwatch," 2019, URL: https://cyware.com/news/european-commission-orders-mass-recall-of-creepy-leaky-child-tracking-smartwatch-e61468b3 [retrieved: may, 2019].

[41] J. P. Carrascal, C. Riederer, V. Erramilli, M. Cherubini, and R. de Oliveira, "Your browsing behavior for a big mac: Economics of personal information online," in Proceedings of the 22Nd International Conference on World Wide Web. ACM, May 2013, pp. 189–200. [Online]. Available: http://doi.acm.org/10.1145/2488388.2488406

[42] "Amazon Key asks users to trade privacy for convenience," 2017, URL: https://money.cnn.com/2017/10/26/technology/business/amazon-key-privacy-issue/index.html [retrieved: may, 2019].

[43] "DuckDuckGo," 2019, URL: https://duckduckgo.com/ [retrieved: may, 2019].

[44] "The Privacy Flag Project," 2019, URL: https://privacyflag.eu/ [retrieved: may, 2019].

[45] G. J. Tomko, D. S. Borrett, H. C. Kwan, and G. Steffan, "Smartdata: Make the data "think" for itself," Identity in the Information Society, vol. 3, no. 2, 2010, pp. 343–362.